In my life time I have murdered 21 human beings. I have committed thousands of burglaries, robberies Larcenys, arsons and last but not least I have committed sodomy on more than 1,000 male human beings. For all of these things I am not the least bit sorry. I have no conscience so that does not worry me. I dont believe in Man, God nor devil. I hate the whole damned human race including myself.

Carl Panzram.

"In my life time I have murdered 21 human beings. I have committed thousands of burglaries, robberies, larcenys, arsons and last but not least I have committed sodomy on more than 1,000 male human beings. For all of these things I am not the least bit sorry. I have no conscience so that does not worry me. I don't believe in Man, God nor devil. I hate the whole damned human race including myself." - *Carl Panzram, writing his life story to his friend, Washington D.C. corrections officer Henry Lesser.*

PANZRAM AT LEAVENWORTH

By John Borowski

Waterfront Productions

PANZRAM AT LEAVENWORTH

Published By:
Waterfront Productions
Chicago, IL
U.S.A.

ISBN
978-0-9976140-7-7

Book Consultants: Ken LaMaster and Joel Goodman

Images/Documents courtesy of: Mark Gado, Joel Goodman, Ken LaMaster, and San Diego State University.

Book Funding Donors:
Thane Ahrens
Natalie Ballard
Jason Cohen
Stephen Giannangelo
Ian Hanslope
Richelle Hildebrand
Steven Isaacs
Kristen Kurek
Wanda Richmond
Cynthia Townsend
Merry VanRyn

Special Thanks:
Fredy Rocha
Dimas Estrada
Lou Rusconi
Andrew Dodge
Renick Wooley
Herlaka Rose
Robert Ray
Angel Eyedealism - angeleyecon.com
Jay Gray/The STD's - facebook.com/J.Gray666 - facebook.com/The-STDs-123061337744352
Amanda Howard - amandahoward.com.au
Josh Cullen -Etsy.com/shop/heythisguydoesart

THE CARL PANZRAM PAPERS - SDSU
Carl Panzram Papers, Special Collections and University Archives, Library and Information Access, San Diego State University. The collection was donated by Henry Lesser.

Dedicated to Henry Lesser, who brought Carl Panzram's story to the world.

CARL PANZRAM

THE SPIRIT OF HATRED AND VENGEANCE

WATERFRONT PRODUCTIONS PRESENTS

VOICE OF CARL PANZRAM JOHN DIMAGGIO STARRING TOM LODEWYCK DAVID WEISS BRETT JETMUND DAVID SALMONSON

FEATURING HENRY LESSER JOE COLEMAN KATHERINE RAMSLAND SCOTT CHRISTIANSON JOEL GOODMAN KEN LAMASTER

DR. THOMAS GITCHOFF MARK GADO ROBERT RAY ASSOCIATE PRODUCER MARK BERRY EXECUTIVE PRODUCER DOUGLAS WYNNE

NR

PRODUCER-WRITER-DIRECTOR JOHN BOROWSKI

PANZRAM.COM

JOHN BOROWSKI'S FEATURE DOCUMENTARY FILM

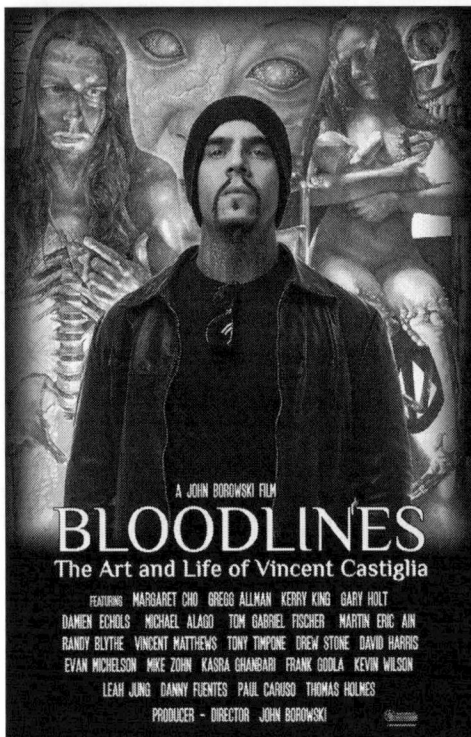

OTHER FILMS BY JOHN BOROWSKI AVAILABLE VIA STREAMING

SERIAL KILLER CULTURE TV - The Web Series
A TV Show by filmmaker John Borowski

Serial Killer Culture TV is a continuing episodic true crime TV series featuring intimate interviews with those involved in the culture of serial killers and true crime. Included are collectors, artists, survivors, authors, forensic psychologists, museums, universities, and more.

CONTENTS

INTRODUCTION

In 2012 my film, *Carl Panzram: The Spirit of Hatred and Vengeance* was released. Spanning five years, the film took me on a journey of production, filming at several prisons, traveling to numerous American states, losing footage on a crashed hard drive, and a move back to my hometown of Chicago from Los Angeles. The subtitle of the film is taken from Panzram's own writings where he called himself the spirit of hatred and vengeance personified while writhing in pain at Clinton Correctional Facility in Dannemora, NY. He is correct in his self-assessment. But I always felt Panzram was an enigma, as he seemed to wear different masks, becoming many archetypes such as the jester, philosopher, intellect, strong-man, teacher, muse, and many more. One thing is for certain: Panzram's life story is extremely important to study.

While researching for my film, I read the book, *Killer: A Journal of Murder*, the only book, at the time, devoted completely to Panzram's life story. *Killer* is filled with many explanations about the historical details surrounding Panzram's life. But I was interested in further details about Panzram's time at Leavenworth.

I see myself as a detective, searching for clues to locate documents, photographs, and information. Similar to a detective, I am on the search for the truth. Can the truths be discovered about a case from the early twentieth century so long after the case has ended? Perhaps the ultimate truths may not be able to find. The primary witnesses are long gone. But, all of the information can be shared, people can make up their own minds about the ultimate truth of a case. When I research my projects, I begin by reading the books which are available on the case. I have discovered that, over time, new information may come to light which other past authors may not have access to. As I researched deeper into the case of Panzram, I met Joel Goodman and Mark Gado. Joel had met corrections officer Henry Lesser and had Lesser's research items. Mark was going to write a book on Panzram which he abandoned before giving me his research materials to use in my film. (Mark was a first responder on 9/11 and he passed away in 2018 from cancer from the effects of his rescue efforts at the World Trade Center.) As I began piecing together the truths of Panzram's life, many aspects did not make sense. Digging deeper into the case, I was careful to study Panzram's actual handwritten autobiography and letters, which are housed at the San Diego State University Special Collections Department. So, with the help of the research materials which I collected and were loaned/donated to me, I investigated deeper and discovered different versions of the events of Panzram's life, especially his time at Leavenworth Penitentiary in Kansas.

One huge piece of the puzzle which I uncovered was Panzram's federal file. The information in the file about Panzram's time at Leavenworth USP was contrary to the information I had read in my researches. As Panzram's incarceration at Leavenworth continued, it seemed the sensationalism of the case took precedence over the possible truths of what occurred at the Penitentiary from February 1, 1929 to September 5, 1930. As I researched, it became apparent that no other author/book had possession of Panzram's federal file, or at least no author or book ever referenced the information I discovered in the file. Another piece of the puzzle which helped clarify Panzram's reasons for murdering Warnke, and Panzram's execution, was the book, *The House of Whispering Hate* by Charles Wharton. After completing and releasing my film on Panzram, I always had the intention of releasing a book containing the documents from Panzram's time at Leavenworth. The documents contained in this book tell many stories including the historical importance of a intimate relationship between a corrections officer and an inmate as well as the changes regarding corporal punishment in federal penitentiaries. Just as Carl Panzram did not want to be found insane, I wanted to clarify whatever I could as to the truths about the incidents which occurred while Panzram was at Leavenworth USP.

When reading the documents, pay careful attention to the following: 1) The reason(s) why Panzram murdered Warnke and 2) Panzram's famous "last words" as he is executed. I have included every official account of Warnke's murder and Panzram's execution including other "witness" accounts and several newspaper articles. It is very interesting that numerous reports paint entirely different pictures of Panzram's execution and his so called "last words". It was my goal to find where Panzram's last words, quoted in the book *Killer*, "Yes, hurry it up you Hoosier bastard! I could hang a dozen men while you're fooling around!" originated from. I never found the provenance of that exact quote in any of my researches. The hangman wasn't even from Indiana, he was Deputy Sheriff H.S. Holliday from Jackson County Missouri. I found every other quote and even a press account which stated Panzram never spoke a word! USP Leavenworth Warden White even quoted Panzram saying he wanted to take a crap on the world! The closest I came to the famous last word quote was in Robert Stroud's (The Birdman of Alcatraz) writings on Panzram, where Stroud states: "Yes! Make it snappy, you hoosierfield c___ s___." Stroud was not present at the execution and heard the story from other officers at the prison. So, what were Panzram's last words? Maybe he said nothing. Maybe he said a combination of all of the stories which were told about his execution. If anyone can locate the provenance of Panzram's famous "last words", I am open to a further discussion on the topic.

If you would like to research Panzram's case further, I highly recommend visiting the San Diego State University Special Collections department. Robert Ray served as the Special Collections Division Head for some time. I can only hope that whoever eventually takes over for Rob realizes the importance of Panzram's writings and treats them with care as much as Henry Lesser and Robert Ray have. As I write this, SDSU is the main repository for Panzram's writings and other documents on Panzram's case. Once I completed my film, Joel Goodman, Mark Gado, and I donated all our research materials on Panzram and Lesser to SDSU, making it the location of the world's largest collection of Panzram research materials. In addition to Joel Goodman, Mark Gado, and Robert Ray, another hero in the story of the archival materials is Thomas Gitchoff, Ph.D., who understood the importance of the Lesser/Panzram relationship and invited Henry Lesser to speak at SDSU. I find it amazing that after Lesser spoke to classes at SDSU, he unassumingly asked Gitchoff if SDSU would like to house Panzram's papers. Panzram's Papers can also be viewed online at: library.sdsu.edu/scua/new-notable/panzram. I would also like to thank my consultants on this book, Joel Goodman and Ken LaMaster. Having held careers in corrections, their clarification on many questions was very helpful to me.

My belief is that every child should read Panzram's story once they hit the age of adolescence, probably around twelve or thirteen years old. Panzram's truth of life cannot be covered with rose colored glasses. Much of his view of the world was formed from his upbringing and the abuses which he suffered. There is a Buddhist concept about "life is suffering". Panzram conveys this aspect 100% in his story. Once we realize where all of the hate and pain comes from, maybe one day as a society we may learn from Panzram's story. Unfortunately, I feel mankind still has a long way to go. But, as long as there are people like Henry Lesser in the world, there is still hope…

A note on the materials: Many of these documents were in surprisingly good shape. I have cleaned up the documents the best I could. Panzram wrote his autobiography and letters to Henry Lesser on yellow paper. Because the interior of this book is black-and-white, it proved a difficult task to convert the letters to black-and-white, and make them look fairly decent and readable. Panzram's letters appear as photocopies due to the conversion, but they are the original documents.

John Borowski, Filmmaker/author

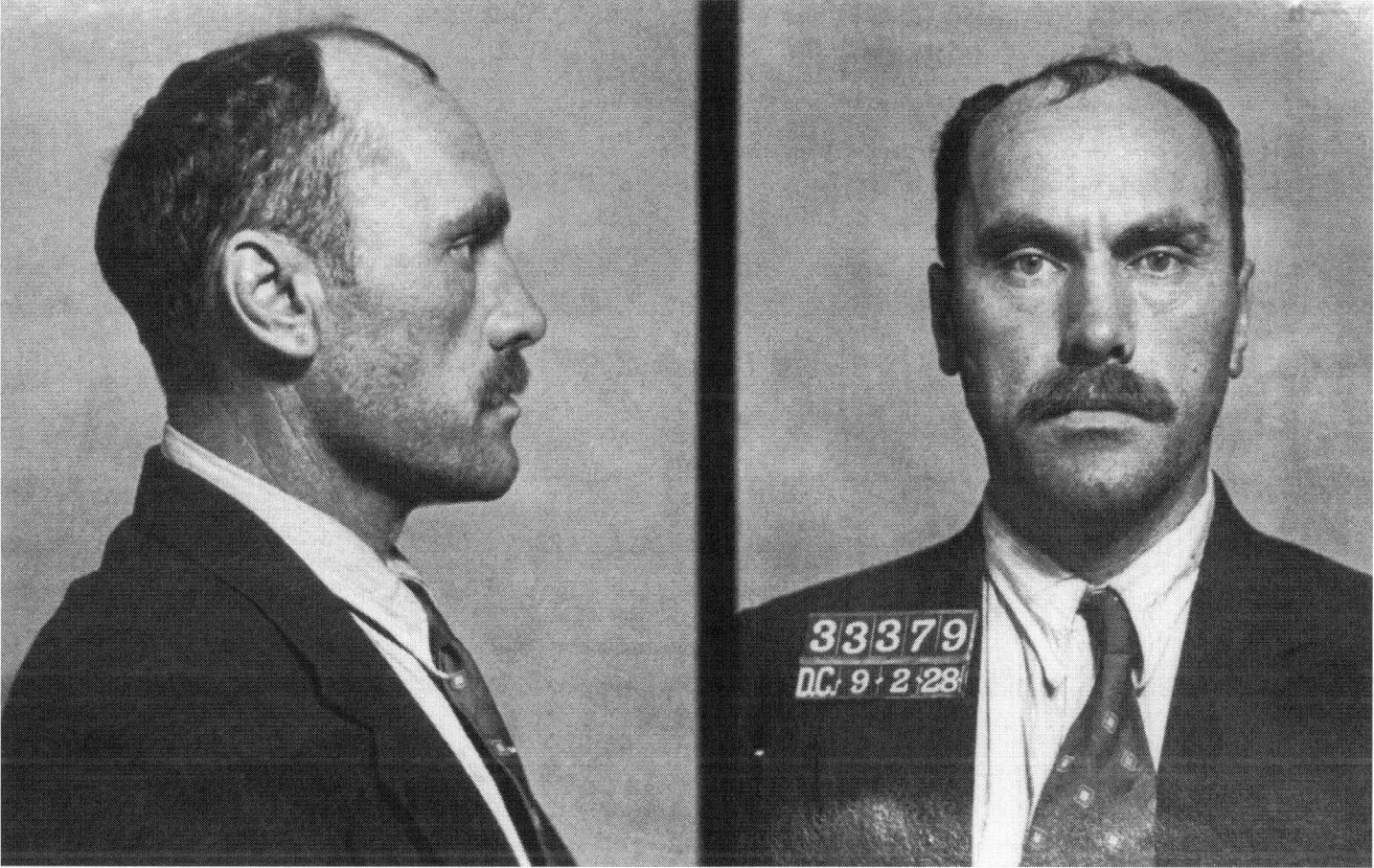

PANZRAM'S WASHINGTON D.C. MUGSHOT, 1928

Name Warden. O.S.P.

Street & No. _____

City Salem. State Ore.

Box B.

Dannemora, N. Y.

May 13. 1928.

Sir;

I write this letter to notify you that I am soon to be discharged from this prison and to ask that you with—draw the warrent which you have lodged against me here.

When I left Oregon in May 1918, I imediatly went to South America and later on to Africa where lived and worked straight and honest for several years, then being sick and a bit discouraged I was fool enough to return to this country and soon after landing in this country I landed in this prison.

Quite soon now I will have finished serving my full sentence of five years here. I recieved this sentence for third degree burglary. I have never been any thing more than a petty larceny crook and now I want to stop living that sort of a life and return to South—America where I have very good prospects to start my life anew.

If you either with-draw the warrent or fail to come here after me, I guarentee to you that as soon as I am released from here, I will be out of this country and be back in South America within thirty days and once there I shall stay and never return to this country.

When the Board of Control of the Oregon State Prison, take this matter up and should my plea recieve

A letter written by Carl Panzram (under two of his Aliases) while he was serving time at Clinton Correctional Facility in Dannemora, NY.

favorable consideration; please inform me as soon as possible so that I can arrange my papers for a passport and transportation in order that I can go there direct as soon as I am released.

If you refuse to grant me this great opportunity to start life over again, no one will be the gainer, neither you nor me, the state of Oregon or any one else, but on the other hand if you look with favor on my plea, every one will be a great deal better off for it.

I hope to recieve a reply from you soon. I am
Sincerely and very truly
John O'Leary 17531.
Alias;   Jefferson Baldwin 7390.

P.S.

If you recieve this letter it will be with the consent and favorable reccomendation of the principle Keeper or the warden of this prison.

John O'Leary.
17531.

CLINTON CORRECTIONAL FACILITY, DANNEMORA, NY

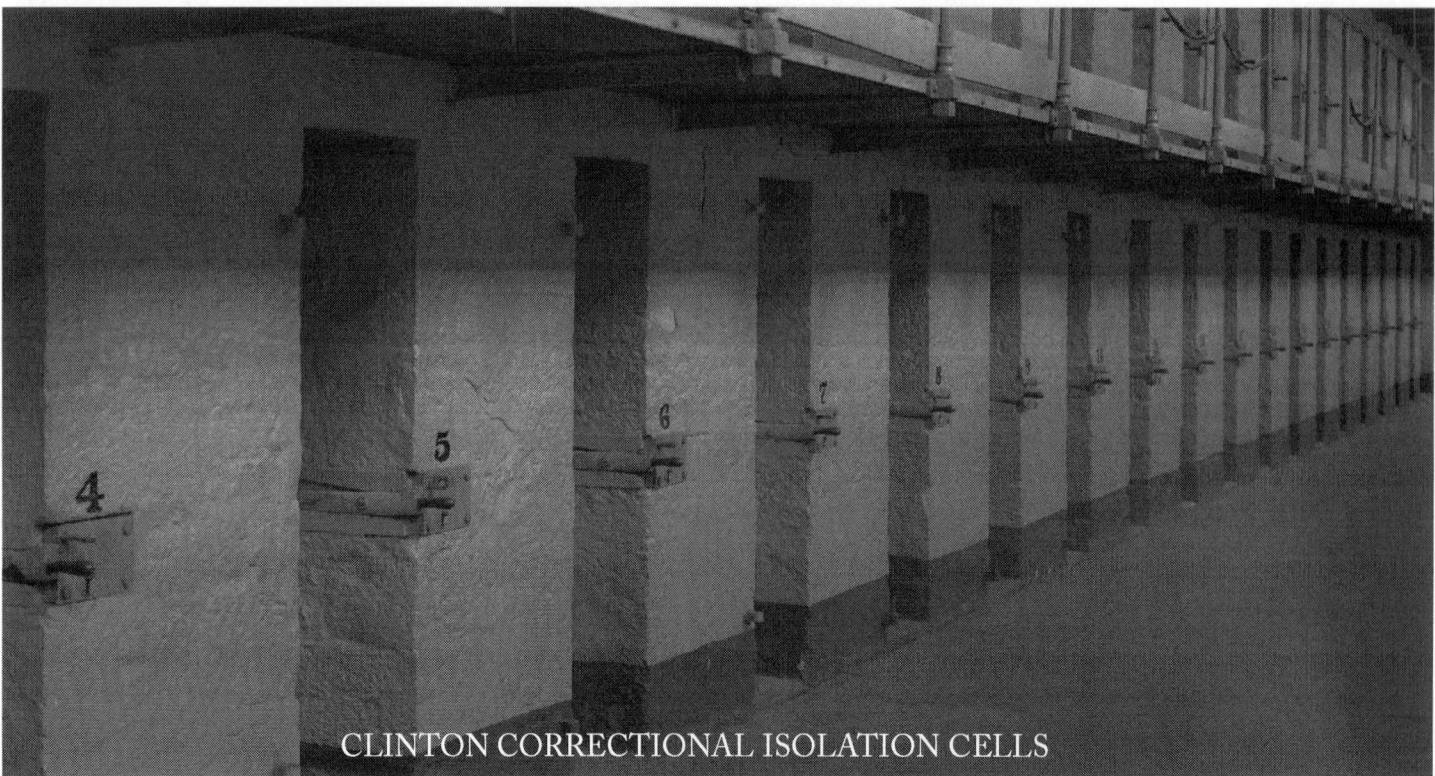

CLINTON CORRECTIONAL ISOLATION CELLS

Box B. Dannemora, N.Y. May 13, 1928

To: Warden O.S.P. Salem, Oregon

Sir,

I write this letter to notify you that I am soon to be discharged from this prison and to ask that you withdraw the warrant which you have lodged against me here.

When I left Oregon in May 1918, I immediately went to South America and later on to Africa where I lived and worked straight and honest for several years, then being sick and a bit discouraged I was fool enough to return to this country and soon after landing in this country I landed in this prison.

Quite soon now I will have finished serving my full sentence of five years here. I received this sentence for third degree burglary. I have never been anything more than a petty larceny crook and now I want to stop living that sort of a life and return to South America where I have very good prospects to start my life anew.

If you either withdraw the warrant or fail to come here after me, I guarantee you that as soon as I am released from here, I will be out of this country and be back in South America within thirty days and once there I shall stay and never return to this country. When the Board of Control of the Oregon State Prison take this matter up and should my plea receive favorable consideration, please inform me as soon as possible so that I can arrange my papers for a passport and transportation in order that I can go there direct as soon as I am released.

If you refuse to grant me this great opportunity to start life over again, no one will be the gainer, neither you nor me, the state of Oregon or anyone else, but on the other hand if you look with favor on my plea, everyone will be a great deal better off for it.

I hope to receive a reply from you soon. I am

Sincerely and very truly

John O'Leary 17531
Alias Jefferson Baldwin 7390

P.S. If you receive this letter it will be with the consent and favorable recommendation of the principle keeper or the warden of this prison. John O'Leary 17531

Written by

Carl Panzram.

Nov. 3. 1928. District Jail
Wash. D.C.

Born June 28. 1892.
East Grand Forks. Minn.

Full List of all
jails, reformatories, Prisons
and State or Government in-
-statutions I have been in.
How I got into them.
How long I stayed in them.
How I got out of them.

No. 1. East Grand Forks. Minn.
Charges, incorrigability and
Burglary. 1903. County Jail.

No. 2. Red Wing, Minn. This is
the seat of the Minnesota
State training School. There
I stayed nearly 2 years.

No. 3. Butte. Mont. Charge Burglary
3 months in the County Jail
there and then tried in County

ONE OF PANZRAM'S AUTOBIOGRAPHY PAPERS

A MOST UNUSUAL FRIENDSHIP

Lifelong career criminal Carl Panzram entered the Washington D.C. jail in the fall of 1928. Not long after arriving, Panzram and jail guard Henry Lesser became friends and Lesser convinced Panzram to write his autobiography so others may learn from Panzram's life story.

Many serial killers and other cirminals have written while in jails and prisons. The focus of the film, "H.H. Holmes: America's First Serial Killer", Dr. H.H. Holmes, wrote "Holmes' Own Story" while sitting in prison awaiting his trial. Serial killer Dennis Rader, whose moniker was B.T.K for Bind, Torture, and Kill, wrote "Confession of a Serial Killer" with Katherine Ramsland, P.H.D by sending her letters while Rader was incarcerated. One of the Moors murderers, Ian Brady, wrote a book entitled "The Gates of Janus", in which he studys other serial killers and includes a chapter on Panzram. Brady writes:

"There is no question that Lesser must be given full credit for the astonishing revelations Panzram was about to commit to paper. Had Panzram hated him as much as he did the other prison guards, he would not have given Lesser the time of day, let alone the privilege of being the first person to be told the homicidal details of his life."

Carl Panzram is definitely unique in many ways, including the fact that he only had a sixth grade education level. In Panzram's autobiography, he tells of all of his incarcerations and the murders of 21 human beings. Throughout his world travels, his hatred grew within him to a point where he not only hated the entire human race, but also hated himself.

In Panzram's own words, here is a list of his incarcerations, which have been verified:

Written by Carl Panzram
Nov. 3, 1928, District Jail, Washington, D. C.
Born: June 28, 1892, East Grand Forks, Minnesota.
Full list of all jails, reformatories, prisons and state or Government institutions I have been in.

How I got into them,
How long I stayed in them,
How I got out of them.

No. 1. East Grand Forks, Minn. Charges: incorrigibility and burglary. 1903. County Jail.
No. 2. Red Wing, Minn. This is the seat of the Minnesota State Training School. There I stayed nearly two years.
No. 3. Butte, Mont. Charge: Burglary--three months in the county jail there and then tried in County Court and sent to the Montana State Reform School at Miles City, Mont. where I was held about 1 year and then made a successful escape. This was in 1905 under my right name, C. P.
No. 5. Joined the U. S. Army in 1906 at Helena, Mont., under the name of Carl Panzram. Stationed at Fort Harrison in the 6th Regular U.S. Infantry in A Company. Practically as soon or very shortly after I joined the Army I was put in the guardhouse for stealing. Several months there and then tried by a U.S. Military General Court Martial and sentenced to 3 years.
No. 6. Sent to the U.S. Military prison at Fort Leavenworth, Kans., where I served 37 months. Discharged.

No. 7. Sometime in 1910 or 1911 under the name of Jeff Davis, I was arrested at Jacksonville, Cherokee County, Texas, the county seat where I was tried for vagrancy, the crime being that I was riding a mail train on top, while being armed with two pistols. For this I was sent to the Country Road Gang where I served 65 days, and escaped. The date I don't remember but the next night I was in Houston, Texas, and that was the night of the big fire there. I think it was early in 1911.

No. 8. Fresno, California, under the name of Jeff Davis, I think. Charge: Petty Larceny. Sentenced to 120 days. Served 30 and escaped.

No. 9. The Dalles, Oregon. Name, Jack Allen. 1912. Charge: Highway Robbery and Assault. Held to await the action for the Grand Jury. Waited about three months and escaped.

No. 10. Seattle, Washington. 1912. Name, Jeff Davis. Charge: Petty Larceny. Served 1 month. Discharged.

No. 11. Moscow, Idaho. 1912. Charge: Petty Larceny and assisting a prisoner to escape. Thirty days. Name, Jeff Davis.

No. 12. Chinook, Mont. Charge: Burglary. Sentenced to one year State Prison under the name of Jeff Davis. 1912. Served 8 months and escaped. Arrested one week later at Three Forks, Mont., for burglary under the name of Jeff Rhodes. Sentenced to one year in State Prison, Deer Lodge, Mont. When I was brought back to the prison I was taken to the County Court at Deer Lodge and given 1 year for escaping from prison. Of these three sentences I served two years and was discharged.

No. 13. Astoria, Oregon. 1914. Name, Jeff Baldwin, Charged with burglary. Given 7 years in the State Prison at Salem, Oregon. Done one year and escaped. While out that time one week I robbed a man and had a gun fight with a deputy sheriff at Eugene, Oregon. For these two crimes I was given two additional sentences, one of two years for robbery and one of 8 years for assault, which made me have altogether a full 17 years to do, in Oregon, but I only done one more year of it and then escaped again. I still owe 14 years to Oregon. After escaping from the State prison at Salem, Oregon, in May, 1918, I changed my name to John O'Leary, took out seaman's papers, passenger's passports and went to South America, Europe and Africa. For the next 5 years, or from 1918 to 1923, I was in 31 different countries, had stole and spent thousands of dollars, committed many murders and robberies and other crimes and the only two times that I was in jail during that 5 years was once.

No 14. I got 10 days for theft in Barlinnie Prison in Glasgow, Scotland, 1919.

No 15. And the other was in Bridgeport, Conn., for burglary and carrying concealed weapons. Six months in 1920 and 1921.

No. 16. My last arrest before this one was in 1923 at Larchmont, N.Y. Sent from there to White Plains, tried in the County Court and sent to Sing Sing prison and from there transferred to Clinton Prison at Dannemora, N.Y., where I served 5 years, being discharged July 6, 1928.

No. 17. Arrested 36 days later in Baltimore, Md., and that's this case. I hope it's my last one as I am pretty damn tired. These are the main places where I have done time but there are about 100 more places where I have been in jail for various offenses for periods of 1 day to a week or so. Altogether, I have served about twenty years of my life in prison and I am 36 years old now.

EXTERIOR D.C. JAIL

at Dannemora N.Y. where
I served 5 years. being
discharged July 6. 1928.
17. Arrested 36 days later
in Baltimore Mcl. and
thats this case. I hope
its my last one as I
am pretty dam tired.
These are the main places
where I have done time
but there are about 100 more
places where I have been
in jail for various offences
for periods of from 1 day to
a week or so. All together
I have served about
twenty years of my life
in prison and I am 36
years old now.

JEFF DAVIS. 4194.

JEFF DAVIS. 4194.

PANZRAM'S FIRST MUGSHOTS FROM BUTTE, MONTANA, 1905

JEFFERSON RHOADES. 4396.

JEFFERSON RHOADES. 4396.

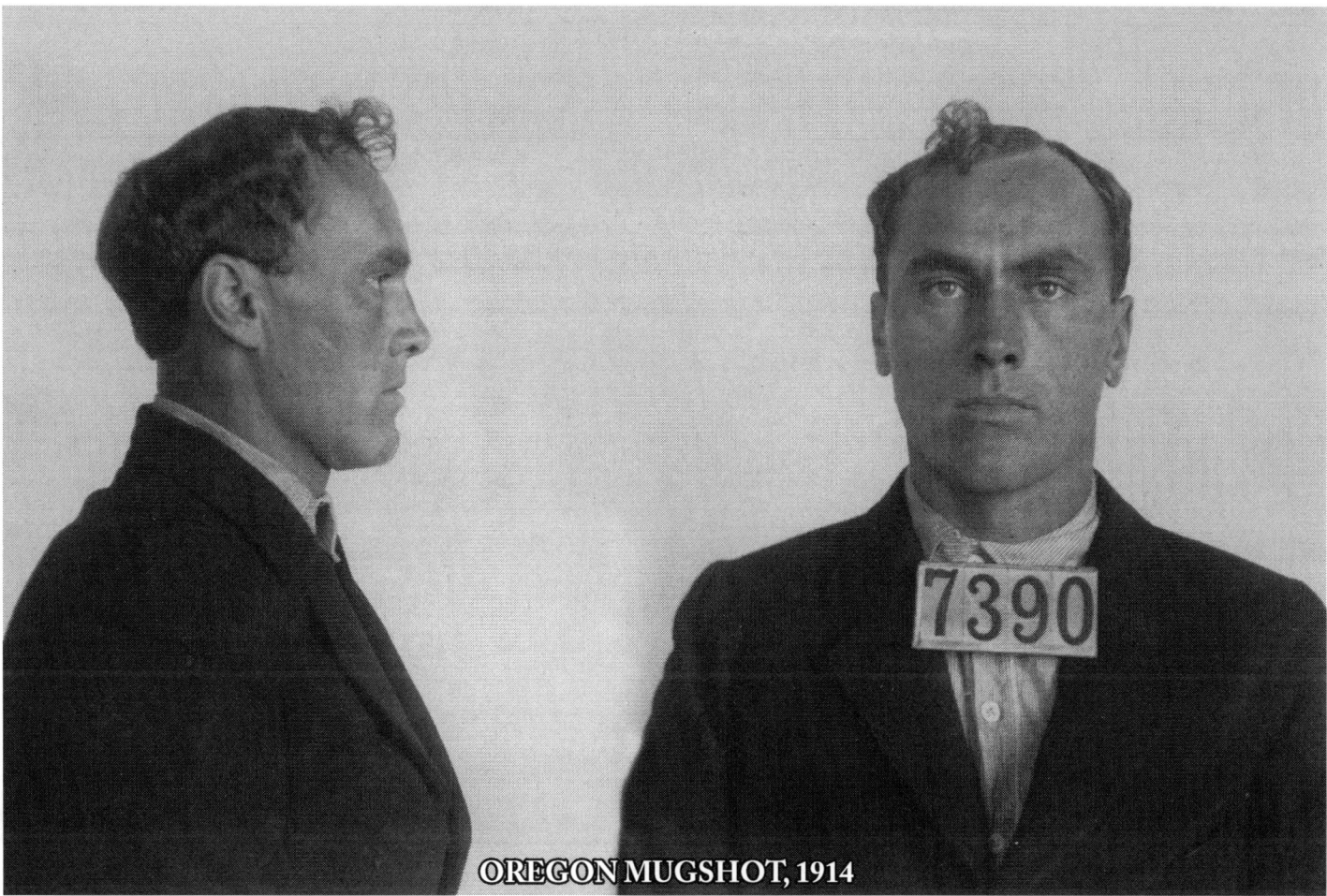

OREGON MUGSHOT, 1914

Oregon State Penitentiary

SALEM, OREGON

NO. 7390

Name Jefferson Baldwin

Alias

Crime Ley. in Dwelling

Age 27   Height 5-9½"

Weight 168   Build Heavy

Hair Med Brown Eyes Gray Blue

Complexion Med. Moustache

Born Alabama

Occupation Thief

Arrested

Received from Clatsop

Sentenced 7 years

HEIGHT	HEAD LENGTH	L. FOOT
76.7	19.3+	27.1
OUTER ARMS	HEAD WIDTH	L. MIDDLE FINGER
87.0	15.9	11.6
TRUNK	CHEEK WIDTH	L. LITTLE FINGER
97.5	15.0	9.7
37 MO	R. EAR LENGTH	L. FOREARM
37 77	6.6	47.4

REMARKS

GENERAL

INFORMATION

NAME, *John O'Leary*

Identification No. B **75182** Color, *W*

Aliases,

Term, *5 - 0*

Date of Sentence, *Oct 1st 1923*

County, *Westchester*

Date of Reception, *4 2nd NYC*

Crime, *Cr. Burg 3d*

Residence (HOME),

Criminal Act, *Express office*

J. J. 3 days   *Jur. Blakley*

ORDER	MARKS, SCARS, MOLES, DEFORMITIES, ETC.
I	Tat anchor fish & heart frm port star @ shea
II	Vac.
	Flag cut @ wt post
	Tat dagger passing thru chinemansd
	frm ant rose ~ anchor & sm butterfly
	frm port star @ shed
III	Sm hor cic ind dx cheek.
	Rd cic ment snake bite dx cheek.
IV	Tat Am. eagle & Later woods ~
	Liberty Justice @ chest

Criminal History

Reform Sch. Montana 1-0 Lar. 1898
Ft Leavenworth Kan. 3-0 Burg 1907
Deerlodge Mt 23 mos Burg 1913

Peculiarities of Habit and Action

State Oregon Prison Salem 3-0 Burg 1914
Escaped by assaulting sheriff awg 8-0 to
Prison tender probaly sentence for assault

SING SING PRISON ⓈⓂⓁ OSSINING, N. Y.

Height	1 m 223	Head lgth	196	L Foot	27.0	Class	1	Age 42 Born in 18—81
Stretch	1 m	Head wdth	16.0	L Mid F	11.7	Areola	lt ble	Apparent Age 42
Trunk	519¾	Cheek wdth		L Lit F		Periph	ORR	Nativity Charlotte Nevada
Curve		R Ear lgth		L Cubit	47.5	Pecul		Occupation

Color L. Eye

Remarks relative to Measurements. 32/32 MO/ S / II

Forehead	Inc	Nose Profile	Bridge	R Ear	Border	lge	Hair	ltch	Beard
	Hght		Base		Lobe		Complexion	peg san
	Width		DIMENSIONS	Teeth		Weight	185
			Height Projection Breadth				
	Pecul			Chin		Build	Lt
			Pecul				

E 75182

STATE OF NEW YORK
Office of Superintendent of State Prisons
BUREAU OF IDENTIFICATION
Capitol, Albany.

Examined Oct 3 – 1923 1
By Tuffo at SS
Reexamined 1,
By at

SING SING PRISON MUGSHOT/IDENTIFICATION CARD, 1923

15

Panzram suffered many tortures at the hands of his captors, who were supposed to keep watch on Panzram and not incite the flames of hatred and anger in him. It is true that Panzram was not an angel. He was a troublemaker. But the ways of dealing with extreme criminals in the early part of America's history was through beatings and tortures. This was the norm.

Panzram describes some of the many tortures inflicted on him:

During my twenty years in all the various prisons and jails I have been in, I have undergone every kind of abuse and punishment that the ingenious minds of many men could devise and, believe me, men can surely figure out some horrible tortures to impose on other men. I have had the whip, the Paddle, the Snorting-pole, the Humming Bird, the Hose, the Jacket, chained up frontwards, backwards, bucked and gagged, spread-eagled, water-cured, starved, beaten, thrown into sweat boxes and half-cooked, thrown into ice-cold dungeons and half frozen. I have been in solitary confinement for years at a time where I could have no privileges or pleasures of any kind. Every single thing in life that men hold worth while and that go to make life worth living for, I have been denied and deprived of. I have gone through every conceivable kind of torture that one man or body of men can impose on another man. I started out in life enjoying it and hating no one. I am winding it up now by hating the whole human race including myself and having no desire to live any longer. I have no desire whatever to reform myself. My only desire is to reform people who try to reform me. And I believe that the only way to reform people is to kill 'em. My motto is: 'Rob 'em all, rape 'em all and kill 'em all.

Panzram describes how he murdered sailors in New York:

I went up to New Haven, Connecticut. There I robbed the home of some one in that place. I got about $40,000 worth of jewelry and liberty bonds. They were signed and registered with the name of W.H. Taft, and among the jewelry was a watch with his name on it, presented to him by some congress or senate while he was the Governor General of the Philippine Islands. So I know it was the same man who had given me my three years in the U.S.M.P. when he was secretary of War about 1906. Out of this robbery I got $3000 in cash and kept some of the stuff. With that money I bought a yacht, the Akista. Her initials and registry numbers were K.N.B.C., 107,296.

On my yacht I had quarters for five people but I was alone for a while. Then I figured it would be a good plan to hire a few sailors to work for me, get them out to my yacht, get them drunk, commit sodomy on them, rob them, and then kill them. This I done. Every day or two I would get plenty of booze by robbing other yachts there. The Barbra II was one of them. I robbed her, and a dozen or so others around there. I was hitting the booze pretty hard myself at that time. Every day or two I would go to New York and hang around 25 South Street and size up the sailors whenever I saw a couple who were about my size and seemed to have money I would hire them to work on my yacht. I would always promise big pay and easy work. What they got was something else. I would take them and all their clothes and gear out to my yacht at City Island. There we would wine and dine and when they were drunk enough, they would go to bed. When they were asleep I would get my 45 Colt Army Automatic I stole from Mr. Taft's home, and blow their brains out. Then I would take a rope and tie a rock on them and put them into my row boat and row out in the main channel about 1 mile and drop 'em over board. They are there yet, 10 of 'em.

Panzram never had a physical address. His places of residence were either rail cars, jails, or prisons. Panzram mentions some of the types of people he has encountered on his journeys:

I have met every kind of a crook there is. I have worked and lived both with and against them. Coppers the same. I know their tricks inside and out. I have associated with every sort, both in prison and on the street. They and their works and their thoughts are like an open book to me. I know them well to my sorrow. I have been mixed up in every kind of a crooked deal there is with every kind of a crook there is. Con-men and gang men. Prowlers and boosters, stick-up artists, can-opener artists and sometimes face artists, peter-men and box-men, paper-hangers and crape-hangers, hustlers and rustlers, pimps and McGimps, hooks from the big town and hooks from the sticks, big shots and pikers, dynamiters and sodomiters, fruiters and poofters, dingbats and gay-cats, shiv-men and gun-men, needle pumpers and snow sniffers, hop heads and jug heads, wise guys and dumbbells, bootleggers and rumrunners, wolves and gunsells, dips and short-card gamblers, home guards and boomers, booze fighters and cop fighters, and last but not least muzzlers and guzzlers. I have put in 35 years in the game of hooks and crooks. I have been from top to bottom and everywhere in between. There is no angle of this game that I haven't tried at some time or other.

In his autobiography to Henry Lesser, Panzram states he murdered 21 people. These murders cannot be verified nor disproved. Panzram always tried to make himself larger than life. He knew he was going to be sentenced to the Federal Penitentiary at Leavenworth, his first in a Federal Penitentiary, which was filled with real bad guys. Panzram most likely created the story of murdering 21 people because he knew he would be around other tough guys and had to build up his reputation to be more than just a common thief.

PANZRAM'S BALTIMORE MUGSHOT, 1928

This most unusual friendship between a prisoner and jail guard is best described by the jail guard himself, where Lesser writes about how he first met Panzram and how he convinced the hate filled criminal to write his autobiography by befriending him:

Recollections of Carl Panzram
By Henry P. Lesser

This is an attempt to set down my recollections of Carl Panzram at the time he was a prisoner at the District Jail, Washington, D., C. awaiting trial and until he entered the gates of the Federal Penitentiary at Leavenworth, Kansas, with a sentence of 25 years on a charge of house- breaking and grand larceny.

Panzram was at the Jail a few weeks before I paid any-particular attention to him. One day as I passed his cell, I struck up a conversation with him. For some reason or other, I thought that he was a habitual and hardened criminal so I asked him, in the midst of the conversation, as to what was his racket. He said, "How do you know?" I answered him diplomatically by saying that I just had such an idea. When I inquired as to the charge placed against him, he replied that he was being held for investigation. He answered me civilly throughout the brief conversation. I may have thought that he was a habitual and hardened criminal because of his physiognomy which did not seem to indicate that he was as kind as the bishop portrayed by Victor Hugo in Les Miserables.

After being at the Jail about two months, he was caught tampering with the bars of his cell window. He had succeeded in prying loose two of the bars. That very day, an hour before this discovery, all of the guards had been gathered together in the office of W. L. Peak, who was in charge of the institution, and warned to watch closely Carl Panzram as there had been received reports from different prisons advising the Warden of the very dangerous criminal in our midst.

W.L. PEAK, D.C. JAIL

Panzram was put into a punishment cell immediately and a few hours afterwards, about 7:00 PM, he was escorted by four Jail guards to the basement of the institution. In the basement are many posts which support iron beams that run directly underneath the ceiling. Each post is about 18 inches in circumference and about 9 feet in height. Panzram was placed with his back against a post, and his hands were handcuffed behind him. A rope was slipped through the cuffs and then tied around the post a few feet above his head so as to extend his arms upward. He was kept in this position for about 12 hours. Eyewitnesses narrated how all night long he shrieked, cursed, and blasphemed. He cursed his mother for bringing him into the world and said that he wished he had a chance to tear her to pieces. He hurled the vilest epithets at the prison officials and a few prisoners who happened to be present. He expressed his desire, in no uncertain terms, to kill them. He wanted to tear their hearts out and throw them in their faces. The Jail physician, Dr. Harris Berman, examined Panzram's heart to make sure that he would not die while at the post because, if that happened, it might create a terrible scandal, and perhaps would result in the removal of the sanctimonious Warden if the truth came out.

While the examination was going on, Panzram taunted the doctor with the charge that he was guilty of committing sodomy upon the body of his assistant, a prisoner. The doctor, of course, resented this unfounded and ridiculous charge and voiced his extreme disapproval in words which only fanned the flames of intense hatred which Panzram held for him. The next morning, the prisoner was taken back to the cell, which happened to be one on the first tier of the South Wing. This cell was one of about six which were only used heretofore for men who were awaiting execution. He was placed in the very first cell that one came to after entering the Wing, so that he could be watched very carefully.

During the course of that day, he called one of the officers who escorted him to the post the night before a "son of a bitch." This officer - knowing him as I do - must have been overjoyed at the opportunity which this offered to have further torture administered to Panzram at the post. A written report of insubordination was made out. The Warden ordered the recalcitrant prisoner be placed at the post again. Four burly guards, anxious and waiting for an opportunity to use physical violence, came into the cell to get Panzram. On the preceding night, he offered no resistance, unaware of where he was going. When the menacing forms of the guards approached, he knew exactly what was contemplated. Offering resistance, he was hit on the head with terrific force by an officer wielding a black-jack. Eyewitness prisoners say that he was kicked and punched by the other guards. A love tap with a blackjack is almost

WASHINGTON D.C. JAIL

WASHINGTON ASYLUM AND JAIL,

Washington, D. C.

CONDUCT   RECORD

CARL PANZRAM   October 4, 1928

CHARGE: Attempted escape.

SPECIFICATION: This prisoner attempted to escape by removing
                 iron bars from his cell window.

DISPOSITION: Cuffed to the post twelve (12) hours. When re-
                 turned to his cell was still cursing his keepers
                 apparently none the worse off from his night
                 spent at the post.

                                                October 4, 1928

CHARGE: Assaulting three officers.

SPECIFICATION: This prisoner, while being removed from his
                 cell, became angry and started fighting. He
                 struck one officer and kicked two others. It
                 was necessary to strike him with a blackjack
                 in order to remove him from his cell and in
                 defense of the three officers.

DISPOSITION: Cuffed to the post for one (1) hour.

                                                October 4, 1928

CHARGE: Cursing an officer.

SPECIFICATION: This prisoner called the Captain of the Watch a
                 "god-damned son-of-a-bitch", and stated that he
                 would like to knock the Captain in the back of
                 the head and then forget about it, like he had
                 done to other men.

DISPOSITION;   Cuffed to the post for one (1) Hour.

20

enough to make one dizzy, so you can believe that the prisoner was knocked out completely. He was put to the post again and stood there all night. When I came to work the following morning, Panzram was sprawled out on a mattress which had been placed on the cell floor.

I learned from the head tiersman, a prisoner, who was in charge of celling men and other work of a routine nature, a full account of the previous night's happening. It was verified by guards who had witnessed all the details. The narration of the brutalities visited upon this defense-less man kindled in me strong indignation and built up a feeling of sympathy for him. I found out that he did not possess any money. A man with money in jail is in a dire predicament; one without money, is indeed unfortunate. I gave the head tiersman a dollar for Panzram. When the tiersman told Panzram that I sent in a dollar, he thought that a joke was being played upon him. "What? A guard sending me a dollar? ! Don't try to kid me." When the tiersman reassured him that it was so, tears came into Panzram's eyes. Here, after being tortured and mistreated by everyone, a guard takes a sympathetic interest in him. Later in the day, when I passed his cell, he stopped me and offered profuse thanks for my gift. I forgot to mention that when the head tiersman said the dollar was from me, Panzram inquired as to how long I had been an officer at the Jail. When the tiersman replied that I had been there over a year, Panzram said that I would become as cruel and obtuse as the others, in time.

If it were not for the fact that I befriended him at this particular time, I Don't think that I would have been able to gain his respect, confidence, and good will which led to his acceding to my request that he write his autobiography for me. We became very friendly, and a spirit of entente cordiale prevailed between us. We discussed the new ideas in penology advocated by such men as Sheldon Glueck, Harry Elmer Barnes in this country, Processor Lippman in Germany, and others. We discussed books, religion, and life in general.

D.C. JAIL CELLS

Panzram most likely did commit sodomy on other men as a form of revenge, but there is no proof that he murdered the people who he confessed to killing when he entered the DC jail.

Even though Panzram was served a warrant for the homicide of Alaxendar Uzzake (Uzzoke) in Philadelphia, the District Attorney in DC, Rover, was smart enough to realize there was not enough evidence to charge Panzram in the Philadelphia murder. "His conviction followed a series of sensational confessions to Maj. William Peak, superintendent of the District Jail, in which he declared that he had killed a boy in Salem, Mass., and another in Philadelphia. Details of the confessions were sent to the police of those cities and officers came here to question Panzram. In Philadelphia he was indicted and extraditing proceedings started. District Attorney Rover, however, insisted that Panzram be tried here first on the housebreaking charge as the evidence in the murders was not regarded as conclusive as that in the burglary case here." -Washington Evening Star, June 20, 1929, p.1. Newspaper accounts can be (and usually are) inaccurate as they operate on quick deadlines for stories. As Panzram was an avid reader of periodicals, he could have easily read about these murders in newspapers when he was in those cities.

Panzram most likely read about the unsolved child murders and remembered them, so if he ever received a long conviction, he could pull them out of his back pocket. He knew the prison system and law well enough that he knew he would be facing a long stretch of time to serve in a federal prison. Panzram's intention is to definitively state his own version of the facts. But when a reader researches into Panzram's entire case, it is easy to wonder what part of his writings are fact and which are fiction.

Newspaper articles talk about a witness who saw Panzram with the McMahon boy in Salem, Massachusetts but witnesses have proven to be wrong on many occasions. In the Albert Fish case, a court trial was undertaken against Charles Edward Pope, who Delia Budd identified in a line up as the kidnapper of her daughter, Grace Budd. Pope resembled Fish, but he was not the kidnapper of Grace Budd as years later Mrs. Budd received a letter written by Albert Fish describing how he killed and ate her daughter. In his claim of murdering a boy in New London, Connecticut, the police stated: "Police today are inclined to view the confession made by Carl Panzram that he murdered a boy here in 1922 a hoax, as records fail to show any violent deaths of children during that year."

CITY OF PHILADELPHIA, SS.

THE COMMONWEALTH OF PENNSYLVANIA

TO ANY POLICE OFFICER OR CONSTABLE OF SAID CITY, GREETING:

You are hereby commanded to take the bod y of Carl Panzram ....

....

If ....he............be found within the said City, and bring ..him............before EDWARD J. HOLLAND,

a Magistrate of the said City, sitting as Committing Magistrate at the Central Police Office, to answer the

Commonwealth of a charge founded on the oath of Joshua H. Hepburn, #Room 666 ....

With Homicide on one Alexander Uszacke, by Strangling and Choking, on

July, 26th, 1928 at Point House Road.

....

and for so doing this shall be your warrant.

Witness EDWARD J. HOLLAND, a Magistrate of the said City, who hath hereunto set his

hand and seal the ....27th.............day of....October.......................

in the year of our Lord one thousand nine hundred twenty eight

Edward J Holland [SEAL]

COMMITTING MAGISTRATE

BELIEVE PANZRAM MAY BE SLAYER SALEM BOY

Washington Prisoner Confesses to Slaying Boy in Greater Boston

Description of Prisoner Corresponds with Suspect—May Seek Extradition

Carl Panzram's booking photo from the Salem Police Department, Mass.

Ex-Convict Gloats Telling Of Boys' Fiendish Murders

By JOHN E. NEVIN

WASHINGTON, Oct. 27. — Carl Panzram, who confessed here last night that he had committted "several" murders, told detectives that had he been able to obtain a barrel of arsenic he would have murdered all the guards and officials of Dannemora Prison in New York.

Panzram, a bitter sour man of 40, confessed to the murder of 14-year-old Alexander Luszzock, a Philadelphia newsboy, last August, and also that of 12-year-old Henry McMahon, of New Salem, Conn. He promised detectives that later he would give them the details of other murders.

Panzram was committed to the Dannemora prison in 1923 for a five-year term. In discussing his stay there, he said to detectives:—

"I like to murder. If I ever had some money I would have given the cops plenty of murder to talk about. Why, when I was in Dannemora prison in New York, if I had had $1,000, I would have poisoned every ——— in the place.

"I found out where the prison reservoir was, and if I could have bought a barrel of arsenic I would have dumped it in and killed all of them, especially the cops. I hate cops, but not as bad as stool pigeons."

Panzram had just finished telling of attacking a boy and then wrapping a belt around his neck.

"Was he dead when you did this?" a detective asked.

"You're damned right he was," Panzram answered.

"If all this ain't enough," he continued, "I'll give you plenty more. I've been all over the world and I've seen everything in the world but hell, and I guess I'll see that now. I don't care for any ——— anywhere, and I want to die."

SAYS HE MURDERED BOY

Confession by Carl Panzram Believed to Be Hoax

New London, Conn., October 26.— Police today are inclined to view the confession made by Carl Panzram that he murdered a boy here in 1922 a hoax, as records fail to show any violent deaths of children during that year.

No date.
(Approx. 10-25-28)

Prosecuting Attorney,
Salem, Mass.

About three weeks ago I made a voluntary confession to you about a murder that I committed near Salem in July 1922.

I heard nothing more about it until yesterday when I was called from my cell to the Wardens Office here where I was told that two of the men present were from Massachusetts.

I was asked to tell my story in detail. This I refused to do. Then I was asked about 11,000 questions most of which had no bearing on the point at issue. Most of these questions I refused to answer at all.

I am willing to answer and give a truthful answer to any questions concerning this case of murder at Salem, Mass.

There is always a proper place and time for everything to be done and the place for me to tell my story is in open Court and the time for it is when I am being tried for the crime.

I do not change my story or retract my confession in any way. I am guilty of the murder of a young boy whose name I dont know but who I believe was McMahon. This boy was about 11 or 12 years old and his home was about 2 or 3 miles from where his body was found. I believe that his home was at Salem. I was told by him that his Aunt ran a store on the right hand side of the street going up the hill from the car tracks about 3 or four blocks from the main street. When I first saw this boy he was near his Aunts store. He had a small pail or basket and was going to the store for something. When I met, him, I offered to give him 50¢ to help me do a small errand, to carry some luggage for me. This he promised to do but first he had to leave the pail or basket in the store. I walked with him to the store where I waited outside the door while he went inside for a moment or two. There were several people there who saw us both at that time. When he came out of the store we walked down the street to the street car tracks and waited for a car. Plenty of people saw us there while waiting for the car. When we got on the car the conductor took particular notice of us. Some of the passengers also. We rode the car for a mile or so, got off at a quite a lonely spot near a slough which we walked thru for several hundred yards and then went into the woods. When we got into the woods I grabbed him by the arm and told him I was going to kill him. I stayed there in the woods three hours with him and during that time I had sexual intercourse with him 6 times. Then I took a rock and beat him over the head until he was dead. I left him there and went away. The next day or so I read in the papers where he had been found. The police were looking for his murderer dressed in a blue suit and a green cap. I was in Newport, Rhode Island at that time and there I broke into a house thru a window where I cut my hand which left blood all over the house. I tore up a sheet from one of the beds wrapped my hand up in it. I then threw away my green ca

(OVER)

picked up another one there. When I left that house I went to Providence.

These are the true facts of the case and the main points at issue. I do not care to talk to anyone here but I am willing to talk to you or anyone else in open Court.

I have not talked to any newspaper reporters although there have been a dozen of them here who have tried to talk to me.

The main reason why there is so much misunderstanding here is because there are a number of people here who are out after the reward and some of them have made mistakes which can and will be explained at the proper time. I did not make this confession to anyone but you, the Prosecuting Attorney at Salem, Mass.

I am Yours truly,

/s/ Carl Panzram.

Alleged Robber Admits Two Murders

Says He Killed Boy in Boston, Philadelphia and Robbed a Newport Home

Washington, Oct. 5 —A voluntary confession of the alleged slaying of two young boys in eastern cities and the robbery of the New Haven, Conn., home of Chief Justice Taft was announced yesterday by Washington police to have been made by Carl Panzeca of East

Criminal No. 47446

Supreme Court
District of Columbia

UNITED STATES
v.
CARL PANZRAN

RECORD OF CONVICTION

TRIAL BY JURY

FEB 1 1929

U. S. GOVERNMENT PRINTING OFFICE: 1936   196596

5319

Hq ____ Precinct.

No. ____ 315101

UNITED STATES

-vs-

#1

Carl Panzran

#2

Joseph Czeswenski

Nolle

WARRANT   House Breaking

WITNESSES:

Louis H Wilson M P Hq

I W Forster

3620 Macomb St N W

9/18/28

9/22/28.

Aug 27 1928

over

SEP 22 1928 ____ 192

#1 Plea ____ Not ____ Guilty

Held to await the action of the Grand Jury.

Committed to Jail in default of recognizance

in the sum of $ ____ 10,000 ____ to appear

in the Supreme Court, D. C. entered in

____,192

Robert E Bradley

Baltimore M. A. Hq.

Police Headquarters, D C

AUG 27, 1928

Received and forwarded for Service.............

FILED

SEP

PANZRAM'S TRIAL FOR HOUSE BREAKING

Note one of the first misspellings of Panzram's name as PANZRAN.
Could Panzram have given the fake name as an alias, or was it just a mistake?

I remember once while I was guarding him in the bathroom, where he was taking his weekly shower, he made the observation that, although be was guilty of inflicting cruelty upon others practically all his life, he resented others treating him likewise and squawked about such treatment continuously.

One day I entered his cell to make the weekly inspection which included the testing of bars. A heavy piece of iron was used to test bars. When he saw me enter his cell, he immediately jumped up from the mattress which was on the cell floor. Then he said, "I guess you are all right; you won't harm me." He resumed his former position.

On another occasion when I entered his cell to inspect the bars, my back was turned to him while I was making the inspection. He could have jumped and relieved me, if he so desired, of my iron bar with which he could have terminated my penological career. When I was ready to leave his cell, he said, "Gee! You're brave to turn your back on me." I didn't reply at the time but later I spoke to him. I said, "Carl, I did not turn my back to you because I was brave. I turned my back to you because I had confidence that you would not harm me. We have been getting along so nicely together." He replied, "I don't want to harm you but you better be careful because I am so erratic that I'm liable to do anything."

He said at times that he was a disciple of Schopenhauer, believing in the philosophy of pessimism. Carl was of the opinion that everyone was selfish and looking out for his own welfare. He believed that people who were good or kind or generous couldn't act otherwise if they wanted to.

It was Christmas Eve. A choir in the rotunda, within hearing of Panzram, had just completed singing carols. I passed his cell and, looking in, I noticed that Panzram was standing with the fly of his trousers unbuttoned. His penis was in plain sight of anyone who might look. It was told to me many times by prisoners who were allowed out on the first tier and who were able to pass Panzram's cell in performing their duties, that Panzram used to pace the cell, jingling a few stray coins in his pocket and repeating all the while, "I would give everything I had for a nice hole." He would work his fingers to represent one while making this assertion.

Christmas cards were being distributed to the offenders. Z., a prisoner, gave them out. He wanted to have a little fun with Carl, so instead of telling him that the Episcopal City Mission presented it, he informed Carl that it was a gift from the Warden, Excitedly, Carl threw it out of his cell door. Carl was very anxious to send a Christmas gift to Warden W. L. Peak in the form of a pineapple. At that time, not knowing what was meant by a "pineapple", I asked him to explain. He looked at me with a haughty air. He said that in the jargon of the criminal a "pineapple*"was a bomb.

One day as I was talking to Panzram through the bars of the cell door, I called his attention to a beautiful sunset which could be seen through his cell window. As I said, "Look over there, Carl," he jumped away from where he was standing and appeared very frightened and excited. When I asked him the reason for this reaction, he said that he thought for the moment that I was trying to divert his attention in order to assault him with some object. He had been used to having his attention diverted in the past, for this reason. Upon second thought, I apologized to him for pointing out the beautiful sunset because he couldn't have been in a mood to appreciate it.

Panzram's brother, who lives in the State of Washington, hired a counsel for Carl. In a letter to Carl, he said that newspapers at home were carrying accounts of his criminal activities. He implored Carl to trust in Jesus Christ and give up his criminal career. Carl reminded the brother of the time when the family gathered a sum of $75 with which Carl was to leave for South America and try to behave. The brother to whom Carl was writing this reply kept the money instead of forwarding it as arranged. He reminded the brother of the brutal manner in which he was treated by him after Carl, when a boy of about 12, attempted to shoot a German preacher in revenge for whippings administered by him. He told his brother that he had killed 21 human beings during his life and had further violated all the laws of man and God. He complained in the letter that no one ever had pity on him. Carl suggested that the brother use the pilfered $75 with which to purchase a gun. Carl said, "As you are a nut on religion like our father, go out into the woods, read your fool Bible, and then blow your brains out." He ended the letter by requesting the brother not to write any more.

In the Supreme Court of the District of Columbia

HOLDING A CRIMINAL TERM

District of Columbia | *to wit:* _____ October _____ Term, A. D. 19 2 8

We, the Grand Jurors of the United States of America, in and for the District aforesaid, upon our oaths, do **Present** _____

Carl Panzram

Housebreaking & Larceny

at the District aforesaid, on the 26th *day of* _October_ , A. D. 19 2 8

This presentment made on the evidence of _____

Dr. Louis W. Eugster,

George F. Klennick,

Joseph Czerwinski,

David Schloss

Louis M. Wilson, M. P.

William E. Mothershead

Foreman.

31

Supreme Court of the District of Columbia

HOLDING A CRIMINAL TERM

THE UNITED STATES

31614   *v.*

CARL PANZRAN

Criminal No. 47446

INDICTED FOR Housebreaking and Larceny

Come as well the attorney of the United States as the defendant , in proper person, in custody of the Superintendent of the Washington Asylum and Jail, and by _____ attorney , _____

Defendant acted as his own attorney

and thereupon the defendant , being arraigned upon the indictment, plead **s** thereto not guilty, and for trial put **a** himself upon the country, and the attorney of the United States doth the like; whereupon comes a jury of good and lawful men of the District of Columbia, to wit:

1. Ernest H. Ehlis
2. Harry Feldman
3. Gus Galamis
4. Albert Jaeger
5. Charles W. Johnston
6. Clarence A. Langley
7. Abraham C. Luber
8. Malcolm Reintzel
9. Millard T. Thodes
10. Mrs. Alice L. Gilchrist
11. Mrs. Audrey E. Koons
12. Mrs. Jeanne L. Fensterer

who, being sworn well and truly to try the issue above joined, upon their oath say that the defendant is guilty in manner and form as charged in the indictment; whereupon it is demanded of the defendant what further he has to say why the sentence of the law should not be pronounced against him , and he says nothing except as he has already said; whereupon it is considered by the Court that for his said offense the defendant be taken by the Superintendent aforesaid to the Washington Asylum and Jail aforesaid whence he came, thence to the Penitentiary (as designated by the Attorney General of the United States), there to be imprisoned for the period of FIFTEEN (15) Years on the 1st count of the indictment, and TEN (10) YEARS on the 2nd count of the indictment xxxxxxx said sentence _____, to take effect from and including this date, and to run consecutively. (In all 25 Years)

I HEREBY CERTIFY that the foregoing is truly taken from the record of proceedings of the Supreme Court of the District of Columbia.

IN TESTIMONY WHEREOF, to this exemplification, I hereunto subscribe my name and affix the seal of the said Supreme Court, this 12ª day of November, in the year of our Lord one thousand nine hundred and twenty-eight, and in the one hundred and Fifty-third year of the Independence of the United States of America.

WITNESS, the Honorable WALTER I. McCoy, Chief Justice of said Court, the

12ª day of November, 19 28

FRANK E. CUNNINGHAM
Clerk.

By _____
Asst Clerk

IN THE POLICE COURT OF THE DISTRICT OF COLUMBIA

Aff. No. ....

District of Columbia, ss:

To the Major of Police of the District of Columbia, Greetings:

Whereas   Louis M Wilson   hath upon oath before me, Presiding Judge of the Police Court of

the District of Columbia, declared that on the ...8th... day of August A.D. 192 8 , at the District

aforesaid, that one... Carl Panzram   and   Joseph Czeswenski

did feloniousiy break and enter the ..premises, 3620 on Macomb Street North West.

of... L W Eugster
in the ..night.... time, and did feloniously steal, take, and carry away ....

..one radiola 18, radio........................ of the value of ..seventy five.............. Dollars,
.... of the value of .... Dollars,
.... of the value of .... Dollars.
.... of the value of .... Dollars,
.... of the value of .... Dollars,
.... of the value of .... Cents,
.... of the value of .... Cents,
.... of the value of .... Cents,
.... of the value of .... Cents.

all lawful money of the United States, of the goods and chattels...
of L W Eugster

against the form of the statute in such case made and provided, and against the peace and Government of the

United States of America.

    You are therefore hereby commanded to take the said....................................
Carl Panzram   and   Czeswenski

and bring .. them .... before the Police Court forthwith to answer charge.

    Witness   The Hon. GUS A. SCHULDT, Presiding Judge of the Police Court of the

District of Columbia, and seal of said Court, this ....27th...

day of........august......................................in the year of our Lord one thousand

nine hundred and twenty....eight

....
Clerk, Police Court, D. C.

BY..
Deputy Clerk, Police Court, D. C.

OCT 1 1928

IN THE SUPREME COURT OF THE DISTRICT OF COLUMBIA

Holding a Criminal Term.

District of Columbia, ss: October Term, A. D. 1928

The Grand Jurors of the United States of America, in ahd for the District of Columbia, aforesaid, upon their oath, do present:

That one Carl Panzran, late of the District of Columbia aforesaid, on, to wit, the eighth day of August, in the year of our Lord one thousand nine hundred and twenty-eight, and at the District of Columbia aforesaid, the dwelling of one Louis W. Eugster, there situate, feloniously did enter, with intent to commit therein the crime of larceny, to wit, with intent the goods, chattels and property in the said dwelling, then and there being, feloniously to steal, take and carry away; against the form of the statute in such case made and provided, and against the peace and government of the said United States.

SECOND COUNT:

And the Grand Jurors aforesaid, upon their oath aforesaid, do further present:

That the said Carl Panzran, on, to wit, the said eighth day of August, in the year of our Lord one thousand nine hundred and twenty-eight, and at the District of Columbia aforesaid, one mechanical devise commonly known as a radiola receiving set, of the value of one hundred dollars, three suits of clothes, each of the value of thirty dollars, two cuff links, each of the value of five dollars, and one watch, of the value of five dollars, of the goods, chattels and property of one Louis W. Eugster; one watch, of the value of thirty dollars, one chain of the value of thirty dollars, one finger ring, of the value of fifty dollars, one comb of the value of ten dollars, two combs, each of the value of five dollars, and six earrings, each of the value of five dollars, of the goods, chattels and property of one Alice R. Eugster, then and there in the said dwelling being found, feloniously did steal, take

and carry away; against the form of the statute in such case made amd provided,

and against the peace and government of the said United States.

Attorney of the United States, in
and for the District of Columbia.

Walter M. Shea, being first duly sworn, deposes and says:

That during the month of November, 1928, he was an Assistant United States Attorney in and for the District of Columbia; that on November 12th, 1928 one Carl Panzran was tried in the Supreme Court of the District of Columbia, Criminal Court No. One, in case No. 47446, on a charge of housebreaking and larceny; that during the trial of said case in said Court Panzran acted as his own attorney; that during the trial of said case one Joseph Czerwinski of Baltimore, Maryland testified as a witness on behalf of the United States and testified that certain jewelry involved in the case on trial was given to him in Baltimore by Panzran. At the conclusion of direct examination of the witness Czerwinski, Panzran was asked by Assistant United States Attorney Collins if he wished to ask any questions of the witness. Panzran then had the following conversation with the witness Czereinski: "Do you know me? Take a good look at me." When the witness looked at Panzran, Panzran drew his fingers across his throat and said in effect to Czerwinski: "I promise you that you'll get it." At the conclusion of the Government's case, the defendant took the stand and admitted breaking into the man's house and stealing the property in question and further stated that he remained in the house for several hours with the hope that the owners or occupants of the house would return so that he might kill them.

This affidavit is made at the suggestion of Chief Justice McCoy before whom the case was tried so that the parole will not be granted this defendant during the twenty-five year sentence he is now serving in the case.

s/s Walter M. Shea.

Subscribed and sworn to before me this seventh day of December, 1928.

s/s Milford F Schwartz,
NOTARY PUBLIC, D.C.

SEAL

COPY:

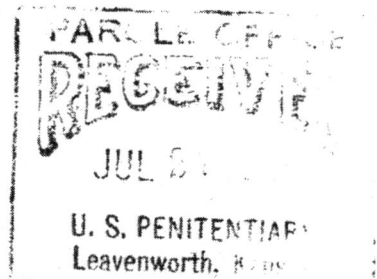

Panzram wrote a letter, asking for his salary, to a man for whom he had worked as a farm hand for a while before being arrested on the charge which led to his incarceration at the District Jail. According to Carl, the man owed him about $10. The former sent him about $2, instead. Panzram returned the money order and suggested to the farmer that he buy some cyanide of potassium with the money, to swallow one-half of it himself and send the remainder of it to the writer.

I don't know how true it is but I was told that, when Carl was in a cell with other prisoners, he administered to one of them, a sick man, with great tenderness.

I happened to be one of the officers named to accompany 32 prisoners, among whom Panzram was included, to the Federal Penitentiary at Leavenworth, Kansas. Panzram, on the way out of the Jail, passed the Warden's secretary, a prisoner who took down Carl's confession to the murder of three boys. Carl made this confession on the second night of his torture at the post. Carl spat upon this prisoner. Carl was heard to remark to a prisoner, while on the way in a police van from the District Jail to Union Station to board the train, that he would try to cause a train wreck. Before we boarded the train. Warden W. L. Peak, who also made the trip, advised the railroad authorities. The emergency cord which runs beneath the ceiling of the coach was disconnected. I understand that pulling the cord while the train was running fast would cause some cars to leave the track.

Panzram was shackled and handcuffed to a prisoner by the name of S. who was very disappointed in getting Carl as a partner. S., you see, was very much like the rest of us, only he liked and did steal keisters (luggage). Like nearly all the prisoners on the train, Carl spent his time playing cards, for money. Whenever Warden Peak got in sight of Carl, he made all kinds of disparaging remarks of a sexual nature in order to taunt the Warden. He gazed intently at the Warden, with eyes burning with hatred, seething with a lust to kill him. He also reacted this way whenever he caught sight of Dr. Berman who, by the way, stood up all night watching Panzram closely, fearing to go to bed lest some- thing direful should happen to him at the hands of the prisoner. As Panzram's legs were securely shackled and his hands cuffed, and as the guards watched him every second, there was very little possibility of anything like this happening.

I remember Carl's thumbing his nose at boys while the train was at a standstill at one of the stations en route. He talked to me in a friendly manner and smiled occasionally at me while on this journey. When he left the train, he gave me a warm hand-shake.

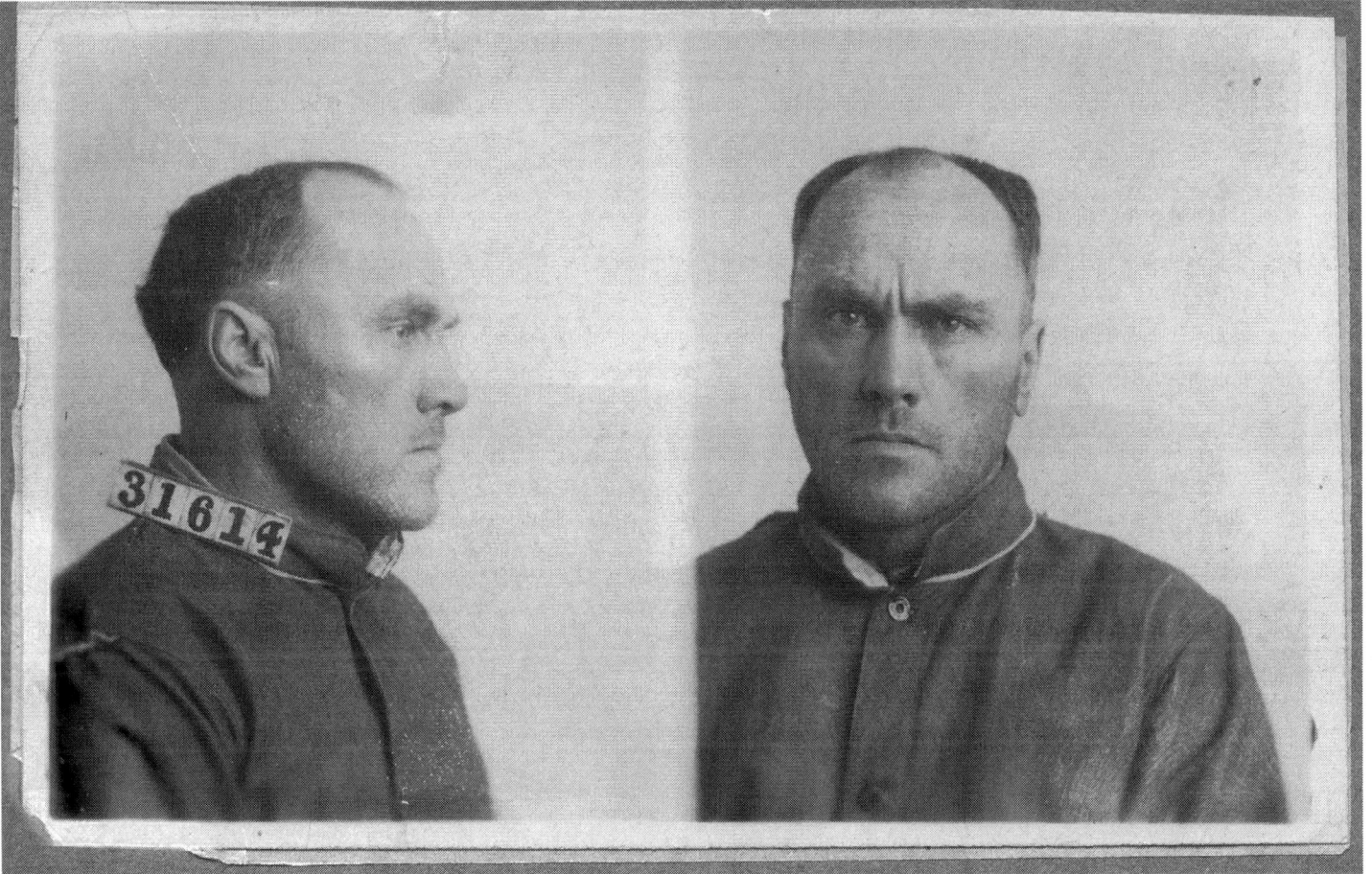

PANZRAM'S LEAVENWORTH PENITENTIARY MUGSHOT

"...when I came here, I told every one I came into contact with that I would surely knock off the first guy who ever bothered me."
- Carl Panzram

LEAVENWORTH PENITENTIARY, LEAVENWORTH, KANSAS

USP LEAVENWORTH GROUNDS AND GATE

CELLS AND GALLERIES - USP LEAVENWORTH

TOM WHITE, USP LEAVENWORTH WARDEN, 1926-1931

"After Panzram's admission I had several conferences with the Deputy Warden about Panzram, and advised the Deputy what word Major Peak had passed to me, and to endeavor to assign to him to some part of the institution where he would be under close supervision, and the Deputy Warden accordingly assigned him to the laundry, about the best place we have for such supervision."
                                                                        -Warden White

Name Carl Pangram
Alias

Classification No. 32 O O I
                    32 I I M

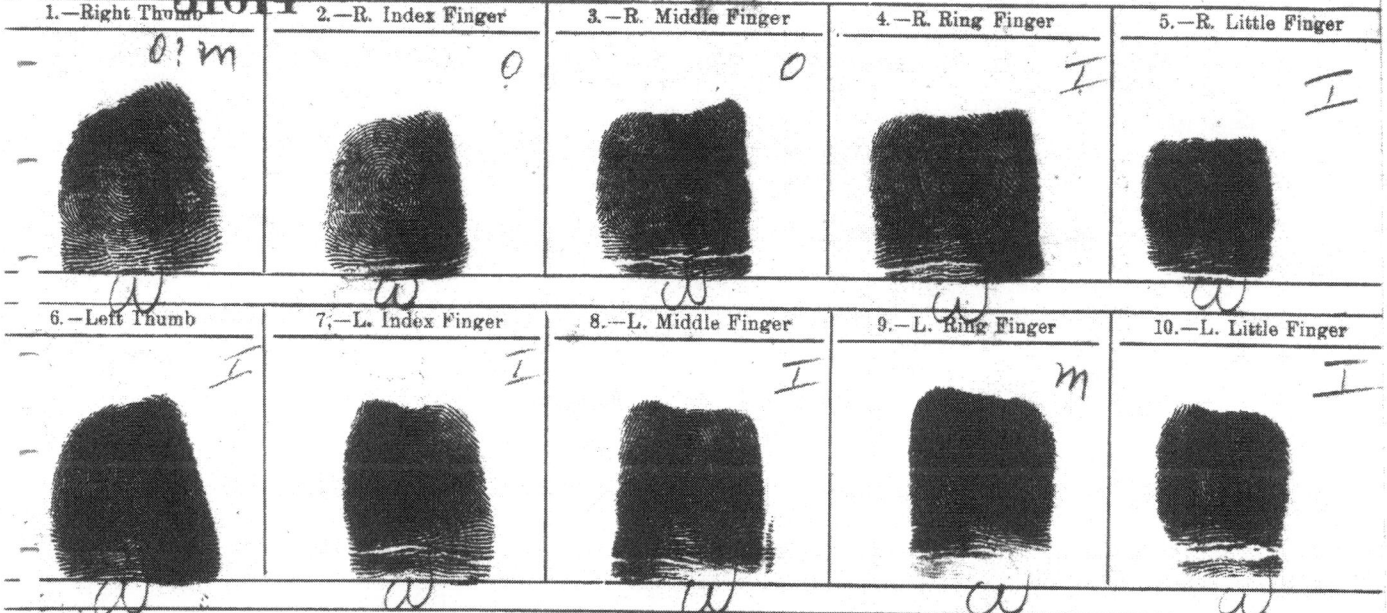

No. 31611   Color White

1.—Right Thumb	2.—R. Index Finger	3.—R. Middle Finger	4.—R. Ring Finger	5.—R. Little Finger
O ? m	O	O	I	I

6.—Left Thumb	7.—L. Index Finger	8.—L. Middle Finger	9.—L. Ring Finger	10.—L. Little Finger
I	I	I	m	I

Age 36   Sex Male   Height 5'-9-3/8"   Weight 185

Hair Blk tr gy   Eyes Med sl.   Comp. Lt.

Build Muscl.   Chin Med proj.

Taken by .... Date ....

Classified by .... Date ....

Carl Pangram.
Prisoner's Signature

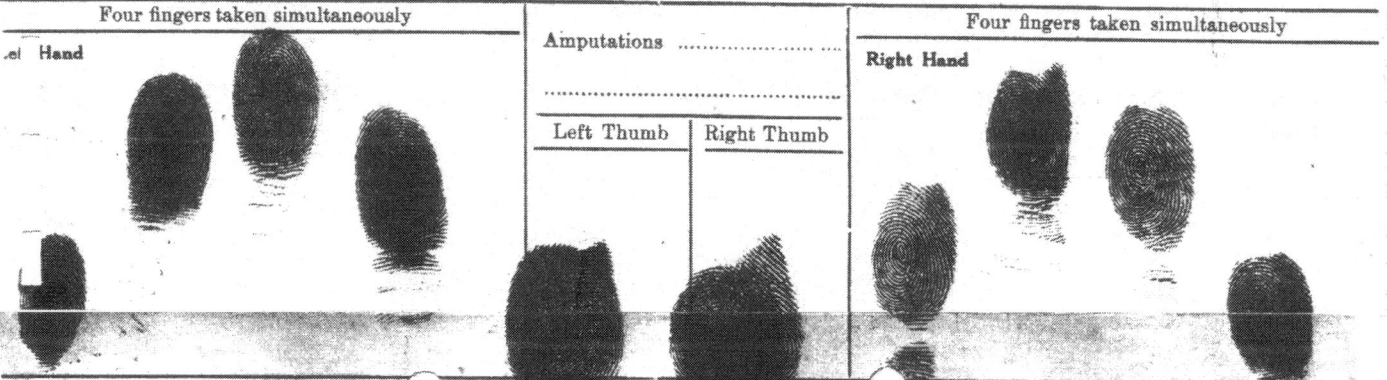

Four fingers taken simultaneously — Left Hand

Amputations ....

Left Thumb	Right Thumb

Four fingers taken simultaneously — Right Hand

Received Feb 1 1929
From D-Washington, D.C.
Crime House breaking and larceny.
Military or Civil Prisoner Civil
Sentence 25 Yrs. .... Mos. .... Days
Date of sentence Nov 12 1928
Sentence begins Nov 12 1928
Sentence expires Nov 11 1953
Good time sentence expires Aug 25 1945
Date of birth Parole date Mar 11 1936
Birthplace Minn.
Religion None.
Occupation Sailor.
Education 5 th grade

3556

Physical Scars
Ears med lge. Teeth 1 go low lft frt.
3 out up lft.

Tattoo 5 pt star on pt lft shldr. Anchor on lft
fore arm. Rose & leaves and stem. Navy anchor
head of Chinese Mandaran pierced by dagger on
rt fore arm/ Five pt star on rt pt shldr.
Double eagle. 5 pt star and words in print,
" Liberty- Justice" on chest.

Previous convictions over.

45

UNITED STATES PENITENTIARY
LEAVENWORTH, KANSAS

Name   Carl Panzran.   Register No. 31614   Color white.

Alias   ▬▬▬▬ John O'Leary- Jefferson Baldwin-
Jeff.Davis-Jeff Rhodes-

Crime   House Breaking and Larceny

Received   Feb. 1, 1929   From D-Washington, D.C.
(1-10 yr and 1-15 yr sent consec)

Sentence   25 years   Fine, costs, etc.

Date of Sentence   Nov. 12, 1928   Sentence begins   Nov. 12, 1928

Maximum term expires Nov. 11, 1953   Minimum term expires Aug. 25, 1945

Good time allowed   3000   days.   Eligible for parole   Mar. 11, 1936

Civil or Military   Civil   Occupation Sailor.   Age 36

Where arrested Baltimore,Md.   When   August 13th.1928.

How long in jail before trial since arrest.   Nativity Minn.

How long in U.S. all but 5 yrs.   Citizen of U.S. yes.

Father living?   no.   Mother living? no.

Name of Father   Name of Mother

Present address of parents

Nativity of Father ??   Nativity of Mother ??

Married no.   Wife living   Children   Boys   Girls

Wife's name and present address

Your residence   ??

In case of sickness or death, notify No one.

Education: Read   Write   Common school 5th grade High school   College

Religion   Preference none

Chew tobacco yes.   Smoke   yes.   Drink   yes.   Use Opium or Morphine no.

Ex-Service Man Yes. Army 1 month.

(OVER)

46

FORMER CONVICTIONS

Where served   U.S.D.B., Ft.Leavenworth,Kansas.   No.   1874

What name   Carl Panzram.   Crime   62nd article of war

Term of sentence   3 yrs.   When and where sent from   Ft. Harrison Helena Mont.
                                                                      1906

Released, when and how   Exp. 1910

Where served   Minn State Training School   No.   2532

What name   same name.   Crime   Stealing.

Term of sentence   until 21.   When and where sent from   East Grand Forks,Minn.
                                                                     1902 Or 1903.

Released, when and how   Paroled 1904 or 1905.

Where served   State Reform School Miles City,Mont.   No.   ??

What name   Same name.   Crime   Larceny

Term of sentence   1 yr.   When and where sent from   Butte,Mont. 1905

Released, when and how   Escpaed 1906.

Where served   State Pen. Deer Ldge,Mont.   No.   ??

What name   Jeff Davis.   Crime   Burglary

Term of sentence   1 yr.   When and where sent from   Chinook,Mont.
                                                                     1913 or 1912

Released, when and how   Escaped   after 8months.

In the event of my death while in the Federal Penitentiary, Leavenworth, Kansas, I hereby direct that my personal effects, including any money remaining to my credit in, or due me from, said penitentiary, shall, immediately after my death, be transmitted to

No one.

whose address is —————————————————————————————————————

x Carl Panzram.

Register No. —————————————————————————————————

Witnesses   D.E. Winterburg
             T.R. Rowan

47

United States Penitentiary
Leavenworth, Kansas
CHAPLAIN'S OFFICE

No. 31614   Date Feb. 1-1929

Name Carl Panzram   Color White   Age now 36

Address _____   Alias Jeff Davis

Committed from Washington, D.C.   Occupation Seaman

Nationality American   Descent German

Sentenced to 25 yrs. _____ mos. For House Breaking & Larceny   Pleaded guilty not

Reason for the act _____

Born in {City / Country} Country Yes   Read Yes   Write Yes   School 5th   Where Minnesota

Where were Parents born? Germany   Left home at 11 yrs.

Religion Agnostic   Preference _____

Mother alive no / Father alive no   died when inmate was { don't remember years of age / " years of age } Brother alive none / Sister alive none

Married now no   Divorced no   Widower yes   Children ___   Living ___   Dead ___

Is your family provided for? ___ Have you a business or position waiting for you upon release? ___

If so, what? ___

If not, what do you intend doing? ___

Available cash upon entering here 1.00

Chew Yes   Smoke Yes   Used liquor moderately Yes to excess no abstainer no

Narcotics {Dealer no / User no}

Wishes to correspond with no one relatives ____ friends

RECORD

Penitentiary Dannamora 5 yrs. Reformatory Red Wing Minn

Jail ___ yrs. ___ mos. (If Alien note here) Yes

Ex-Service man Yes   Army-Navy Detachment Army 6th Inft

Length of service 1 month   Serial Number ____

48

UNITED STATES PENITENTIARY

Leavenworth, Kansas

Date __Febry 5thm1929.__

Examination of __Carl Panzran__   Register No. __31614__

Received __February 1st,1929__ From __Washington, D.C.__ Age __36__ Race __White__

Crime __Larceny__   Sentence __25 Years__   Exp. Short Time ....

Eligible for Parole ....   Occupation __Sea Man__

Married: ~~Yes~~ No ...... Height __5__ feet __8½__ inches   Weight __172__ Lbs.

General Physical Condition: Good ~~Fair~~ ~~Poor~~   Posture __Slightly stooped.__

Head __Negative__	Pupils { Regular ~~Irregular~~	Equal ~~Unequal~~	React to Light and Distance	Yes ~~No~~

Ears __Negative__   Nose __Negative__   Throat __Negative__

Teeth: ~~Good~~ ~~Fair~~ Poor   Chest __Negative__   { Inspiration __41½__ / Expiration __39__

Abdomen __Negative__   Back __Negative__   Hernia __No__

Heart __Negative__   Pulse { Regular / Irreg. } In F & R { Good / Fair / Poor } In T & V ......

Genitalia __See Remarks.__ ~~Negative~~   Gonorrhea { ~~Yes~~ / No / ~~Doubtful~~ }   Syphilis { ~~Yes~~ / Denied / ~~Doubtful~~ }

Legs __Negative__   Feet __Flat__   Use Tobacco { Yes / ~~No~~ }   Liquors { Yes / ~~No~~ }

Drugs { ~~Yes~~ / No } C M O H { Grains per day for .... yrs. .... mos. } Treatment { Yes / No }
  Off habit for .... yrs. .... mos.

Wasserman .... Urinalysis .... Blood Count ....

REMARKS. Tattoo both arms and shoulders and chest.
None on Back.
Right Testicle extracted.

For previous Record
See reverse side
of sheet

Examined by _[signature]_
Physician

Feb. 9, 1929.

31614

District Attorney,
Room 666 City Hall,
Philadelphia, Pa.

Re: Nos. 1457-8

Dear Sir:-

Notations have been made on our records showing that Carl Panzram, our Register No. 31614, will be wanted by you upon the expiration of his sentence here. His minimum term expires Aug. 25, 1945.

You will be notified thirty days prior to the release of this prisoner in order that you may have an officer here to take him into custody.

Respectfully,

McC/r

Warden.

REGISTER NO. **31614**

UNITED STATES PENITENTIARY
LEAVENWORTH, KANSAS

Panzram — 2 — 1 — 192 *9*

Name	Crime	Years	Months	Days	Color
Carl Panzram	Robbery	25			

Money $1.00   Stamps *none*

Watch _____

Knife _____   Shaving Brush _____

Ring _____   Safety Razor _____

Purse _____   Books _____

Cuff Buttons _____   Coins _____

Collar Buttons _____   Fountain Pen _____

Keys _____   Metal Pencil _____

Frat. Pin

Miscellaneous   *1 pipe delvd*

Prisoner's Signature: *Carl Panzram.*

Officer Searching *Vincent Harper*

Panzram had a one dollar bill on his possesion when he entered Leavenworth USP. The 1$ be may be the same dollar which Henry Lesser gave him.

51

Previous arrests and convictions:

As Carl Panzran, U.S.D.B. Ft. Leavenworth, Kan. NO. 1874, 62 Article of war, from Ft. Harrison, Ind. 1906 3 yrs.

As Carl Panzran, Minn. State Training School, Stealing, from East Grand Forks, Minn. 1902 Or 1903, Until 21. Paroled 1904 or 1905.

As Carl Panzran, State Reform School, Miles City, Mont., Larceny, 1 yr, from Butte, Mont. 1905.

As Jeff Davis , State Gen. Deer Lodge, Mont., burglary, 1 yr, from Chinook, Mont. 1912 or 1915.

As Jeff Rhodes, from State Pen., Deer Lodge, Mont. Burglary, from Three Forks, Mont. 1912, 1 yr.

As Jeff Davis, State Pen , Deer Lodge, Mont., Escape from foret conviction,1914 1 yr.

As Jefferson Baldwin, Oregon State Prison, Burglary, 7 yrs., from Asroria, Ore. 1914. Escaped 1915.   No. 7390

As Jefferson, Baldwin, Oregon State Prison,   2 yrs Robbery, 8 yrs Assault, 10 yrs, from Eugene , Ore. No.7390. Escaped 1918.

As John O'Leary, Barlinnie Prison, Glasgow Scotland, Theft, from Glasgow, Scotland, 1919. Served 10 days and deported.

As John O'Leary, Sing Sing, N.Y. No. 75182, Burglary, 5 yrs, from White Plains, N.Y. August 1923.

As John O'Leary, Bridgeport Conn., Fairfield County Jail, Burglary, 6 months, from Bridgeport, Conn. 1921.

3 6 4

Leavenworth, Kansas Feb. 16. 1929.

Warden.—

When I arrived here on Feb. 1, 1929, I brought with me, one sea-bag and one hand-bag. which contained my personal belongings.

among my things was.

1 = Ingersol watch and small chain

1 = mirror

1 = Gem Safty razor.

1 = Fountain Pen

and also a number of other things.

I would like to have everything that I am permited.

I have been given to understand that it is permited to have such things here in this place.

If this is the case, will you please allow me to have my things.

The officer in charge of the Package Room advised me to write this note to you because there has been some sort of a mix up in the property belonging to me and some other man.

I am

Carl Panzram.
No. 31614.
Cell 138. D.

Not Permitted.
B.W.
Warden

Warden White furnished a photostat copy of a letter addressed to District Attorney Clark, Salem Mass, under date of February 19, 1929, signed by Carl Panzram, Register No. 31614, reading as follows:

"In my reading of the newspapers lately I noticed that you have made a statement that you are going to have me brought to trial for the murder of George Henry Mc Mahon of Salem about seven years ago.

I write you this letter to notify you that I waive all of my extradition rights and am quite willing that I should be brought back to Massachusetts for trial for murder.

I made a full confession of this murder of Mc Mahon, while I was in the Jail at Washington, D.C. You sent a number of witnesses from Salem to identify me, which they done.

Now I have since then been sentenced to 25 years and am now confined here in this prison.

I do now change my former confession in any way. I commited that murder. I alone am guilty. I am not sorry. My consicence does not trouble me. I sleep sound and have sweet dreams. I am not insane. I not only committed that murder but 21 more besides and I assure you here and now that if I ever get free and have the opportunity I shall sure knock off another 22.

I am very truly Carl Pangram #31614."

Leavenworth, Kansas *March· 12,* 1929·

Deputy Warden·

I understand that there are a number of warrents against me here. Several for murder and one for being an escaped convict from Oregon.

Will you please let me know how many warrents there are against me, Where they are from and what charges?

I believe that I am legaly entitled to this information but if not then I should like to have whatever information on this subject, that you see fit to allow me to have.

I am very truly

Carl Panzram.
#31614
Cell 138. D.

Laundry

31614

MAR 14 1929

ACTING

THE PRISON LAUNDRY

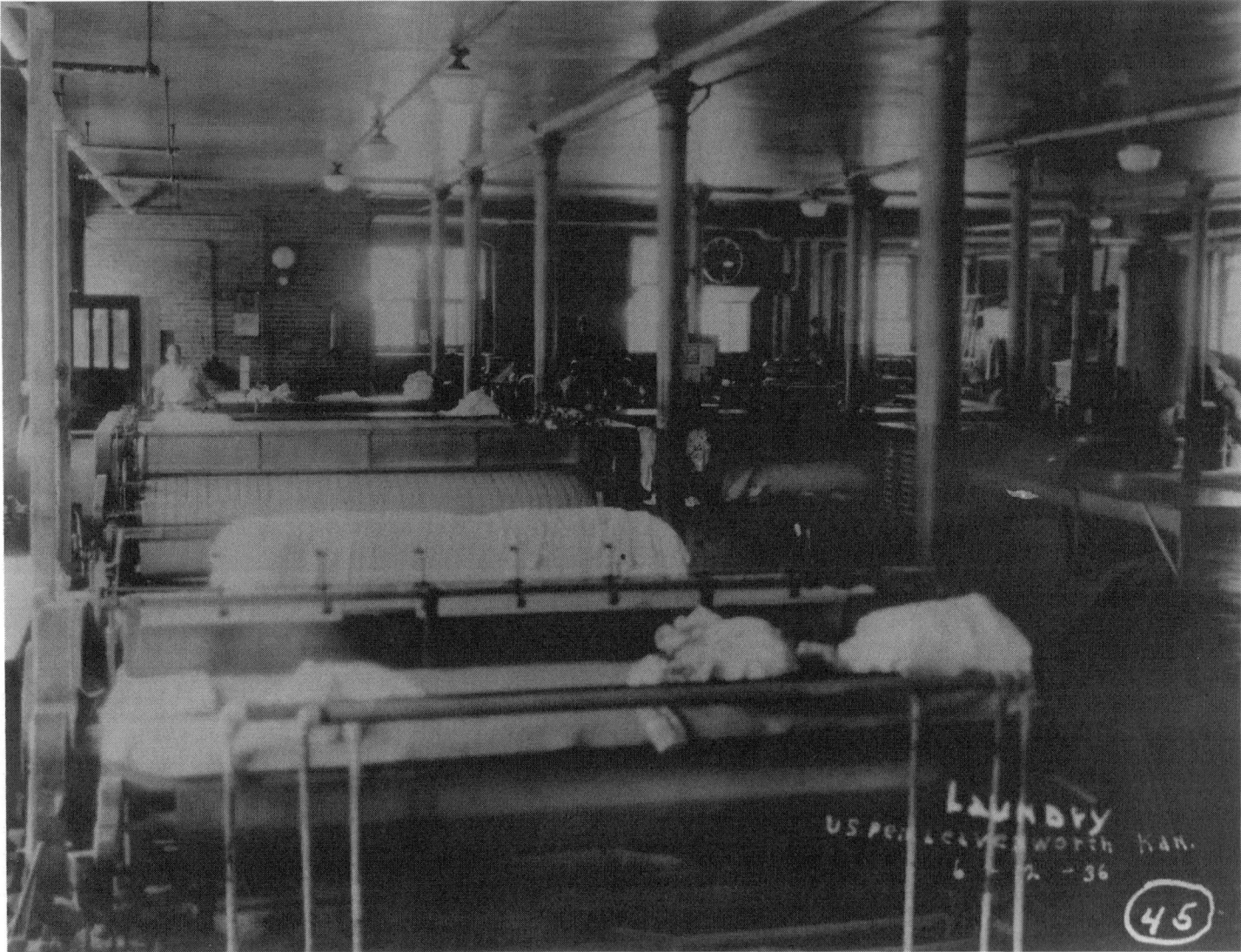

INTERIOR LAUNDRY BUILDING

EXTERIOR LAUNDRY BUILDING

ROBERT WARNKE
Leavenworth's Prison Laundry Foreman.

Leavenworth, Kansas March 26, 1929.

Deputy Warden.

I respectfully ask that you give me the job in the Cement Shed from which you today changed Ben Craven to the laundry.

I want that job because I am doing a long time and I am an old crank and I want to be by myself. I am a cripple and the job I have now I don't like; standing on my broken ankles bothers me.

I am very truly

Carl Panzram
31614
Cell 138. D.

31614

P.S.

You can watch me on that job just as well as you can where I am now and I wont be any more apt to get into mischief any quicker there than where I am now.

Leavenworth, Kansas April 1, 1929.

Mr. Henry James.
  % Miss Elanor Trott.
    The Lenmar. Apt 4 7.
      2100. N. St. N.W.
        Washington.
          D.C.

Mr. James:

Your letter of March 30th was handed to me this evening and I am answering at once to thank you for it and its enclosure of one dollar. Your letter was quite short but straight to the point as usual. I enjoyed reading it and I expect to enjoy the spending of your dollar. I never got the post card which you sent me.

This is my first letter since I have been here. I shall be glad to hear from you at any time you care to drop me a line. You can write to me without sending me any money. I'll be glad to hear from you just the same and I'll allways answer you.

There is very little news that I can give you because there is none to give so far as I know. I have been here 2 months today. Nothing very unusual has happened to me so far. I have been treated just the same as every-body else here. I have no complaints of any kind. What the future may have in store for me I dont know or very much care. Your postscript in regards to Allen was the natural result to be expected considering the conditions and circumstances in which he was situated. He will be the gainer in the long run. That sort of a man will allways be up in front sooner or later.

I believe you know the regulations about my privilege in letter writing. So please dont ever send me any thing unless your sure I'll get it. I dont need anything. I can manage all right. My wants are very little and I think

62

On April 1, 1929, Panzram sends his first letter to Henry Lesser from Leavenworth USP. Lesser assumed the alias of Henry James, creating a fictitious identity so his position at the DC jail would not be compromised if it was discovered that he was corresponding with Washington D.C.'s former inmates, especially a prisoner as controversial as Panzram. Lesser would surely have had a stern reprimand, especially under Peak. Panzram asks about Lesser's ladyfriend, who was Eleanor Trott, Lesser's girlfriend. Mrs. Trott was typing all of Panzram's letters into manuscript format for Lesser.

April 1, 1929

Mr Henry James
c/o Miss Elanor Trott
The Lenmar Apapt. 47
2100 N. St. N.W.
Washington D.C.

Mr. James:

Your letter of March 30th was handed to me this evening and I am answering at once to thank you for it and its enclosure of one dollar. Your letter was quite short but straight to the point as usual. I enjoyed reading it and I expect to enjoy the spending of your dollar. I never got the post card which you sent me.

This is my first letter since I have been here. I shall be glad to hear from you just the same and I'll always answer you.

There is very little news that I can give you because there is none to give so far as I know. I have been here 2 months today. Nothing very unusual has happened to me so far. I have no complaints of any kind. What the future may have in store for me I don't know or very much care. Your postscript in regards to Allen was the natural result to be expected considering the conditions and circumstances in which he was situated. He will be the gainer in the long run. That sort of a man will always be up in front sooner or later.

I believe you know the regulations about my privilege in letter writing. So please don't ever send me any thing unless your sure I'll get it. I don't need any thing and I think I can manage all right. My wants are little and I think I can satisfy them. I have met a number of my old pals in here who knew me years ago. I still have my perpetual grouch and I don't believe it will ever wear off until I pass out completely. That time can't come too quick for me. Just at present I pass my time in sleeping, eating, working, reading, and thinking. And the last is not the best.

I have wondered about you a number of times and since reading your letter, the thought has occurred to me that you may be keeping house or getting ready to. The name sounds English. Kind of musical too. I had hopes though that you by this time would have found yourself in a better job with more congenial surroundings and a cleaner atmosphere. Take my tip and drop that job like you would poison. That's no kind of a job for you. your built for better things than that. How is your lady friend and yourself getting along in your writing the Biography of the meanest man you ever knew. I have been passing my time away by scribbling a bit now and then. So far I have written about 30 or 40 thousand words. Should you ever come to this and if you cared for it I would gladly make you a present of my little contribution to the worlds worst literature. You owe me nothing but I consider myself under some obligation to you. Well, I'll wind up this tale of woe, by saying So Long and best wishes.

I am very truly

Carl Panzram. #31614
Box. 7. Leavenworth.
Kansas.

I can satisfy them. I have met a number of my old pals in here who knew me years ago. I still have my perpetual grouch and I don't believe it will ever wear off until I pass out completely. That time cant come too quick to suit me. Just at present I pass my time in sleeping, eating, working, reading and thinking. And the last is not the least.

I have wondered about you a number of times and since reading your letter, the thought has occured to me that you may be Keeping house or getting ready to. The name sounds English. Kind of musical too. I had hopes tho that you would by this time have found yourself in a better job with more congenial surroundings and a cleaner atmosphere. Take my tip and drop that job like you would poison. That's no kind of a job for you. Your built for better things than that. How is your literary lady friend and yourself getting along in your writing the biography of the meanest man you ever knew. I have been passing my time away by scribbling a bit now and then. So far I have written about 30 or 40 thousand words. Should you ever come to this place and if you cared for it I would gladly make you a present of my little contribution to the worlds worst literature. You owe me nothing but I consider myself under some obligation to you.

Well, I'll wind up this tale of woe, by saying So Long and best wishes.
I am very truly

Carl Panzram #31614.
Box. 7.
Leavenworth.
Kansas.

THE AMERICAN MERCURY

H. L. Mencken, EDITOR . Alfred A. Knopf, PUBLISHER · Samuel Knopf, BUSINESS MANAGER

730 FIFTH AVENUE · NEW YORK

Cables: KNOPF NEW YORK
Telephone: CIRCLE 7670

April 6, 1929.

Dear Mr. Lesser:

I doubt that I could use the Panzram manuscript in The American Mercury, and so I hesitate to ask you to send it to me. It seems to me that the story of such a man ought to get scientific attention, and so I suggest that you get into communication with Doctor Carl Murchison, of the Clark University at Worcester, Massachusetts. As you probably know, he wrote a book on criminal intelligence two or three years ago. He is now in charge of the University publications at Clark, and it is probable that he'd be greatly interested in the Panzram manuscript. There should be no difficulty about sending it. Let it go by express. In any case, the postoffice would certainly not scrutinize such a thing too closely. Its scientific value would undoubtedly protect it against attack.

Have you ever thought of doing any articles yourself? If so, I'll be delighted to get a chance at them. Certainly there should be some good stuff in your observations of criminal ways. If any definite ideas occur to you, let me hear of them.

Sincerely yours,

Henry Lesser wrote to H.L. Mencken, American journalist and scholar, about publishing Panzram's autobiography.

Copy of my letter to H. L. Mencken written sometime in 1929

Dear Mr. Mencken

I waited to answer your very kind letter of April 6, 1929 until a duplicate copy of the Panzram manuscript came again into my possession. I am mailing it to you today.

My only purpose in submitting the writings is because I sincerely believe you will be profoundly interested in its contents.

As you suggested, I will get in touch with Dr. Carl Murchison of the Clark University at Worcester, Massachusetts concerning the manuscript.

If I ever write about my observation of criminals, anything which I consider significant and of sufficient merit to meet the high standard required of articles appearing in the American Mercury, I shall certainly let you know.

Sincerely and Admiringly,
Henry P. Lesser

THE AMERICAN MERCURY
730 FIFTH AVENUE
NEW YORK

SPF · NEW YORK   Telephones: CIRCLE

May 25, 1929.

Dear Mr. Lesser:

This is one of the most amazing documents I have ever read. Obviously, printing it in a general magazine would be impossible. Moreover, I doubt that it could be done as a book for general selection. The man to handle it effectively is Dr. Murchison. I hope that you let him see it. Meanwhile, my best thanks for sending me the manuscript. I can't recall reading anything more shocking.

Sincerely yours,

GEORCE G. HENRY
CHIEF INSPECTOR

JOHN J. SANTRY
STEPHEN G. NELSON
GEORCE E. LURZ
INSPECTORS

31614

4/26/29

Warden,
    U.S.Penitentiary,
      Laevenworth,
        Kansas.

Dear Sir:-

    Kindly send me a copy of the criminal record of one
Carl Panzram, your #31614; Received from Washington. D.C. 2/1/29;
I am writing his complete record, and have one record that states
he served a term of three years, crime Burglary, in 1907.

    I will send you a copy when record is complete.

        Ypur Respectfully.

George G. Henry,

        Chief Inspector.

(W.P.B.)

P.S. Send reply to Bureau of Identification, Police Head quarters,
Baltimore, Md.

Leavenworth, Kansas April 23. 1929

Mr Henry James.
℅ Miss. E. Trott.
Lenmar Apts.
No 2100 N. St. N.W.
Wash. D.C.

Your letter of April 18th reached
me today. I found the one dollar enclosed or at
any rate I got it to my credit here on the books.
Many thanks for both. I have only had your
letter about an hour and I have read it three
times allready and liked it better each time.
Pretty nice letter all right and quite interesting
too. I am glad to hear that your all right and still
feel a bit interested in me. You asked me what
sort of work I am doing. Well to tell the truth I have an
easy job. not very much to do and that little easy.
I dont mind it much but I am trying to get a diff
job where I'll be more by myself. Perhaps later on
I'll manage it. It makes me feel better to hear
that your autobiography is going to get a reading
by such a man as Mencken. Should he accept
it and publish it, I would like to get a subscription for 6 months or so. Can you manage
that for me? I will be permitted to recieve the
magazine if it comes direct from the publisher.
You ask if I would care for some books. Well
yes I would like to get some good books but
the kind I want I cant have. One thing I would
like to have and that will be permitted me is

Leavenworth, Kansas April 23, 1929

Letter from Carl Panzram to Henry Lesser.

Your letter of April 18 reached me today. I found the one dollar enclosed or at any rate I got it to my credit here on the books. Many thanks for both. I have only had your letter about an hour and I have read it three times already and liked it better each time. Pretty nice letter all right and still feeling a bit interested in me. You asked me what sort of work I am doing. Well to tell the truth I have an easy job. Not very much to do and that little easy. I don't mind it much but I am trying to get a different job where I'll be more by myself. Perhaps later on I'll manage it. It makes me feel better to hear that your autobiography is going to get a reading by such a man as Mencken. Should he accept it and publish it, I would like to get a subscription for 6 months or so. Can you manage that for me? I will be permitted to receive the magazine if it comes direct from the publisher. You ask if I would care for some books. Well yes I would like to get some good books but the kind I want I can't get. One thing I would like to have that will be permitted me is a dictionary one about 100,000 words will be all right. But there is no rush about it. I can manage that all right by and by. I am earning a little money by making some bead, necklaces, and curios which I am thanking you for. The money which you sent to me I used in buying the material I used in making these things. Now what I wanted to ask of you was this, if I send you some of the things I make, can you and will you sell them for me and send me the money? Let me know about this will you? I have done a good bit of writing and up to date I have written about 60,000 words. But I am afraid that it is all a wasted effort as I don't know what to do with it now that I have written it all out. Should you ever come here and have an hour or two to spare, then maybe you could have me called out for a visit. Use your own judgement about that. You probably won't have time but if you could spare an hour or two I should be glad to see you and talk to you. I have been here about three months now and so far I haven't been in any jams yet. I am getting along all right but I am still pretty hostile and I might blow up any time. I am awful, awful weary and I am hoping that I'll find some way of getting a rest. I hope it won't be too long to wait. You better take my tip and ditch that lousy job you have right now. There's lots better ways for you to make a living. Well I'll have to ring off for this time so. So Long and good luck.

I am Carl Panzram
No 31614 Box 7
Leavenworth. Kansas

a dictionary. one about 100,000 words will be all right. But theres no rush about it. I can manage that all right by and by. I am earning a little money by making some bead, necklaces, and curios which I am thanking you for. the money which you sent to me I used in buying the material I used in making these things. Now what I wanted to ask of you was this, If I send you some of the things I make, Can you and will you sell them for me and send me the money? Let me know about this well you? I have done a good bit of writing and up to date I have written about 60,000 words. But I am afraid that it is all a wasted effort as I don't know what to do with it now that I have written it all out. Should you ever come here and have an hour or two to spare, then maybe you could have me called out for a visit. Use your own judgement about that. You probably wont have time but if you could spare an hour or two I should be glad to see you and talk to you. I have been here about three months now and so far I haven't been in any jams yet. I am getting along all right but I am still pretty hostile and I might blow up any time. I am awfull, awfull weary and I am hoping that I'll find some way of getting a rest. I hope it wont be too long to wait. You better take my tip and ditch that lousy job you have now. Theirs lots better ways for you to make a living. Well I'll have to ring off for this time so, So Long and good Luck. I am   Carl Panzram.
No 31614 Box 7.
Leavenworth. Kansas.

70

Panzram's April 23, 1929 letter to Lesser mentions wanting to work by himself. Panzram could have wanted a job change and makes sense as he was a loner and despised other people. Panzram may have been asking for a job change so he could attempt to escape from another area of the prison.

In mid-April, inmate Louis Kelly witnessed a verbal altercation between Panzram and the laundry foreman, Robert Warnke, in regards to Panzram's bleaching handkerchiefs. Bleach is a controlled substance inside correctional facilities because it is corrosive and caustic. Panzram may have been bleaching handkerchiefs for other inmates to gain extra money, cigarettes, or other items. Exchanging a service for something of value is highly prohibited. Panzram's actions seemed to be overriding Warnke's rules. There was definitely a power struggle going on between Warnke and Panzram in the laundry. Prisoner Louis Kelly relates:

> Panzram and Mr. Warnke had a few words over three handkerchiefs which Panzram had and was washing in a bleacher in the laundry. Warnke told him that he was not permitted to use that bleacher, and that he was not any better than any of the rest and that no one was allowed to use that bleacher. Panzram argued, saying that he was only trying to bleach three handkerchiefs, but Mr. Warnke said he could not have his rules run over and repeated that Panzram was no better than the rest of the prisoners employed in the laundry. He, Panzram, remarked that if Warnke did not "lay off him" he would "get" Warnke.

UNITED STATES PENITENTIARY
LEAVENWORTH, KANSAS

May. 18. 1929.

Undersigned Prisoner requests audience with the

Deputy Warden.

for the following reason:

Change of job.

Name Carl Panzram.

Reg. No. 31614.

MAY 18 1929

Audience held_____192

DISPOSITION OF CASE

This man wants a job in a bath room. No change.

May 18, 1929 – Panzram requests another job change to a bathroom. "No change" written by the Deputy Warden, Fred Zerbst. It may have been easier for Panzram to escape from Leavenworth while working in another location within the prison.

Leavenworth, Kansas May 19. 1929.

Deputy Warden,

Yesterday I had an interview with you. At that time you told me to let you know if I could suggest any jobs in this prison which I could handle and where I would be by myself.

Now I have 3 different jobs in view either of which I would like to have.

One job is in the basement of A. Cell House. Running the hot-air blower. The man who has that job now is a crippled white man.

Another, and a similar job is in the basement of B. Cell House. The fellow who has that job now is called Bill, his number is 20725 and he has only a short time left to serve and then his job will be vacant.

Another job is in the tool room of the steel shop. The man who has that job now has 8 months left to serve.

Should I have any choice in this matter, I would preffer the job in the basement of either A. or B. Cell-House running the blower.

In any case I would like to get out of the Laundry where I am now.

I am.
Carl Panzram.
No 31614
Cell 138. D.

72

May 19, 1929

Panzram letter to Deputy Warden Zerbst.

Deputy Warden:

Yesterday I had an interview with you. At that time you told me to let you know if I could suggest any jobs in this prison which I could handle and where I would be by myself.

Now I have 3 different jobs in view, either of which I would like to have.

One job is in the basement of Q. Cell House. Running the hot-air blower. The man who has that job now is a crippled white man.

Another and similar job is in the basement of B. Cell House. The fellow who has that job now is called Bill, his number is 20725 and he has only a short time left to serve and then his job will be vacant.

Another job is in the tool room of the steel shop. The man who has that job now has 8 months left to serve.

Should I have any choice in this matter, I would prefer the job in the basement of either A or B Cell House running the blower.

In any case I would like to get out of the laundry where I am now.

I am
Carl Panzram
No 31614
Cell 138 D.

31614

Leavenworth, Kansas May 19. 1929.

Mr Henry James.
℅ Miss E. Trott.
Lenmar Apts.
No 2100 N. St. NW.
Washington
D.C.

I recieved your last letter on April 23. and
since then I have been impatiently waiting
for another. This is my third letter since
you wrote me. But I have enough time to write
letters but I suppose you have a few other things
to do besides troubling yourself about me.
When you do write me again I wish you would
tell me as much as possible about Mr
Menchens reply to your. In your last letter
to me you asked me if I wanted any books
or reading matter, and if it would be permitted
to recieve any. The type of reading matter which
I prefer is taboo here and I can manage pretty
well with what I get now. I intend to get myself
a dictionary and encyclopedia in 6 volumes
as listed in Montgomery Ward Co. catalog
It costs 8 dollars and if I ever get that
amount of money together I intend to get
one of those sets -
      While browsing thru an old batch of
misselanous magazines the other day, I struck
an exceptionaly interesting article in th
American Magazine of the March, 1929 issue
Look it up and let me know what you think

74

Leavenworth, Kansas May 19, 1929

Letter from Carl Panzram to Henry Lesser.

I received your last letter on April 23, and since then I have been impatiently waiting for another. This is my third letter since yours to me. But I have enough time to write letters but I suppose you have a few other things to do besides troubling yourself about me.

When you do write me again I wish you would tell me as much as possible about Mr. Menchems reply to you. In your last letter to me you asked me if I wanted any books or reading matter and if I would be permitted to receive any. The type of reading matter which I prefer is taboo here and I can manage pretty well with what I get now. I intend to get myself a dictionary and Encyclopedia in 6 volumes as listed in Montgomery Ward Co. catalog. It costs 8 dollars and if I ever get that amount of money together I intend to get one of those sets.

While browsing thru an old batch of miscellaneous magazines the other day, I struck an exceptionally interesting article in the American Magazine of the March 1929 issue. Look it up and let me know what you think of it. It's title is, "My seven minutes in Eternity" and it was written by Bill Pelley. I think it will be of interest to you.

If I send you a bead hand-bag which I have made in my spare time would you be good enough to either buy it yourself or sell it for me and send me the money? I'll leave the price to you. Any thing you say goes.

That's all for this time.

So Long and Good Luck. I am,
Carl Panzram
Leavenworth, Kansas.

Leavenworth, Kansas May 25. 1929.

Mr Henry James.
% Miss E. Trott.
Lemmas Apts.
2100 N St. N.W.
Wash. D.C.

Enclosed in this letter you will find a small hair watch chain and charm. It only took me a week to make it, in my spare time, a few minutes or an hour at a time. I am allowed to send out but one package each month. I would send more if I could. I spend my spare time doing such things as this, with a little reading throwed in with a lot of thinking. Next month I'll send you a bead neck-lace. I recieved your letter of May 20th. Pretty short all right. but, let's hope your next will be longer and contain more. this one was full of paper but the only interesting thing in it was your comment about Sinclair's aroused interest in his oil well at Bocas Del Toro, Panama. Tell him not to blame me even tho I am the one who touched it off. A big sham by the name of Morriss was the real cause. He canned me when I was doing all right and everybody else was satisfied. His mistake cost Harry a hundred grand. Years later I heard from other fellows like myself that Harry was and is a pretty good old scout to my kind of people. But being sorry didn't rebuild his oil rig. Maybe I earned a part of it back for him by the work I done for him on his oil field

May 25, 1929 - Leavenworth, Kansas

Letter from Carl Panzram to Henry Lesser.

Enclosed in this letter you will find a small hair watch chain and charm. It only took me a week to make it, in my spare time, a few minutes or an hour at a time. I am allowed to send but one package each month. I would send more if I could. I spend my spare time in doing such things as this. With a little reading throwed in with a lot of thinking. Next month I'll send you a bead neck-lace. I received your letter of May 20th. Pretty short all right. But lets hope your next will be longer and contain more. This one was full of paper but the only interesting thing in it was your comment about Sinclair aroused interest in oil well in Bocas Del Toro, Panama. Tell him not to blame me even though I am the one who touched it off. A big man by the name of Mowriss was the real cause. He canned me when I was doing all right and everybody else was satisfied. His mistake cost Harry a hundred grand. Years later I heard from other fellows like myself that Harry was and is a pretty good old scout to my kind of people. But being sorry didn't rebuild his oil rig. Maybe I earned a part of it back for him by the work I done for him on his oil field down in Angola, Portugese West Africa. If you will take the trouble to look up the back files of the Saturday Evening Post for 1923 or 1924 you will find a series of articles written by a Mr. Marcosson about the oil business, among them you will find my picture, taken at Quimbazie way up the Quanza River. I was driving a tie of big buck cannibals and they were hauling a boiler on a long rope, hooked up two abreast just like oxen. Only they didn't have as much brains as an ox. If you look these things up you must remember that at the time I was sailing under the name of Capt. John O' Leary. Harry may not know me but surely will have heard of me from a Mr. Crandell one of his Directors in his Co. or Mr. Williams his Supt in Loanda, Angola. Old man Mowriss sure knows me to his sorrow. He must have wanted me pretty badly when he offered $500.00 for me. I would like to hear him roar when, "If ever he does", hear that I am the one who put such a crimp in his plans. I done it because he was bull-headed and wouldn't let well enough alone. Well I have gossiped enough now so I'll quit writing and start walking up and down the floor talking to myself, cursing a blue streak and every once in a while having a good hearty giggle. But what I got to giggle about I cant figure out yet. But that cuts no ice So

Carl Panzram.
31614 Box 7
Leavenworth, Kansas

down in Angola, Portuguese West Africa.

If you will take the trouble to look up the back files of "The Saturday Evening Post" for 1923 or 1924 you will find a series of articles written by a Mr Marcosson about the oil business, Among them you will find my picture, taken at Quimbage way up the Quanga River. I was driving a team of 80 big buck canibals and they were hauling a boiler on a long rope, hooked up two abreast, just like oxen. only they didn't have as much brains as an ox. If you look these things up you must remember that at that time I was sailing under the name of Capt. John O'Leary. Harry may not know me but he surely will have heard of me from a Mr Crandellon, one of his directors in this Co. or Mr Williams his Supt in Loanda. Angola. Old man Mowriss sure knows me to his sorrow. He must have wanted me pretty badly when he offered $500.00 reward for me. I would like to hear him "roar, when, if ever he does, hear that I am the one who put such a crimp in his plans. I done it because he was bull headed and wouldn't let well enough alone. Well I have gossipped enough now so I'll quit writing and start walking up and down the floor, talking to myself cursing a blue streak and every once in a while having a good hearty giggle. But what I got to giggle about I can't figure out yet. But that cuts no ice to

Carl Panzram.
31614 Box 7.
Leavenworth.
Kansas.

PHOTO FROM *THE SATURDAY EVENING POST*

The "Saturday Evening Post" photo which is featured in an article in the January 26, 1924 issue where Panzram states that there is a photo of him with workers in Africa. The person leading the African natives in the photo MAY be Panzram, but it is impossible to tell for certain as his face is obscured in the photo.

31614

Leavenworth, Kansas June 15, 192 9.

Mr Henry James
% Miss E. Trott.
The Lenman Apt 47.
No 2100 N. St. N.W.
Washington
D.C.

Your Letter of June the 8th reached me the other day. That was a pretty nice letter all right. Full of news, and all of it good. I was a bit surprised to read what Mencken wrote to you. I didn't have much faith in the thing being worth while, but when any one like Mencken says its good I must believe it. You use your own judgement and do just as you like about it. The Yours and what you do with it is O.K. by me. I should like to read the article by The Nation about Older but Thats out of order here. Send no clippings. I am still on my same job and like it less each day. I am getting all set for a change. It wont be long now. I think your out of luck for the other 15,000 words I wrote her. Thats out of order also. Glad your friend was pleased with the watch chain and charm. I made it out of an old fiddle-bow and a peach-stone. Next Month I'll send you a Bead-necklace. That wont be worth any thing either. But the following month I shall, if all goes as usual, send you a Bead Hand bag which should be worth something over 15 or 20 bucks. These same sort of bead bags sell in the stores for around 35°° and up to 100°° according to the material used and the quality of the work -manship.

June 15, 1929

Letter from Carl Panzram to Henry Lesser.

Your letter of June the 8th reached me the other day. That was a pretty nice letter all right. Full of news, and all of it good. I was a bit surprised to read what Mencken wrote to you. I didn't have much faith in the thing being worth while, but any one like Mencken says it's good I must believe it. You use your own judgement and just do what as you like about it. It's yours and what you do with it is O.K. by me. I should like to read the article by The Nation about Older but that's out of order here. Send no clippings. I am still on my same job and like it less each day. I am getting all set for a change. It won't be long now. I think your out of luck for the other 75,000 words I wrote here. That's out of order also. Glad your friend was pleased with the watch chain and charm. I made it out of an old fiddle bow and a peach-stone. Next month I'll send you a bead-necklace. That won't be worth any thing either. But the following month I shall, "if all as usual", send you a bead hand bag which should be worth something over 15 or 20 bucks. These same sort of bead bag sell in the stores for around $35.00 and up to $100.00 according to the material used and the quality of the workmanship. On my bag I have a silver handle which cost $2.75, Lining .75 and the beads $2.50, that's not counting such items as the silk thread, bead needles and wax and my 2 months labor on it. Considering every thing I think I should be justified in looking for at least $15.00 for it. But when you get it you must use your own judgement. Whatever you do with it will be OK. by me. The necklace as you will see I put in the initial T so I guess you'll know what to do with that. That should be some compensation to her for all of the work she must have done in deciphering and typing all of my scribbling. Did you take the trouble to verify any or all of my statements. I think you should. Don't you? I met an old friend of mine here by the name of Reynolds, an old, old timer. I wish you knew him and that he knew you. He sure could spin you some weird yarns. It's pretty hot here just now. I have been expecting to see old boy Sneek down here with a new lot of bums. There are a number of people here who would be glad to see either one or both of 'em. What's Allen doing? Why the heck don't you take my tip and drop that job your on surely your not going to wait until you get the same as Allen got. your the same type as him and you must expect the same kind of deal if you stop in your same line of business. So Long and good Luck.

I am
Carl Panzram

When Panzram writes: "I think your out of luck for the other 75,000 words I wrote here. That's out of order also." Does this mean they were confiscated? Did the prison give those papers back to Panzram eventually? We may never know. It is very interesting to note that even in 1929, inmates were attempting to sell items or artwork which they created so they may have some spending money in the prison commissary.

On my fag I have a silver handle which cost $2.15, Lining 75 and the beads $2.30, that's not counting such items as the silk thread, bead needles and wax and my 2 months labor on it. Considering every thing I think I should be justified in looking for at least $15.00 for it. But when you get it you must use your own judgement. Whatever you do with it will be O.K. by me. The necklace as you will see I put in the initials J so I guess you'll know what to do with that. That should be some compensation to her for all of the work she must have done in deciphering and typing all of my scribbling. Did you take the trouble to verify any or all of my statements. I think you should. Don't you? I met an old friend of mine here by the name of Reynolds an old, old timer. I wish you knew him and that he knew you. He sure could spin you some weird yarns. Its pretty hot here just now. I have been expecting to see old boy Sneak down here with a new lot of bums including Wilcox. There are a number of people here who would be glad to see either one or both of em. Whats Allen doing? Why the Heck dont you take my tips and drop that job your on. Surely your not going to wait until you get the same as Allen got. Your the same type as him and you must expect the same kind of a deal if you stay in your same line of business. So long and good luck.

Dan

Carl Panzram.
31614. Box. 7.
Liavenworth. Kansas.

82

-B-
Cell House
2 Bunk - Cell
6-12-36
U.S. Pen. Leavenworth Kan.

83

UNITED STATES PENITENTIARY
Leavenworth, Kansas

6-19 ___ 1929

Prisoner Carl Panzram

No. 31614 Employed Laundry

Offense ~~trafficking~~

Specification 31614 admitted giving 8 pkg of camels and four bags of bull durham to 31750 and he had not purchased any cigarettes through Chief Clerk. I ask him where he got them and He said He didn't care to tell me.

W. Adkins.
_____
Guard

Action: This man before being given a hearing on above report on June 20, 1929 about 8 o'clock A. M. assaulted and killed foreman Warnke in the laundry. He is to be confined in segregated cell on regular diet until further disposition is made of this case.

F. B. Zerbst
Deputy Warden
192___

JUN 20 1929

Form 30L

84

A sample offense write up. When prisoners would commit a violation of the rules or an offense, they would be formally written up. The prisoner would then be given a hearing. But before Panzram could have a hearing, he murdered the laundry foreman Warnke. This was Panzram' had not committed any violations at Leavenworth prior to June 16, 1929. The best way to describe these form would be like a speeding ticket. The officers would write the incident up on these forms and take the form along with the inmate to the Deputy Warden's Clerk, where the incident would be recorded in the Deputy Warden's ledger of inmates and offenses. The deputy warden was like the institution judge, he would listen to the officers side of the story ask the inmate questions, and then pass judgment. This was the only offense on record in Panzram's federal file. The discrepancy typed in the federal file is listed as June 22, but the true date was June 19 when the offense occurred.

June 19, 1929
Prisoner: Carl Panzran
No: 31614 Employed: Laundry
Offense: trafficking
Specification: admitted giving 8 packages of camels and 4 bags of bull durham to 31750 and he had not purchased any cigarettes through Chief Clerk. I ask him where he got them and he said he didn't care to tell me.

Guard: Watkins.

Actions: This man, before being given a hearing on above report, on June 20, 1929, about 8 o'clock a.m. assaulted and killed foreman Warnke in the laundry. He is to be confined in segregated cell on regular diet until further disposition is made of this case.

Signed by Deputy Warden Zerbst

DATE	VIOLATIONS	day: lost
1929		
June 22	Violation of prison rules: Trafficking. #31614 admitted giving 8 pkg of Camels and four bags of Bull Durham to 31750 and he had not purchased any cigarettes through Chief Clerk. I ask him where he got them and he said he didn't care to tell me. (Watkins) This man before being given a hearing on above report, on June 20, 1929 about 8 o'clock A.M. assaulted and killed Foreman Warnke in the Laundry. He is to be confined in segregated cell on regular diet until further disposition is made of his case. (F. G. Zerbst, D.W.)	—
June 22	Released from Isolation and placed in Segregation.	
4-16-30	Released from segregation to attend court.	

Letter confiscated by Leavenworth USP Warden – June 22, 1929 - The original handwritten letter missing. It is not known whether the letter was written by Panzram on June 22 or confiscated on June 22. The letter most likely came before the Warden's attention on June 22, prior to the letter being mailed out as Panzram does not make any mention of the murder of Warnke. Panzram begins talking about his own death here as he began planning to either escape, die trying to escape or commit an offense which would bring along a sentence of execution.

Letter from Carl Panzram to Henry Lesser.

I wrote to you last Sunday and again today. I don't expect you to write as often as I do. I have a little more time to spare that you have, in fact I have so much time to spare that I have a hard job in passing it. You on the other hand, I presume haven't enough time. Well there's a remedy for that. But why worry about time when a guy like Einstein says there is no such thing as time. I don't know about that though. I have my doubts about his theory. He's a pretty shrewd bird all right but when he says there is no such thing as time then I half suspect that he has never been in the Jail House. Then there was another Big Shot who wrote that, "Stone Walls and Iron bars do not a prison make." I think that if he had to pack away 25 boffoes in this Joint, he would soon sing a different song. He wouldn't sing at all but if he ever did it would be, "The Jail-House Blues." Some of these writers spring some queer theories about what they know very little. I guess that's all balled up in grammar, but I guess you capish what I am trying to write in my own dumb way.

The 26th day of this month will be my birthday, should I be unfortunate enough to live that long. But I suppose I'll be still kicking around then. I always have had luck. Anything I want, I seldom get, but if I don't want some certain thing, that thing I am sure to get. I sure would like to know who or what is or was my jinx. I wouldn't harm him or it, much. That is, not too much. I met a poor chump here sometime ago to whom I put this query and his answer was to offer me a bible and prayer book. Yes, you guessed it, he is still alive, but only because I didn't bring my pistols with me when I came here. I must be more dumb than I think I am. He and others like him can get comfort and happiness out of things that I can only get more mad at. I have read everything I could get and that I was able to understand with my limited amount of intelligence but still I am as such in the dark as ever. But anyway to cut out the hot air and get down to what I have been thinking about more or less, is this. If or when you do send me any money, please be sure to send it either by registered mail or in P.O. money order and not in cash. But you better hurry up though, because ever since I read that article in the American Mag by Petty I have been thinking more and more about what a fine little angel I'll make. A Golden Harp, a halo and a pair of wings. Nothing to do but flap my wings and crow like a rooster. Ride the Clouds instead of having to live like –

Carl Panzram

THE MURDER OF WARNKE

R. E. WARNICA KILLED

Prisoner in Federal Penitentiary Uses Flat Iron for Assault

Robert E. Warnica, formerly of this city, but for some years a foreman at the laundry in the Federal penitentiary at Ft. Leavonworth, was killed Thursday morning by a prisoner. He was employed at the Park Steam Laundry here some years ago, and his son, Robert, and daughter, Florence, attended high school here. The press dispatches of Thursday give this version of the attack:

"Leavenworth, Kan., June 20. — Carl Fanzran, 36, a prisoner in the federal penintentiary here, today ran amuck and killed R. E. Warnica, 47, foreman of the laundry, with a flat iron.

"Following the slaying, Panzran pursued other fellow prisoners about the laundry brandishing his weapon, but was overpowered by Phil Holgrave a guard.

"Panzran, received in the prison February 1, 1929, from Washington, D. C., was reported yesterday by a guard for an infraction of institution rules. Fellow prisoners said he made threats to obtain revenge then.

"The slaying occurred early this morning. The foreman was struck while his back was turned.

"Warden Thomas White immediately began an investigation following the slaying.

"Warnica is survived by his widow, Florence, and a son, Robert, 23, of Phoenix, Ariz."

TELEGRAM

TELEGRAM	✓
DAY LETTER	
NIGHT MESSAGE	
NIGHT LETTER	✓
GOVT. RATE	✓
COMMERCIAL	

WESTERN UNION	
POSTAL	
GOVT. RADIO	
COLLECT	
PAID	✓
NO. WORDS	

DEPARTMENT OF JUSTICE
UNITED STATES PENITENTIARY
LEAVENWORTH, KANSAS

June 20, 1929.   31614

Superintendent of Prisons,

Department of Justice,
Washington, D. C.

Laundry Foreman R. G. Warnke was fatally injured
this morning by Carl Panzran thirty one six fourteen
committed here from Washington February first nineteen twenty
nine for twenty five years for housebreaking and burglary.

Iron bar used in infliction of injuries.
Prisoner being held in Isolation and Warnke being given
all medical attention possible but his condition is
hopeless.   Will investigate thoroughly and report.

T. B. White,
W A R D E N.

91

REPORT MADE AT:	DATE WHEN MADE:	PERIOD FOR WHICH MADE:	REPORT MADE BY:	
Kansas City, Mo.	6-25-1929	6/20 - 22, 1929	J. R. BURGER	ebc

TITLE	CHARACTER OF CASE:
CARL PANZRAN, Prisoner, Reg. No. 31614	MURDER OF CIVILIAN R. G. WARNKE at Federal Penitentiary, Leavenworth, Ks., June 20, 1929.

62-꒰

SYNOPSIS OF FACTS: BEGINNING.   70-47

Investigation predicated on information furnished
this office by T. B. White, Warden, Federal Peni-
tentiary, Leavenworth, Ks. Subject CARL PANZRAN,
Prisoner, Register No. 31614, Federal Penitentiary,
Leavenworth, Ks., murdered R. G. Warnke, civilian
foreman of the laundry at the Federal Penitentiary,
Leavenworth, Kansas, June 20, 1929. Statements obtained from Warden T. B. White, Captain of Guards
Fred L. Morrison, Guards Phil Holtgraves, Charles
Rossie and Louis W. Guenther; inmates Jim Kasoff,
Louis Kelly, Neil Maxwell, Harry Howard, Raymond
Thomas, Rolla Pombles, Jack Shapiro, Amos B. Malone
and Jesse C. Cooper, with reference to said murder;
also statement from Dr. C. A. Bennett, prison physician, describing condition of R. G. Warnke, when received at hospital and transfer of body from prison
hospital to institutional mortuary; also certificate
of death of R. G. Warnke. Subject admitted to this
Agent that he struck R. G. Warnke with iron bar with
intention of killing him for cause of his own which
he would tell in Court.

P.

DETAILS:

This investigation was predicated on telephone call from T. B. White, Warden of the
Federal Penitentiary at Leavenworth, Kansas, reporting that Subject had murdered
R. G. Warnke, Civilian Foreman of the Laundry, located in the Federal Penitentiary,
Leavenworth, Kansas, on June 20, 1929.

-At Leavenworth, Kansas.-

Agent interviewed and conferred with Warden T. B. White of the Federal Penitentiary,

DO NOT WRITE IN THESE SPACES

APPROVED AND FORWARDED:				RECORDED AND INDEXED:
R. E. Vetterli	SPECIAL AGENT IN CHARGE	62-21811-1		
		BUREAU OF INVESTIGATION		CHECKED OFF:
COPIES OF THIS REPORT FURNISHED TO:		JUN 28 1929 A M		JUL 8 - 1929
5-Bureau		DEPARTMENT OF JUSTICE		JACKETED:
1-U.S.Atty., Topeka, Ks.				
1-Warden, U.S.Prison, Leavenworth, Ks.		ROUTED TO: Div. Two	FILE	
3-Kansas City				

THE F.B.I. INVESTIGATION INTO THE MURDER OF WARNKE

Leavenworth, Kansas, and obtained from Mr. White all information possible, together with letters and documents incorporated herewith, at which time Mr. White made signed statement and Agent interviewed and took statements from prison guards, the prison physician and inmates of the institution, whose statements as set forth in the order named in the synopsis of this report:

*June 22, 1929.

Statement made and certified to by Thomas B. White, Warden of the United States Penitentiary, Leavenworth, Kansas: -

Shortly after I arrived at my office June 20, 1929, at about, I think, 7:50 or 7:55 A.M. Guard Dave Watkins came running into the office and made the statement that a prisoner by the name of Carl Panzram had killed R. G. Warnke, civilian foreman of the Laundry which is in and a part of the United States Penitentiary, Leavenworth, Kansas, and which is located on a Government reservation, and that Panzram was running amuck and probably had injured or killed others. I immediately got a pistol from the Armory and, thus armed, went to the Yard. As I passed down the hallway one of the prisoners told me that the man who committed the murder had passed over into the East Yard, and I therefore went to the East Yard and, thinking Panzram had probably gone to the Brick Yard, I proceeded to ask the foreman of the Brick Yard if he had seen the man come that way. He said he had not, and as I was returning to the West Yard I was told that Panzram had given up and was placed in isolation. I then proceeded to the Isolation Building and verified this report.

Immediately thereafter I sent a telegram to the Superintendent of Prisons, of the occurrence, and began an investigation, and got all prisoners in that I had information were in the Laundry at the time of the murder and saw it, and questioned them and took all preliminary statements. I called the Bureau of Investigation, Department of Justice, Kansas City Office, and had an agent proceed to the prison to make an investigation.

On the admission of Carl Panzram to this prison, I was told by Major Peak, in charge of the group of prisoners that came with him, that Panzram was a very desperate man and that I would have to keep close tab on him. After Panzram's admission I had several conferences with the Deputy Warden about Panzram, and advised the Deputy what word Major Peak had passed to me, and to endeavor to assign him to some part of the institution where he would be under close supervision, and the Deputy Warden accordingly assigned him to the Laundry - about the best place we have for such supervision. I had reports from the Deputy Warden on two or three different occasions afterwards and he told me that he had had a number of talks with Panzram in an endeavor to advise him that the best thing he could do for his own interest and the best interests of the institution was to behave himself. The Deputy Warden reported on all occasions of his interviews that

Panzram was rather surly, but the Deputy was of the opinion that his advice was having some effect. Some time after Panzram was admitted to the prison, there was a letter came to my attention which was written by Panzram and addressed to the Prosecuting Attorney at Salem, Massachusetts, and concerned the case of murder that was against Panzram at Salem. A photostatic copy of this letter was made by our Record Office and I kept it in the files for future references. Today I have turned over the copy of this letter to the Department of Justice Agent making the investigation, Mr. John R. Berger. After Panzram had murdered Mr. Warnke, another letter which was written by Panzram and addressed to Mr. Henry James, care of Miss E. Trott, The Lenman Apts., No. 2100 N. St., N.W., Washington, D.C., was brought to me, and it was reported that it was taken from Panzram's person after his apprehension for the murder. This letter in the original I am turning over to Mr. Berger, also. Both of these letters, while the composition is very good show that Panzram had the vilest of dispositions, as he discussed murder in them as if it was a pastime.

I have never had a personal conversation with Carl Panzram, but from what I know of his actions and from the good composition of his letters I would take it that he is sane. I am having Dr. B. Landis Elliot of Kansas City, a visiting psychiatrist, examine Panzram on his next visit to the institution.
(Signed) T. B. White."

"June 21, 1929.
Statement Made and Certified to by Fred L. Morrison, Captain of the Guards, United States Penitentiary, Leavenworth, Kansas:

On June 20, 1929, I was acting as Deputy Warden in the absence of Deputy Warden F. G. Zerbst. After the usual relief was made by the day guards and after the men had gone to breakfast, I attended to the usual routine duties pertaining to that time. I took my usual station at the corner of the Carpenter Shop about 7:30 A.M. After the men had come out from the dining room, I went to the outside East Gate for the purpose of passing the various outside gangs out. This I had done and had started to return to the inside prison. While I was between the two East Gates, Guard George Cross shouted to me, telling me that a man had been killed in the Laundry, and I would judge this time was about 7:45 or 7:50 A.M. I came on through the inside gate into the yard and I met Warden T. B. White and Guards Dave Watkins and John Krautz and William Haag. I learned from them that the foreman of the Laundry, R. G. Warnke, had been killed by a prisoner, Register No. 31614, Carl Panzram. The Warden was under the impression, for some reason, that Panzram had gone towards or into the Brick Yard, which accounted for th

AERIAL OF LEAVENWORTH PENITENTIARY

LEAVENWORTH USP POWER HOUSE

U.S.P. LEAVENWORTH, KANS.
DINING ROOM = LOOKING SOUTHEAST.
9-10-37
93

LEAVENWORTH USP DINING ROOM

guards and himself being there where I met them. In company with them,
I proceeded on to the Brick Yard and upon reaching the paper shed which
is on the line of the Main Yard and the Brick Yard I suggested to the
Warden that we run all men into the cells and get eight or ten guards
with guns to look for Panzram. He agreed to this and ordered me, with
the aid of Lieutenant Schwantz, to do so. Proceeding to carry out this
order, I started through the yard towards the Deputy Warden's Office
and upon reaching the Ice Bant met Mr. Arthur Fowler, Civilian Store-
keeper, who informed me that Panzram was then in Isolation, having
given himself up to someone. I proceeded on to the Deputy Warden's
Office and found this to be true by inquiry of the Isolation guard,
Mr. Edmonds. The Warden had been notified of this immediately after
me and he proceeded to the Deputy Warden's Office and arrived shortly
after me, probably about 8:00 or 8:05 A.M.

In discussing our future actions, we decided that Mr. Phil
Holtgraves, the guard in the Laundry, should secure the names and numbers of as many prisoners as possible who may have seen all or some part
of this killing. The Warden then returned to his office, and I held the
usual morning Court Call while Mr. Holtgraves, the guard, was finding
these various prisoners who knew something about this crime. About
9:00 A.M., same date, the Warden returned to the Deputy Warden's Office
and proceeded to hold an investigation of this crime. By the time
Warden White came, Guard Holtgraves had secured the names and numbers
of the men to be interviewed and the Warden proceeded to question them
concerning their knowledge of the killing, the evidence of which I
understand the Warden has since handed you.

The Laundry in which R. G. Warnke was employed as formean is a
part of the United States Penitentiary located on a Government reservation
in the County of Leavenworth, State of Kansas, and the murder of R. G.
Warnke was committed by Carl Panzram, Register No. 31614, at said Laundry on
said reservation on June 20, 1929, about 7:50 A.M.

(Signed) Fred L. Morrison
Capt. of Guards U.S.P."

"June 21, 1929"

Statement Made and Certified to by Phil Holtgraves, Guard,
United States Penitentiary, Leavenworth, Kansas:

I am employed as a guard at the Federal Penitentiary,
Leavenworth, Kansas, and on June 20, 1929, I was standing at
the front office of the Laundry located in the Federal Penitentiary and I saw Carl Panzram, Register No. 31614, come in the
door and as he went down to his place of work as he came in, I
was writing passes. I heard a disturbance and when I looked up
towards that direction I saw Panzram with an iron bar in his hand
about two feet long and about an inch or an inch and a quarter in
diameter, and I rant down towards him and before I got there Panzram
ran after another prisoner, Register No. 30534, and as he ran after that
man I followed him. Then the other prisoner ran around and passed Mr. R. G.
Warnke, civilian foreman of the Laundry, lying on the floor, and took
his bar and hit Mr. Warnke. Then Panzram ran after another prisoner, then

they all started running. Panzram would start running after one
man, then change and start running after another. The rest of the
men were out of the Laundry - they all ran   out. I still followed him
and he went into the Deputy Warden's Office and he did not stay in there
but just a few seconds and he came back out. Then Panzram ran down the
street after Guard Guenther until he got along about the Power House, and
then he saw another prisoner pass there and Panzram ran after that prisoner
with his iron bar, then went a little further and turned and came back by
the Dining Room. I walked into the street and he came over to within a
distance of about fifteen feet from me, threw the bar down in the street
and said, "Here I am. Do whatever you want to with me. I can't get no
more of them." So I took him into Isolation and locked him up.

From my acquaintance with Panzram since his arrival here and confinement in this institution since February 1st this year, in my judgment he
is sane and knows right from wrong, and is of a revengeful temperament, also
high tempered. I have noticed Panzram's previous actions and his actions
at the time, or immediately after the killing of R. G. Warnke, in which
Panzram was defiant until he saw that he was in a position to be overpowered and probably killed, when he immediately threw down the bar that
he had killed Mr. Warnke with and submitted to arrest.
                    (Signed)Phil Holtgraves
Witness:
Fred L. Morrison, Capt. of Guards, U.S.P."

"June 21, 1929
Statement Made and Certified to by Charles Rossie, Guard,
United States Penitentiary, Leavenworth, Kansas.
I am employed as a guard at the Federal Penitentiary at
Leavenworth, Kansas, and was on duty June 20, 1929. I have known
Carl Panzram, Register No. 31614, for the past two months. On
above date while on duty as guard I saw a number of people running
out of the Laundry located in this Federal Prison, some of them
hollering "Fire!," at which time someone remarked to me, "You had
better go in there, " meaning in the Laundry. I immediately
proceeded to the Laundry, and enroute to the Laundry someone
remarked that Panzram had killed R. G. Warnke, civilian foreman
of the Laundry. I then entered the Laundry and saw Panzram waving
in iron bar which appeared to be about three feet long and an inch
or an inch and a quarter in diameter, over his head; and he, Panzram, said to me at this time, "I know you, and I am going to get
you." About that time twenty-five or fifty men came running out
of the door of the Laundry, Panzram following them with the iron
bar in his hand, and Panzram went to the Deputy Warden's office
and then started over to the East Gate. I came out of the Laundry
ahead of him. He chased two or three different prisoners around
the yard, hitting at one of the prisoners and then starting after
someone else. He got as far as the Kitchen when one of the guards,
George Cross, on the East Gate Tower, pointed a machine gun at Panzram. When Panzram saw the guard with the gun he, Panzram, immediately went back to the Deputy Warden's office and threw down this
iron bar and went into the Deputy Warden's Office, and then I
picked up the iron bar and turned it over to Captain Fred L. Morrison. I did not see Panzram after this time.

LEAVENWORTH USP #2 TOWER AND EAST GATE

From my acquaintance with Panzram, Register No. 31614, he is sane, knows right from wrong, and is revengeful and will kill for revenge.

(Signed) Charles Rossie

Witnessed by
Hed L. Morris,
Capt. of Guards, U.S.P."

"June 21, 1929

Statement Made and Certified to by Louis W. Guenther, Guard, United States Penitentiary, Leavenworth, Kansas:

I am a guard employed at the United States Penitentiary, Leavenworth, Kansas.

On June 20, 1929, about 8:00 A.M. Guard John Krautz requested me to look for Register No. 31614, Carl Panzram, and told me that I might find him around the hallway, and while I was up there there was a man who worked in the Laundry located within this prison, came up the hall and said there was a couple of men got killed over in the Laundry. I naturally went over there as quickly as I could get there, and when I got there I saw this Car Panzram, Register No. 31614, coming down the steps with an iron bar in his hand, and he cut across the lawn to the Deputy Warden's Office. There I went in, and I did not know the Deputy was on furlough and thought Panzram was going in to get him, and so I started in to the Deputy Warden's Office right behind Panzram and he took after the Deputy Warden's orderly over there, which gave me a chance to look in the office, and as he had left the door ajar I heard an awful racket, and when I looked in there I attracted his attention. I told Guard Rossie and another guard - I do not remember his name - to "Come on, let's get him," and Panzram heard me say that and turned to me. I did not see any help, so I jumped on out of the office, and he followed me out into the yard. My intentions were to get him up to the tower on the East Gate where we could use the gun on him, but he was wise enough not to get in run range, and stayed behind some box cars on the tracks there. He chased another prisoner, Shapiro, and I started for the tower to get a gun and as soon as I got to the tower he went back and gave himself up because he knew I was coming back with a gun - I think he knew that was my intention. About the time I got to the tower, he dropped the bar and gave himself up.

When I remarked in the Deputy Warden's Office to "Come on, let's get him," Panzram resented this remark and said, "Come on, take me, you Sons of Bitches!" and swung at me with the iron bar in an attempt to hit me.

LEAVENWORTH USP VIEW FROM EAST GATE - FACING WEST

In my honest opinion I think that Carl Panzram is sane, my opinion being based on the fact that when Panzram attacked me or attempted to attack me with the iron bar and followed me for some distance, when he, Panzram, discovered that I was leading him out to an armed guard, Panzram realized that he was liable to be shot, he immediately retreated and returned to the Deputy Warden's Office and threw down the iron bar and gave himself up.

                    (Signed)Louis W. Guenther
Witnessed by Fred L. Morrison, Capt. of Guards, U. S. P."

                              "June 21, 1929.

          Statement made and certified to by Jim Kasoff,
          Register No. 11654, Prisoner in the U.S. Penitentiary,
          Leavenworth, Kansas:

     I have known Carl Panzram, Register No. 31614, for the
past two months. On June 20, 1929, about 7:50 A.M. I saw Carl
Panzram hit Mr. R. G. Warnke, civilian foreman of the Laundry,
over the head with an iron bar about two feet long and about
the size of a broom handle, while Mr. Warnke was standing bent
over in the Laundry located in the prison, the first blow
knocking Mr. Warnke down and Panzram again hitting Warnke
after he had fallen to the floor. I then ran out of this
Laundry and told Mr. Phil Holtgraves, guard in the Laundry,
that Panzram had killed Warnke and to "watch himself." I then
ran on out into the yard out of the way of Panzram.
     I have since also identified the photograph of Carl Panzram
as the man who struck and killed Mr. R. G. Warnke with the iron
var above described.
                    (Signed) Jim Kasoff 411654
Witnessed: Fred L. Morrison, Capt. of Guards, U.S.P."

                              "June 21, 1929

          Statement made and certified to by Louis Kelly, Register
          No. 29150, a prisoner in the United States Penitentiary,
          Leavenworth, Kansas:

     On June 20, 1929, about 7:50 A.M. I was in the Laundry
located at the Federal Penitentiary, Leavenworth, Kansas, sitting
on a bench about ten feet away from the small washer which is
located in said Laundry, and Mr. R. G. Warnke, civilian foreman
of this Laundry, was standing about the middle of the Laundry
near the south side of the building, at which time and place I
saw Mr. Warnke fall to the floor, and Carl Panzram, Register
No. 31614, whom I have known since about February 1, 1929, was
standing bent over Mr. Warnke, hitting Warnke with an iron bar
about three feet long and about the size of a broom handle in
diameter. When I saw what was going on, I ran to the west side
of the Laundry and Panzram started after me and chased me around a
couple of tables. I then got out of his way and ran out of the
Laundry and informed Guard John Krautz of the murder. While I

was talking to Guard Krautz, Panzram came out of the Laundry and started for the Deputy Warden's office with the iron bar in his hand. Panzram immediately came out of the Deputy Warden's Office and again chased myself and seven or eight more prisoners as far as the coal pile about two hundred feet away. Panzram chased us for about two hundred feet, then turned around and returned to the Deputy Warden's office, where he threw the iron bar down near the Deputy Warden's office and then went into that office. I did not see him thereafter.

I have worked with Panzram in the Laundry since February 1st this year, and Panzram has remarked to me on several different occasions, and has often boasted as to what he would do if anyone ever "did him any dirt." Panzram said he did not believe in facing a man and fighting it out. He said the way to get any man was to get him when he is not looking. He, Panzram, said to me, "If anybody does me dirty, I don't forget it. I might appear as if I had forgotten things, but I always remember them. I will never use my hands on anybody." About two months ago, Panzram and Mr. Warnke had a few words over three handerchiefs which Panzram had and was washing in a bleacher in the Laundry. Warnke told him that he was not permitted to use that bleacher, and that he was not any better than any of the rest and that no one was allowed to use that bleacher. Panzram argued, saying that he was only trying to bleach three handerkerchiefs, but Mr. Warnke said he could not have his rules run over and repeated that Panzram was no better than the rest of the prisoners employed in the Laundry. He, Panzram, remarked that if Warnke did not "lay off of him" he would "get" Warnke. Mr. Warnke, I believe, understood this threat as well as any of the rest of us. Carl Panzram has made plenty of threats about all he is going to do to people, and has turned all the men against him, but Panzram had never made many threats towards any one particular man.

From my association with Panzram, in my honest judgment he is sane; however, revengeful to all human mankind, and in my judgment would not harm anyone unless he thought the person had done something to cross his path. The reason I have for thinking the man, Panzram, is sane is that he often remarks, "I am your friend today, but your enemy towmorrow." He says he has been beaten up so much and put through the third degree in different institutions that he has been in until he has got a hatred and a perpetual grouch not only against the officials of the penitentiary, but against all inmates as well. Panzram says he hates the officials like he does a snake, but he has often said that he hated the inmates just as much, because he says they all have "done him dirty."

I know that when Carl Panzram was running amuck in the Laundry he was not a bit excited, but had his head right with him all the time. When he faced the East Gate, as he was getting closer to it he realized what was ahead of him. I think if he was insane - blind with bloodthirst - he would not have seen that gate; but he had seen enough to turn back when he thought of the rifle. When he saw he was being or was going to be closed in on, he had sense enough to drop his bar, too. He passed close enough to some men in the Laundry that he could have killed several, but he seemed to have a list made out for certain persons.

Since Carl Panzram murdered R. G. Warnke I have viewed Panzram's photograph, Register No. 31641, which I positively identified as one and the same Panzram who murdered Mr. Warnke as above stated, and I will willingly testify to this effect in court.

(Signed) Louis Kelly

Witnessed: by Fred L. Morrison."

"June 21, 1929.
Statement made and certified to by Neil Maxwell, Register No. 30534, a prisoner in the United States Penitentiary, Leavenworth, Kansas.

On June 20, 1929, about 7:50 A.M. I saw Carl Panzram, Register No. 31514, walk up behind Mr. R. G. Warnke, civilian foreman of the Laundry located in the Federal Penitentiary, Leavenworth, Kansas, while Mr. Warnke was bending over a washing machine, apparently rinsing clothes. Panzram at this time hit Mr. Warnke in the back of the head with an iron bar about three feet long and about the size or probably a little larger than a broom handle in diameter. The first blow that Panzram struck Mr. Warnke, Mr. Warnke fell to the floor, and Panzram hit him again with his iron bar on the head after Warnke had fallen to the floor. When Panzram first hit Mr. Warnke, I remarked to Harry Howard, another prisoner who was standing beside me in this Laundry, to "look there," and Howard also looked around and saw Panzram hit Mr. Warnke the second blow. Panzram then ran towards Harry Howard, and after prisoner Kelly and chased Kelly out of the building, and I did not see Panzram again until a few minutes later, at which time Panzram ran into the Deputy Warden's office with the iron bar, and I did not see Panzram after that. I then assisted in carrying Mr. R. G. Warnke to the Hospital for medical aid.

The murder of Mr. R. G. Warnke by Panzram was, in my judgment, uncalled for and without any notice to Mr. Warnke, and Panzram had on two or three different occasions prior to the murder of R. G. Warnke talked of different murders and of murdering people, and appeared to be of a murdering disposition; however, sane. For instance, after Panzram had murdered Mr. Warnke he would not submit to arrest until he discovered that he was liable to be killed if he did not surrender at once, and when Carl Panzram saw himself in this position he immediately threw down the iron bar and surrendered, which convinces me of his sanity.

I have since positively identified the photograph of Carl Panzram, Register No. 31614, as being one and the same person who murdered R. G. Warnke as above stated, and will willingly testify to the above facts.

(Signed) Neil Maxwell

Witnessed by Fred L. Morrison, Capt. of Guards, U.S.P."

"June 21, 1929

Statement Made and Certified to by Harry Howard, Register
No. 30615, a prisoner in the United States Penitentiary,
Leavenworth, Kansas:

I have known and worked with Carl Panzram, Register No.
31614, at the Laundry located at the Federal Prison, Leavenworth, Kansas, since about February 1st this year, and have,
previously to June 20, 1929, had conversations with Panzram
at different times on different subjects.

In my opinion, judging from previous conversations with
Panzram, he is of a revengeful nature, high tempered, and
sane.

On June 20, 1929, about 7:50 A.M. while I was sitting in
the above described Laundry talking to Louis Kelly, who is
also an inmate of this institution, Kelly remarked to me,
"Jesus Christ! Look there!" I then turned my head and looked
around and saw Panzram standing over Mr. R. G. Warnke, civilian
foreman of the Laundry, and saw Panzram hit Warnke in the head
with an iron bar about three feet long and a little larger than
a broom handle in diameter. After Panzram hit Warnke, Panzram
then turned and looked at me and said to me, "You are the next
Son of a Bitch I want." Panzram then started running after me
and Kelly then jerked me out of the way, and when Panzram saw
Kelly jerk me to one side he, Panzram, then ran after Kelly
with this iron bar and continued chasing Kelly to the rear, or
west end of the Laundry. I then ran out at the front door and
kept away from Panzram, and later saw Panzram drop the iron bar
near the Deputy Warden's Office and run into the Deputy Warden's
Office, and I did not see him thereafter.

I have since seen Panzram's photograph, Register No. 31614,
and can positively identify Panzram, and will willingly testify
in court as above stated.

(Signed) Harry Howard.

P.S. My term here expires July 28, 1929, and I may be reached
thereafter at 827 Howard Street, Detroit, Mich.

Witnessed by Fred L. Morrison, Capt. of Guards, U. S. P."

"June 21, 1929

Statement made and certified to by Raymond Thomas,
Register No. 31896, a prisoner in the United States
Penitentiary, Leavenworth, Kansas.

I have known Carl Panzram, Register No. 31614, for about six
weeks and have worked with him in the Laundry at Leavenworth Penitentiary during this time.

On June 19th, while at work in the Laundry he, Panzram,
told me he was going to kill Mr. R. G. Warnke, civilian foreman
of the Laundry, and I told him he had better not, and then the next
morning I went and told Mr. Warnke that I had heard threats made
against him, and in about five minutes I saw Mr. Warnke standing
and smoking a cigaret and I saw this man Panzram step out from behind a concrete post and hit Mr. Warnke on the head with an iron
bar about three feet long and about an inch and a quarter in diameter. Then Panzram made a swing at prisoner Harry Howard and
Kelly, another prisoner, told Harry Howard to run; and then Panzram came around the mangle and hit at me with the iron bar, coming
very close to me. Then he went back and hit Mr. Warnke again with
the same iron bar. Then I ran out of the door. In fact, Panzram
hit Mr. Warnke two blows in the first instance, and returned a few
moments later and hit him another blow with the same iron bar on
the head. I then ran out of the way through the door with several
other prisoners, and Panzram chased us for some distance and then
returned towards the Deputy Warden's office, where I understood he
gave himself up.
From my acquaintance with Carl Panzram, in my judgment he is
sane; however, revengeful and high tempered, and a man that will
murder a man that in his, Panzram's judgment has treated him
wrongfully; and in my opinion Panzram murdered R. G. Warnke without
any provication or cause other than he, Panzram, conceived the idea
that Mr. Warnke had at some time done somthing that did not appeal
to him Panzram.
I have since viewed the photograph of Carl Panzram, Register
No. 31614, which is one and the same person who murdered Mr. R. G.
Warnke, as above stated, and I will willingly testify to the above
facts in court.
SignedXRaymond Thomas
Witness J.R.B.
Fred . Morrison, Capt. of Guards, U.S.P."

"June 21, 1929.

Statement Made and Certified to by Rolla Pombles,
Register No. 31366, a prisoner in the United States
Penitentiary, Leavenworth Kansas;

On June 20, 1929, about 7:50 A.M. while I was in the Laundry located at the Federal Prison, Leavenworth, Kansas, where I was working on that date, while I was standing near Mr. R. G. Warnke, civilian foreman of the Laundry, I was dipping water out of a barrel when I heard a noise sounding like a thud, at which time I looked up and saw Carl Panzram, Register No. 31614, standing over Mr. Warnke with an iron bar about two and one half feet long and about the size of a broom handle - maybe a little larger than a broom handle. Panzram later hit Mr. Warnke another blow on the head with this iron. I then ran to the back of the Laundry to get out of Panzram's way, and I heard someone hollering and looked around and saw Panzram chasing a man by the name of Harry Howard, who is also an inmate employee of the Laundry. I then ran downstairs in the Clothing Department room and notified Mr. Harper, who is the civilian Receiving and Discharging Officer in the Clothing Department located in the basement of the Laundry building.

Prior to this time I had two or three converstions with Panzram, at which time he told me of being in different penitentiaries and of raping and murdering children.

Signed)Rolla Pombles

Witness: Fred L. Morrison, Capt. of Guard, U.S.P."

Statement Made and Certified to by Jack Shapiro,
Register No. 24298, a prisoner in the United States
Penitentiary, Leavenworth, Kansas.

I have known Carl Panzram, Register No. 31614, since February
3, 1929.

On the morning of June 20, 1929, while I was walking towards
the Deputy Warden's office looking for Panzram, Register No. 31614,
to notify him of the call from the Deputy Warden's office, I met
Panzram at the Wagon Scales at the corner of the Warehouse and the
old Clothing Department in the Federal Prison yard, and when Panzram saw me he ran towards me in a threatening manner with an iron
bar about three feet in length and about one and one quarter inches
in diameter, and said to me, "You Jew Son of a Bitch, I am going
to kill you. You are the one I want." I ran away and he came
right after me for about one hundred feet and then stopped. He,
Panzram, then walked back to the Deputy Warden's office and threw
down the iron bar which he was chasing me with.

About two weeks ago Panzram told me he was going to kill one
of the prison guards, Dave Watkins, as Guard Watkins had told him
to button up his shirt collar, and Panzram had it in for him. Panzram also told me at this time that he was going to kill Mr. Warnke,
civilian foreman of the prison Laundry, for the reason that he,
Panzram, had asked Mr. Warnke to make a change in his, Panzram's
work, and Mr. Warnke had refused to do so.

From my acquaintance and association with Carl Panzram, I
would judge him to be sane, and is a man of revengeful disposition,
and high tempered, and a man that will kill for revenge.

As above stated, I am well acquainted with Carl Panzram, Register No. 31614, and can not be mistaken as to his identity, and will
willingly testify to above facts in court.

(Signed) Jack Shapiro

Witnessed: by Fred Morrison Capt. of Guards, U.S.P."

"June 21, 1929.

Statement Made and Certified to by Amos B. Malone,
Register No. 28280, a prisoner in the United States
Penitentiary, Leavenworth, Kansas:

I am now an inmate of the Federal Penitentiary, Leavenworth,
Kansas. I have known Carl Panzram, Register No. 31614, for the
past two or three months; in fact, I have been working in the
Laundry with Panzram during this period.

On June 20, 1929, while I was at the Laundry located at
the Federal Penitentiary, Leavenworth, Kansas, Carl Panzram walked by me with an iron bar in his hand, which appeared to be about
32 or 33 inches in length and about the size of a broom handle
in diameter. He walked on past me to where Mr. R. G. Warnke,
civilian foreman of the Laundry, was standing by a small washer
near the middle of the Laundry building on the south side, and
walking up behind Mr. Warnke, hit Mr. Warnke on the back of the
head with this iron bar, and when Panzram hit Mr. Warnke on the
head with this bar, Mr. Warnke fell to the floor out of my sight.
However, I then walked towards Panzram and saw him, Panzram, hit
two more blows, apparently to me on Mr. Warnke. Panzram then
walked away from Mr. Warnke a short distance, and returned to
where Mr. Warnke was lying on the floor and hit him another blow
with this iron bar on the head, remarking at this time, "Here's
another one for you, you Son of a Bitch!" Panzram then ran out
of the Laundry building into the prison yard and I did not see
Panzram again until he had surrendered to the prison guards
near the Deputy Warden's office, at which time Panzram had thrown
this iron bar he had killed Mr. Warnke with down on the pavement.

Since the above mentioned murder I have positively identified photograph of Carl Panzram, Register No. 31614, as the
man above described killing R. G. Warnke at above mentioned date
and place.

(Signed) Amos B. Malone

Witness: Fred L. Morrison, Capt. of Guards, U.S.P."

"June 21, 1929.

Statement Made and Certified to by Jesse C. Cooper,
Register No. 32229, a prisoner at United States Penitentiary,
Leavenworth, Kansas:

On June 20, 1929, about 7:50 A.M., while in the Laundry
located at the Federal Penitentiary at Leavenworth, Kansas, where I
am an inmate employee, the first time I saw Carl Panzram that morning,
he was running amuck. Everyone was running out and I did not know
he had hurt anyone. I did not know it until I saw blood on the
bar which he had in his hands. He was outside of the Laundry
building then. I had run out ahead of him, and he came out. I
said, "This man has hit somebody," because blood was on the bar.
Then I recalled seeing him in the Laundry hitting at something,
but what it was I could not see because of baskets and things in
the Laundry which obstructed my view, although I could see him
hitting down at something twice; and a little later they brought
the dead man, R. G. Warnke, out; of course the men in the Laundry
had all scattered by then. I realized then that it was Mr. Warnke
I had seen Panzram hitting at with the iron bar which he had in
his hand at that time, about two feet long and about an inch and a
quarter in diameter, - a very dangerous weapon -, as Mr. Warnke
was lying in the exact spot where Panzram was hitting with this
iron bar.

I have since identified Carl Panzram's photograph, Register
No. 31614, as one and the same person whom I saw in the Laundry at
the time of the murder as above stated, and I will willingly testify
as above in court.

Signed -Jesse C. Cooper

Witnessed by Fred L. Morrison, Captin of Guards, U.S.P."

STATEMENT MADE BY DR. C. A. BENNETT,
PRISON PHYSICIAN, June 20, 1929:

Mr. R. G. Warneke, Laundry Foreman, was carried into the Hospital about
8:00 A.M. today, on an improvised stretcher, bleeding quite profusely from
numerous gashes in his scalp, ear, nose and mouth; hematoma of both eyes. He
was immediately given a stimulent, hypodermically, for stimulation of his respiration and heart, but with no avail. He came in very weak, with a rapid
pulse and his respiration was slow and stertorous. His clothes were immediately searched for dangerous weapons, but none found.

He had an incision over his frontal region of his scalp 2¾ inches long, which
started about two inches above the base of his nose and midline, slanting 2¾
inches towards the vertex of his skull, pointing a little to the right. This
was a sharp cut with about one tablespoon full of brains hanging from the upper
three-fourths of this laceration.

He had another lacerationfive inches long which started over the mastoid region
of the right ear, 1½ inches, posterior of his righ ear and pointing towards
his vertix.

He had another laceration starting 1½ inches posteriorily towards the occiput
of this second laceration lower point; this last incision extending about one
inch below the second incision, and running into the vertex of the second laceration, and this other laceration is 9½ inches long, and from the upper one
half of these two last lacerations is protruding about two or three tablespoons
of massed brain tissued; lying on top of this massed brain tissue, was a small
piece of skull bone 1¼ inches long and one half inch wide.

One and one fourth inches behind the third laceration, towards the occiput, is a
fourth laceration, 2 inches long which extends from about the middle of the ear
region to the occiput.

Over the crown of the skull is a fifth laceration 2¼ inches long which slants
on an angle of about 25° with the third laceration.

He also had numerous ecchymoses under the skin, over his forhead and about his
eyes; whenever his head is moved, there was numerous crepitation of the bone.

He also had a fracture of the lower jaw; the contour of his forehead was badly
disfigured, and swollen with numerous indentations due to crushing of his skull.

He had one final laceration about 1 inch long at the outer angle of his left
eye ball.

All of these lacerations have either penetrated the brain cavity or dented the
skull bone.

Mr. Warneke was sent to the Institution Mortuary just as he came into the
Hospital with the exception of some hair which was shaved from around the larger
laceration.

Photographs were immediately taken after his death, and the Coroner was called
at 8:30 A.M.   (Signed) C. A. Bennett, Physician."

Bush-Lowe Undertaking Co., Leavenworth,Kansas, took charge of body at Federal
Penitentiary and can testify as to burial.

Photostatic copy of the CERTIFICATE OF DEATH executed in connection with the death of R. G. Warneke, Residence No. 100 North Broadway, Leavenworth, Kansas, which is in and a part of this file, shows place of death: County of Leavenworth, Township Leavenworth, City of Leavenworth; that this Certificate was executed 6-20-29 by (an M.D.) Joseph Skoggs; that he last saw him alive on 6-20-29 and that death occurred on the date sated above at 8:00 a.m; cause of death: A fractured skull. Struck over head by an iron bar by a prisoner at Federal prison Leavenworth, Kansas, that the test that confirmed diagnosis was examination; that R. G. Warneke was of male sex, white, married; wife -Mrs. R.G. Warneke; occupation of deceased: Laundry Foreman, U.S. Penitentiary, Leavenworth, Kansas.

Warden White furnished a photostat copy of a letter addressed to District Attorney Clark, Salem Mass, under date of February 19, 1929, signed by Carl Panzram, Register No. 31614, reading as follows:

"In my reading of the newspapers lately I noticed that you have made a statement that you are going to have me brought to trial for the murder of George Henry Mc Mahon of Salem about seven years ago.

I write you this letter to notify you that I waive all of my extradition rights and am quite willing that I should be brought back to Massachusetts for trial for murder.

I made a full confession of this murder of Mc Mahon, while I was in the Jail at Washington, D.C. You sent a number of witnesses from Salem to identify me, which they done.

Now I have since then been sentenced to 25 years and am now confined here in this prison.

I do now change my former confession in any way. I commited that murder. I alone am guilty. I am not sorry. My consicence does not trouble me. I sleep sound and have sweet dreams. I am not insane. I not only committed that murder but 21 more besides and I assure you here and now that if I ever get free and have the opportunity I shall sure knock off another 22.

I am very truly Carl Pangram #31614."

Warden White also furnished Agent with photostat copy of a letter addressed to Mr. Henry James, % Miss E. Trott, The Lenmar Apts., No. 2100 N. St.N.W., Washington, D.C., which reads as follows:

"Leavenworth, Kansas, June 22, 1929.

I wrote to you last Sunday and again today. I don't expect you to write as often as I do. I have a little more time to spare than you have, in fact I have so much time to spare that I have a hard job in passing it. You on the other hand, I presume havent enough time. Well Theres a remedy for that. But why worry about time when a guy like Einestine says there is no such a thing as time. I don't know about that tho. I have my doubts about his theory. He's a pretty shrewd bird all right but when he says there is no such a thing as time then I half suspect that he has never been in the Jail House. Then there was another Big Shot who wrote that, "Stone Walls and Iron bars do not a prison make." I think that if he had to pack away 25 Boffoes in this Joint, he would soon sing a different song. He wouldn't sing at all but if he ever did it would be, "The Jail-House Blues." Some of these writers sprin some queer theories about what they know very little. I guess thats all balled up in grammer, but I guess you cabish what I am trying to write in my own dumb way.

The 28th day of this month will be my birthday, should I be unfortunate enough to live that long. But I suppose I'll be still kicking around then. I allways have had luck. Anything I want, I seldom get, but If I don't want some certain thing,That Thing I am sure to get. I sure would like to know who or what is or was my jinx. I wouldn't harm him or it, much. That is, not too much. I met a poor chump here sometime ago to whom I put this querry and his answer was to office me a bible and a prayer book. Yes, you guessed it, He is still alive, but only because I didn't bring my pistols with me when I came here. I must be more dumb than I think I am. He and others like him can get comfort and happiness out of things that I can only get more made at. I have read everything I could get and that I was able to understand with my limited amount of intelligence but sill I am as much in the dark as ever. But anyway to cut out the hot air and get down to what I have been thinking about more or less, is this. If or when you do send me any money, please be sure to send it either by registered mail or in P. O. Money Order and not in cash. But you better hurry up tho, because eversince I read that article in the American Mag by Petty I have been thinking more and more about what a fine little angel I'll make. A Golden Harp, a haloe and a pair of wings. Nothing to do but flap my wings and crow like a rooster. Ride the Clouds instead of having to live like -   Carl Panzram No. 31614 Box 7 Leavenworth,Ks."

Agent interviewed Subject CARL PANZRAN in the isolation ward at the Federal Penitentiary, where he is now confined and first advised Subject Panzran of his constitutional rights and asked him if he desired to make a statement, to which he stated he did not. Agent then asked Subject Panzran if he had struck R. G. Wernke with an iron bar and he stated he had. Agent then asked him if he had struck him with the purpose of killing him and he answered: "Hell, Yes, what do you suppose I hit him for, if I did not intend killing him." Agent then asked him his cause or purpose in striking Mr. Wernke and Panzran replied that he "had a cause which he would tell in Court and not before and did not care to be questioned further in this matter."

FRED L. MORRISON, Captain of Guards, and inmate HUGH PEARSON were present when interview was had with Panzran.

At the time of the above interview with Panzran he appeared calm, normal in mind, and before answering any of Agent's questions inquired thoroughly as to Agent's authority in questioning him.

Description and previous criminal record of Subject CARL PANZRAN are as follows:

"NAME: CARL PANZRAN, alias
John O'Leary.-Jefferson Baldwin.

Color	White
Reg. No. 31614	Federal Penitentiary, Leavenworth, Ks.
Age	36
Height	5 ft 9 3/8
Weight	185
Build	Muxc.
Complexion	Lt.
Hair	Blk. tr. grey
Eyes	med. Sl.
Sentenced	Nov. 12, 1928
From	D-Washington D.C. for 25 years
Crime	House-breaking & Larceny

Marks, scars, etc:

Tatoo 5 pt. star on frt lft shldr
anchor on left forearm, Rose & leaves & stem.
Navy Anchor head of Chinese Mandaran
pierced by dagger on rt forearm
5 pt. star on R frt. shldr. Double eagle
& 5 pt star & words in print - Liberty-Justice
on chest

FPC   (O/W)   M
           32   0   0 I
           32   I   I M"

"UNITED STATES PENITENTIARY
Leavenworth, Kansas.

Color

Record of - Carl Panzran   Register No. 31614   WHITE
Alias - John O'Leary, Jefferson Baldwin, Jeff Rhodes, Jeff Davis
Crime - House Breaking and Larceny   Civil
Sentence - 25 years (1-10 yr and 1-15 yr sent consec)
Received at Penitentiary Feb. 1, 1929, from D-Washington, D.C.
Date of Sentence Nov. 12, 1928   Sentence begins, Nov. 12, 1928
Maximum term ends, Nov. 11, 1953   Minimum term ends, Aug. 25, 1945.
Good time allowed, 3,000 days   Occupation, Sailor   Age 36 years
Eligible to parole, Mar. 11, 1936.
WANTED BY: (1) Chief of Police, Salem, Mass.   (2) District Attorney,
       Philadelphia. (3) State Penitentiary, Salem, Oregon.

CRIMINAL HISTORY

1902 As: Carl Panzran, #2532 Minnesota State Training
School for Boys, Red Wing, Minnesota, until
21 yrs of age, from E. Grand Forks, Minn., for
Larceny, Released by Parole 1904

1905 As: Carl Panzran, #?? State Reform School, Miles
City, Montanta, 1 year for Larceny, from Butte,
Montana, Escaped 1906.

1906 As: Carl Panzran, #1874 USDB, EX Fort Leavenworth,
Kansas, 3 years for 62nd Article of War, from
Fort Harrison, Montana, Released by Expiration
1910.

1912 AS: Jeff Davis, #?? State Prison, Deer Lodge, Mont.
1 year for Burglary from Three Forks, Mont.
Escaped.

As: Jeff Davis, #?? State Prison, Deer Lodge, Mont.
1 year for Escape on First Conviction. Released
by Expiration 1914.   #7390.

1914 As: Jefferson Baldwin, Oregon State Prison, Salem,
Oregon. 7 years for Burglary, from Astoria, Ore.
Escaped 1915."

     It may here be noted that the iron bar used by Subject Panzran in murder of
R. G. Warnke is retained and preserved for evidence, if desired, by Warden T. B. White
at the Penitentiary, Leavenworth, Kansas.

     Photograph and fingerprints of Subject Panzran were obtained and are with
and a part of this file.

     Copy of this report is being furnished the United States Attorney at
Topeka, Kansas, for his attention and such action as desired.

PENDING.

The HOUSE of WHISPERING HATE

By

CHARLES S. WHARTON

Ex-Congressman, Ex-Lawyer, Ex-Convict

Edited By
HARRY READ

Former City Editor, Chicago American

MADELAINE MENDELSOHN
CHICAGO

The House of Whispering Hate is regarded as one of the most accurate books on life inside Leavenworth Penitentiary. Wharton's account of the hanging of Panzram is the most accurate and detailed account of an eyewitness account of the execution. (Note the misspelling of Warnke's name.)

THE HOUSE OF WHISPERING HATE

By

Charles S. Wharton

Ex-congressman, ex-lawyer, ex-convict

Edited by
Harry Read
Former City Editor, Chicago American

Madelaine Mendelsohn
Chicago - ©1932

Charles Stuart Wharton (April 22, 1875 – September 4, 1939) was a U.S. Representative from Illinois.

Born in Aledo, Illinois, Wharton moved to Chicago with his parents in 1878, attending the public schools. He graduated from the law department of the University of Michigan at Ann Arbor in 1896. He was admitted to the bar in 1896 and commenced practice in Chicago, Illinois. He served as prosecuting attorney for the town of Lake in 1899, and was appointed assistant city attorney of Chicago in 1903.

In 1904, Wharton was elected as a Republican to the Fifty-ninth Congress (March 4, 1905 – March 3, 1907). He was an unsuccessful candidate for reelection in 1906 to the Sixtieth Congress. He subsequently resumed the practice of law in Chicago, Illinois.

Wharton served as member of the Board of Exemption and Government Appeal Agent at Chicago during the First World War and also served as an assistant corporation counsel in 1919. In 1920 he was appointed Assistant State's Attorney and served in this capacity until December 1923, when he resigned to resume private practice.

Wharton again resumed the practice of law in Chicago, Illinois, but in 1928, he was convicted of conspiracy in connection with the robbery of a mail train in Evergreen Park, Illinois, and was consequently disbarred. He was imprisoned in Leavenworth Prison from 1929 to 1931.[1]

Wharton later operated a restaurant and was author of several books. He died in Chicago, Illinois, September 4, 1939. He was interred in Mount Hope Cemetery.

(Source: Wikipedia contributors. (2019, May 15). Charles S. Wharton. In Wikipedia, The Free Encyclopedia. Retrieved 15:52, May 11, 2020, from https://en.wikipedia.org/w/index.php?title=Charles_S._Wharton&oldid=897219510)

Charles S. Wharton (left) and United States Deputy Marshall Joseph Spizziri boarding the train for Leavenworth Penitentiary.

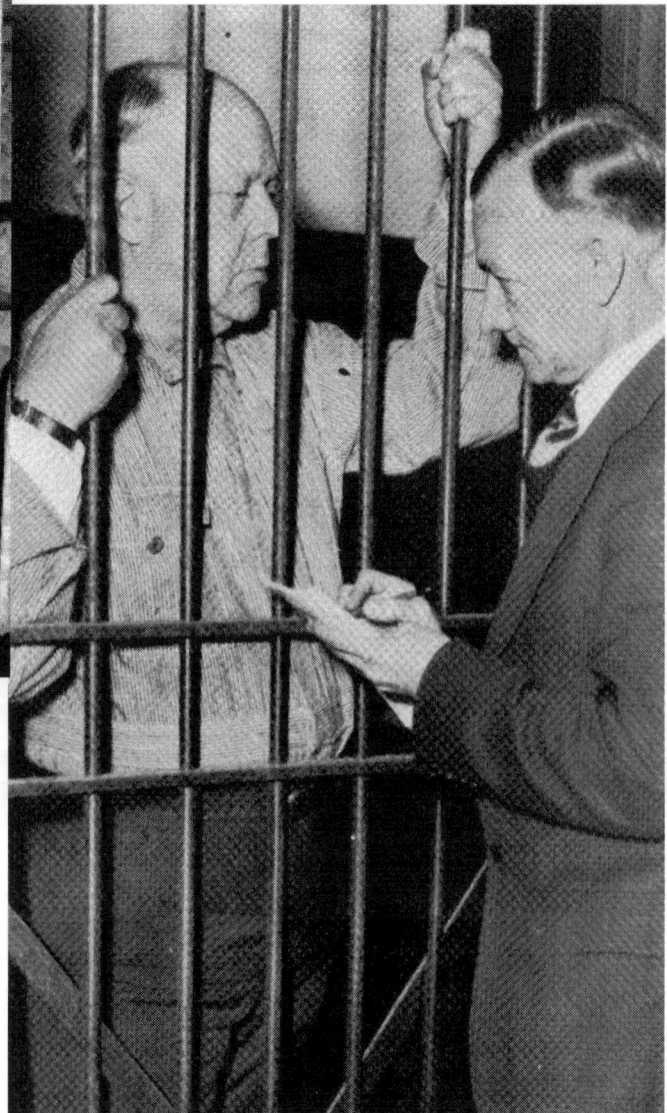

Charles S. Wharton behind bars at Leavenworth.

THE HOUSE OF WHISPERING HATE - Chapter 3 pp 24-25

We had shuffled forth to another breakfast of greasy, tasteless food, when suddenly there was a terrific uproar behind our line, and a moment later guards rushed past, bearing a stretcher. I glimpsed a lumpy form huddled beneath a blanket, and then my legs nearly gave way, for the rear end of the covering failed to conceal a hairy, broken human skull from which a bloody, gelatinous mass exuded forth upon the dirty canvas.

I wanted to turn and stagger back to my cot, but prison discipline doesn't take such things into account. Therefore I kept on to the mess hall where the sight of dirty tin plates, the smell of sloppy food, nearly succeeded in putting me on sick call.

Word of the murder spread like wildfire through the prison. The victim was Warnicke, civilian foreman of the laundry, whom the convicts regarded as a brute and a bully, delighting to torment his prison slaves. It was his favorite diversion to taunt Panzaran, a convict murderer, about his reported moral habits, but the day of his killing he had jeered once too often. Goaded to frenzy, Panzaran picked up an iron bar, and with a single savage swing, smashed off the top of the foreman's head.

For days the prisoners spoke of nothing else, and gradually I managed to overcome the nausea which memory of Warnicke's bloody and battered skull had induced, until I was able to discuss the affair without shuddering. As another aid to forgetfulness, I found myself busy answering the questions of curious prisoners. Phrased in their own peculiar lingo, they provided a few fleeting interludes of amusement, in spite of the irritation they caused me at first.

The Leavenworth Times
June 20, 1929

CONVICT MURDERS R. G. WARNKE

An Early Morning Break at Prison Farm Camp

USES FLAT-IRON
TO CRUSH SKULL
IN MORNING FRAY

**Foreman of Federal Penitentiary
Laundry Victim of Madman
in Surprise Attack.**

A LAUNDRY ROOM BATTLE

**Carl Panzram, Temporarily
Crazed, Runs Amuck and
Threatens Lives of
Other Prisoners.**

R. G. Warnke, 47, foreman of the federal prison laundry for the last eight years, early this morning was slain by a prisoner who attacked him with a heavy-flat iron a few minutes after Warnke had reported for duty.

Warnke's skull was beaten in by the prisoner, who used the heavy iron in dealing a terrific blow on the top of the foreman's head. Warnke died instantly.

After seeing the foreman fall to the floor of the laundry room, Carl Panzram, 36, the prisoner, ran amuck and threatened the lives of three other prisoners who were working in the room. Panzram was held at bay until Phil Hograve, a guard, answered the call of alarm and subdued Panzram, who immediately was placed in the isolation ward.

Warden Thomas B. White announced this morning Panzram was noted as a "bad actor" and was received at the federal prison February 1, 1929, from Washington, D. C. , Panzram's occupation was that of a sailor, Warden White said.

Panzram was convicted of larceny and housebreaking, the warden revealed and is under a sentence of 25 years at the prison here.

Warden White also asserted he understood Panzram was noted as a killer, although the prisoner had given no trouble until yesterday, when he was reported for a minor infraction of prison rules.

Panzram's disobedience was not reported by Warnke, the warden pointed out.

Warnke, as foreman of the laundry, was highly thought of in his line of duty and was reported to be popular among prisoners. He is said never to have reported a man unless the prisoner deliberately violated rules of the institution.

So far as could be learned there was no "bad blood" existing between Panzram and the slain man.

Panzram is reported to have suddenly become enraged a few minutes before 8 o'clock, when Warnke reported for duty. Although accurate details of the killing could not be learned, it is understood Panzram seized the heavy flat iron and buried it in Warnke's head at a moment when Warnke was unprepared for the attack.

Shouting incoherently the crazed man darted across the room toward another prisoner and threatened to strike him over the head with the heavy iron.

Shouting for nearby guards other prisoners managed to keep clear of Panzram, who appeared temporarily crazed, until the prisoner was subdued.

Coroner Joseph Skaggs was summoned to the federal prison a few minutes after the killing and Mrs. Florence Warnke, wife of the slain man, was notified at her home, 712 Dakota Street.

Despite the terrible shock caused by news of her husband's death, Mrs. Warnke controlled herself sufficiently to notify her son, Bob Warnke, 23, whose home is in Phoenix, Ariz.

According to Mrs. Warnke, her husband seldom discussed his work at the prison.

"He wanted to forget it as soon as he got home," Mrs. Warnke sobbed this morning. "But I do believe he had less trouble with the men than any other official there. He always was kind to everyone but there were times when he feared he would be killed."

Mrs. Warnke exhibited a wicked looking blackjack which she said her husband had taken from a prisoner sometime ago.

"He had to watch them constantly; he never knew when he would be stabbed or hit on the head," she said.

Warnke had spoken of no trouble with the prisoners, she said. He left his home this morning in good spirits.

"And a few minutes later they told me he had been murdered," the grief-stricken woman cried.

121

Warden White announced this morning he would notify the Department of Justice immediately and that an investigation into Warnke's death would be made.

The body was removed this morning to the Bush-Lowe funeral home, Sixth and Olive streets, where it will remain until further arrangements are made. Funeral arrangements probably will be completed upon the arrival of Bob Warnke of Phoenix, Ariz., tomorrow afternoon.

Washington, June 20--(AP)--Carl Panzram who killed a prison laundry foreman in Leavenworth today, was regarded as one of the most vicious prisoners ever in the District of Columbia jail.

When he was sentenced to twenty-five years for housebreaking and burglary, Panzram staged a scene in the courtroom, shouting that he hated "the whole human race and would like to kill every person in the world."

Prior to his sentence, Panzram told the jail superintendent that he had killed a boy in Salem, Mass., and another in Philadelphia and also wrote a letter to the chief of police in New London, Conn., in which he said he killed a boy either near New London, or New Haven, adding that he had forgotten because of the number of persons he had murdered.

Two Massachusetts women, Mrs. Bertha M. Luxton, of Marblehead, and Mrs. Theresa Parsons of Salem, identified Panzram as the man last seen with 12 year old Henry McMahon, who was found slain near the outskirts of Salem six years ago. An effort was made to extradite Panzram but authorities here decided to hold him on the larceny and burglary charges.

ROBERT WARNKE TO BE BURIED AT JUNCTION CITY

If Son Arrives in Time Funeral Will Be Saturday Afternoon

TO TRY CONVICT FOR MURDER

Panzram Probably Will Spend the Remainder of His Life in Solitary Confinement If He Is Not Hanged --- The Legal Procedure.

The body of Robert G. Warnke, foreman of the federal prison laundry, who was killed by Carl Panzram Thursday morning, will be taken to Junction City, Kas., for burial. This is the old home of Mrs. Warnke, it is said, and it is desired to have the interment at that place.

The son, Robert Warnke, Jr., is said to be on his way from Phoenix, Arizona, and he is expected in Saturday night. The funeral will be held at the Bush-Lowe mortuary at 2 o'clock Saturday afternoon and the body will be sent to Junction City Sunday.

Mr. Warnke was a quiet unassuming man, who attended strictly to his own busines and he was well liked by the prison officials. They all deeply deplore his sad end. He was also liked by the prisoners. Laundry foreman is one of the most trying positions at the penitentiary and as a rule prisoners do no not lik to work in the hot place. Mr. Warnke handled the men without much friction and he seldom placed reports against them. It is said he did not make a report against Panzram, who murdered him in a brutal manner.

Panzram in Isolation Cell.
Panzram is now held in a solitary cell in the isolation department of the penitentiary. It is said he refused to make any statement about his killing Warnke and he maintains a sullen attitude.

Statements will be secured from all who witnessed the murder of Warnke and they will be embodied in reports that will be sent to the Department of Justice in Washington and the United States attorney for Kansas. This will be followed by giving Panzram a preliminary hearing before United States Commissioner Lee Bond and then a grand jury indictment. If the preliminary procedure is expedited Panzram can be tried on a first degree murder charge at the October term of the United States district court in Leavenworth.

If convicted of first degree murder and he is sentenced to be hanged, the chances are, judging from other federal penitentiary murder trials, he will be commuted to a life sentence and will then be placed in what is termed solitary confinement for the remainder of his life as a "dangerous character." This is done on the recommendation of the warden approved by an order from the attorney general of the United States.

Congenial Companions.

Panzram will have as company Robert Stroud, who killed Guard Andrew Turner by stabbing him in the heart; Ona Manuel, who killed Guard Robert Barr, by stabbing him in the breast with a chisel; John Aday, an Apache Indian, who murdered Thomas Wallace, another prisoner, by hitting him on the back of the head with a baseball bat. These may not be very pleasant companions, but they ought to prove congenial to a revengeful creature with a record of Panzram.

Solitary confinement in the federal penitentiary is not the severe punishment that the designation would imply compared with some state prisons. In many of the state prisons when a prisoner is placed in solitary confinement he never is allowed to leave his cell unless he becomes so sick that he has to be transferred to the hospital. He is not allowed books or newspapers or anything in the form of recreation.

Under the rules governing the federal penitentiary a "dangerous character" is isolated mainly to keep him from injuring an officer or another prisoner. He receives the same food as other prisoners, is furnished books from the library and newspaper if he has the money to pay for the subscription, is allowed out of his cell two hours each day for exercise in the brick wall inclosure 40 feet wide by 17 feet long. If he tries to kill one of his comrades or makes a disturbance he is held in a cell for a week or more until he agrees to behave himself.

Stroud and Manuel put in their time painting pictures, raising canary birds, and in various other ways. They never are allowed out in the main yard with other prisoners or to attend ball games or picture shows.

They are not taken into the chapel Sunday morning, but it is part of the duty of the prison chaplains to visit them at their cells and offer them religious advice. As a rule they do not show much enthusiasm over the visits of the chaplains.

SEGREGATION AND THE BIRDMAN

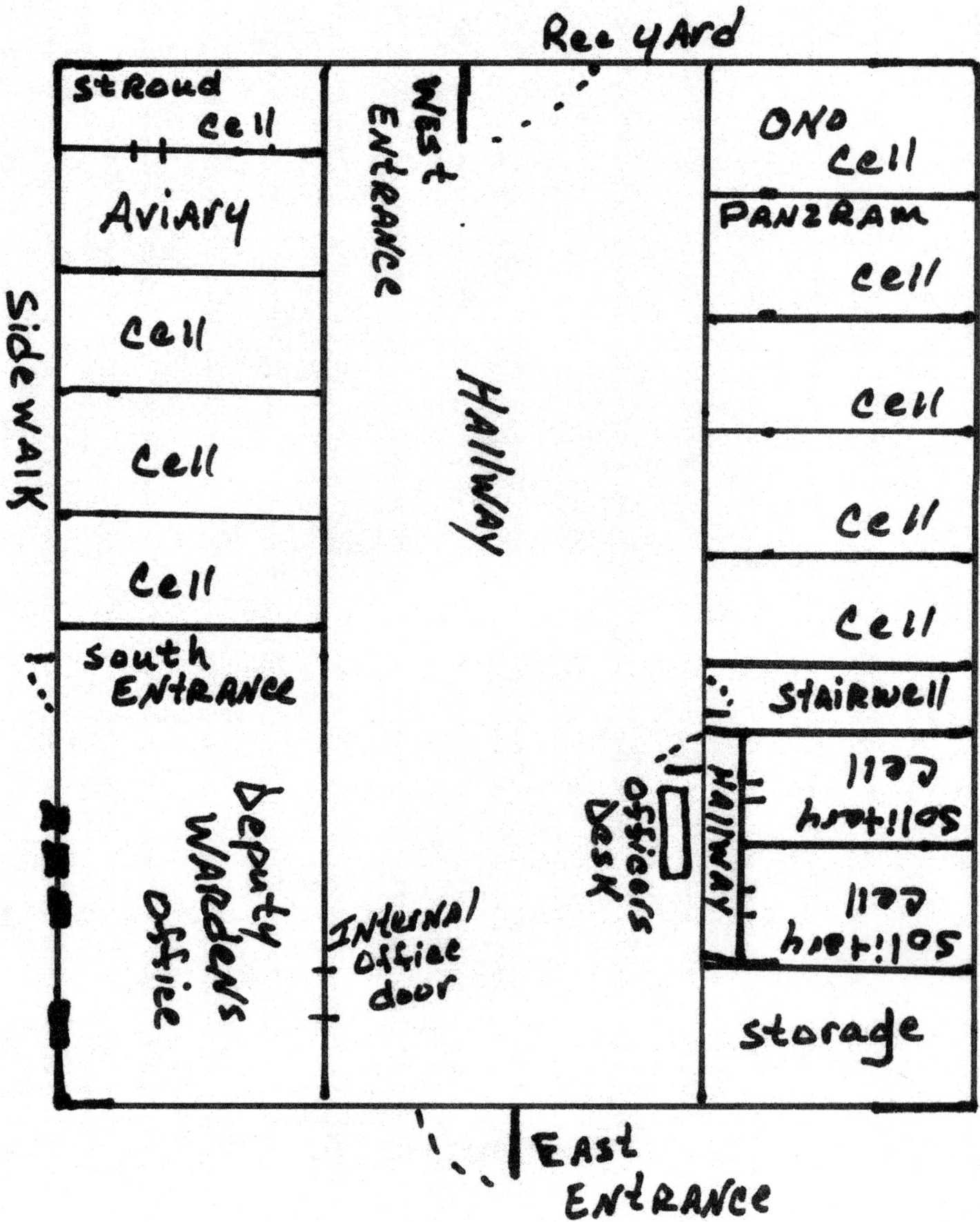

BUILDING 63: DEPUTY WARDEN'S OFFICE & SEGREGATION FIRST FLOOR INTERIOR
(*Courtesy of Ken LaMaster*)

Back in that era there were two Isolation Cells in building 63, they had solid doors on the front of the cells and inmates couldn't communicate with each other. Segregation cells had barred doors and inmates had periods where they could talk from cell to cell. They usually placed inmates like Panzram in isolation when they first entered the segregation building until the Deputy Warden, Warden, and Dr's could evaluate them. After the initial statements were taken and the investigation of the violent incident ended and the inmate was deemed most likely to behave himself he'd be placed in a regular seg cell. Usually the minutes following a violent killing or serious assault the individual is on a massive adrenaline rush and for some it takes a while for them to come down. Those guys are placed in a cell where they can't harm staff or other inmates and usually are left there until they come down. A lot of times we would let them "sleep it off" until the woke up the next day. I've only seen two inmates after a murder that were calm, cool, and collected. Both their blood pressure was normal, neither were hopped up, sweating, nothing. It was like another day at a ho hum job.

Ken LaMaster
Historian/Author
1983 – 2010 USP Leavenworth, Senior Officer Specialist

BUILDING 63 - THE DEPUTY WARDEN/SOCIAL SERVICE & SEGREGATION BUILDING

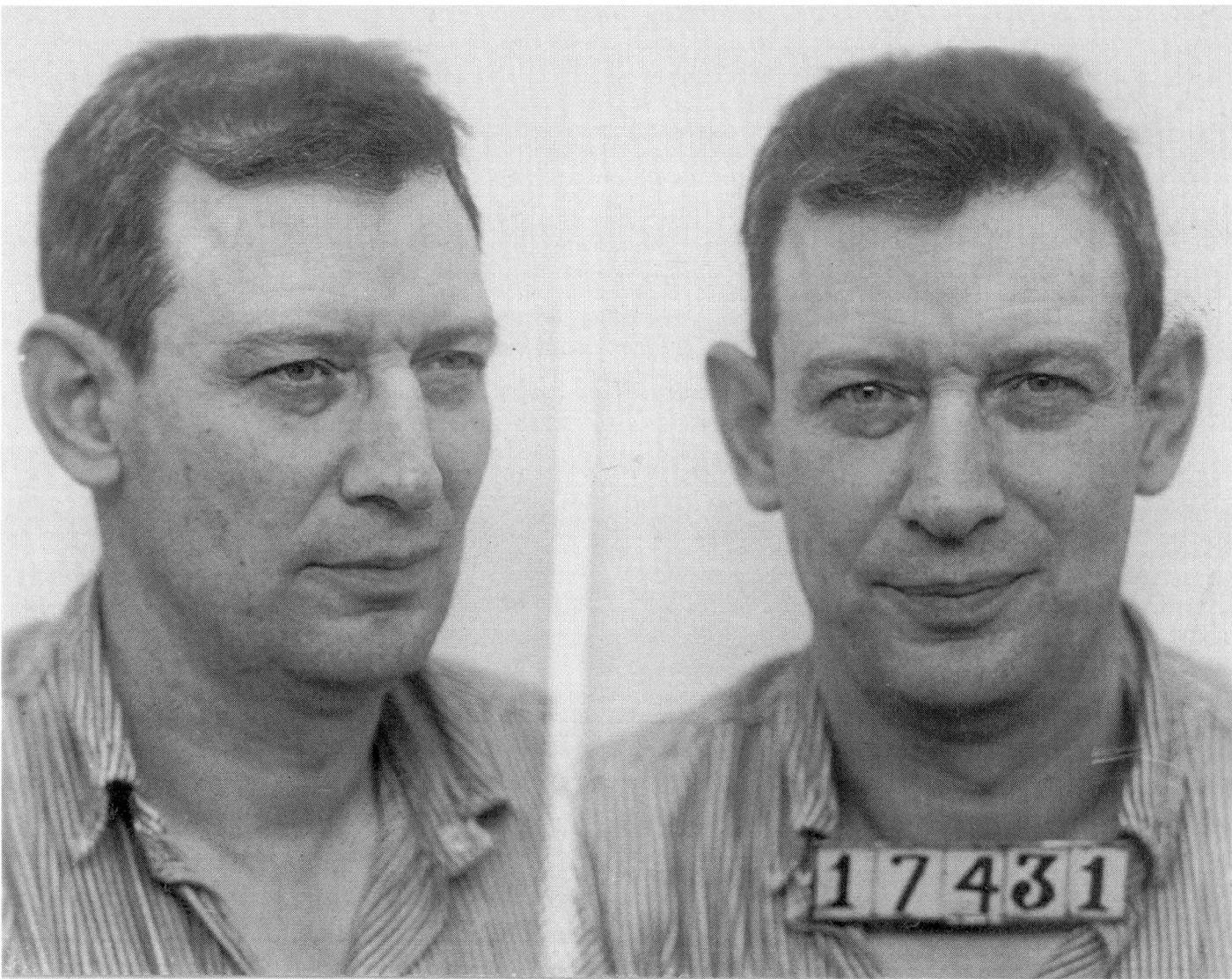

ROBERT STROUD

Robert Stroud is famous for being "The Birdman of Alcatraz", even though Stroud had 2 cells containing his bird aviary in Leavenworth, NOT at Alcatraz. While at Alcatraz, Stroud wrote a manuscript on the history of the penal system, which was a scathing indictment of the practices of prisons and was never published. Through my research, I met and interviewed Charles Dudley Martin, who was Robert Stroud's Springfield, MO attorney. Dudley had all of the hand-written pages of Roberts Stroud's writings and also typed copies in his possession when I met him in October of 2008. In an effort to publish these works, I sent Dudley a proposal, which he declined. In the last conversation I had with Dudley, I was told that the company which had the manuscripts had lost or damaged either the handwritten originals or the typed copies. No more information has been discovered on where these manuscripts are, or if they will ever be published. The truth of Stroud's writings on Panzram will never be known. Stroud seems to take credit for some of Panzram's actions and even writes about Panzram's execution, which he was not even able to see personally as all the windows had been covered in Stroud's cell. As an expert in the field of true crime, I do not place much truth in Stroud's writings of Panzram and feel they must be taken as fiction as there are numerous inaccuracies in Stroud's retelling of events. Although Stroud's writings on Panzram are fascinating, it seemed Stroud wanted all the attention. (Notated are sections of Stroud's writings where Henry Lesser wrote notations. Also note Stroud's misspelling of Warnke's name.)

Looking Outward

Part III

The Seeds Of Destruction

Chapter XIX

Panzeran.
The Man Who Over Played His Hand.

Panzram

The Man Who Over-Played His Hand.

Carl Panzram worked in the Laundry; so, naturally, he was no stranger to the Kluxer's, Robert Warnakey's, vile insults and equally vicious pencil. He had done one stretch in the hole and had gone to Third Grade on one of Warnakey's reports.

Now, as a general rule, most guards and foremen did not want a man back in their shop or gang after having him put in Third Grade, and when men came out of Third Grade, they were sent to other gangs or shops unless their former guard or foreman asked for them. But it was also a general rule that no man would be given a change of work if his foreman asked for him. In such cases, it was presumed that the man was a useful worker and that his foreman was trying to help him.

Back in the old days, many guards asked for men who had struck them, not with the idea of avenging themselves, but in order to assist the inmate and remove any trace of bitterness by returning good for evil.

Normally, this system worked well. Foremen were not responsible for discipline. Most foremen did not report or abuse their men. On the contrary, they were always ready to front for them and stand between them and trouble. They asked for men who had worked for them, when they were coming out of grade, to keep them from being put on worse jobs.

Warnakey, however, being a complete sadist, asked for his men because he could not bear the thought of losing a victim. So, when Carl had come out of grade a few days before the riot, he had gone back to the laundry. He had been one of the men assigned to wrecking the laundry machinery, at which he had done a rather thorough job. He had been taken out after the riot, halted before, given a tongue lashing, rather than a hearing, marched down that long, main corridor, out the left-hand door, to the head of those steps, and he had been hit over the head with a blackjack. But Carl Panzram was heavily-built, thick-set man of medium hight, with heavy bones and a thick skull.

He was of German extraction, about forty years old; he had been a sailor on windjammers; and he had powerful hands and arms. He had not gone down under the blow. He had swung around to face his assailants with extended arms and craping fingers. And no one had wanted to step within within reach of these thick, stubby fingers, which had power enough behind them to crush an ordinary man's bones. So there had been no further attempt to beat him. He had been march to the isolation and chained to the door, and, as this was being done, he had addressed the man who had struck him.

"Listen, punk!" Panzram had said. "I have strangled many better men than you, and if I ever get my hand on you or that monkey-face Zerbst, I will ring your necks like I would a chicken's. That

Carl Panzeran worked in the Laundry; so, naturally, he was no stranger to the Kluxer's, Robert Warnakey's, vile insults and equally vicious pencil. He had done one stretch in the hole and had gone to Third Grade on one of Warnakey's reports.

Now, as a general rule, most guards and foremen did not want a man back in their shop or gang after having him put in Third Grade, and when men came out of Third Grade, they were sent to other gangs or shops unless their former guard or foreman asked for them. But it was also a general rule that no man would be given a change of work if his foreman asked for him. In such cases, it was presumed that the man was a useful worker and that his foreman was trying to help him.

Back in the old days, many guards asked for men who had struck them, not Not with the idea of avenging themselves, but in order to assist the inmate and remove any trace of bitterness by returning good for evil. Normally, this system worked well. Foremen were not responsible for   discipline. Most foremen did not report or abuse their men. On the contrary, they were always ready to front for them and stand between them and trouble. They asked for men who had worked for them, when they were coming out of grade, to keep them from being put on worse jobs.

Warnakey, however, being a complete sadist, asked for his men because he could not bear the thought of losing a victim. So, when Carl had come out of grade a few jays before the riot, he had gone back to the Laundry, he had been one of the men assigned to wrecking the laundry machinery, at which he had done a rather thorough job. He had been taken out after the riot, hailed before Zerbst, Given a tongue lashing, rather than a hearing, marched down that long, main corridor, out the left hand door, to the head of those steps, and he had been hit over the head with a blackjack. But Carl Panzeran was heavily built, thick-set man of medium height, with heavy bones and a thick skull.

He was of German extraction, about forty years old; he had been a sailor on windjammers; and he had powerful hands and arms. He had not gone down under the blow. He had swung around to face his assailants with extended arms and groping fingers. And no one had wanted to step within reach of those thick, stubby fingers, which had power enough behind them to crush an ordinary man's bones, so there had been no further attempt to beat him. He had been marched to the Isolation and chained to this door, and, as this was being done he had addressed the man who struck him.

"Listen, Punk!" Panzeran had said. "I have strangled many better men than you, and if I ever get my hand on you or that monkey-face Zerbst, I will ring your necks like I would a chicken's. That long, scrawny neck of yours will pop like a pipe stem." And Carl focused his pale-blue eye on the guard's neck, like a connoisseur studying a strange and interesting work of art, and even though his hands were chained, no one wanted to hit him.
Panzeran had been put in D-cellhouse, and he had been one of the last men turned out.

All of this had made Carl Panzeran extremely unhappy, but other things made him even more angry. He was serving thirty or forty years the writer had forgotten which and he did not think that he could serve out his sentence. He had no intention of trying to do so under conditions unacceptable to him. He was a yegg. He had been a passive and active pederast since before his twelfth birthday, and following the riot, instead of putting him back with the boy he had been celling with before he went to Third Grade, Freddy had forced him to cell alone.

Naturally, that had made Panzeran more angry than anything else. He was a vigorous and powerful man, still in the prime of life, and he was not exactly a fool. He knew that to be forced to cell alone under his circumstances, to see youth and pulchritude all around him; yet, to be forever denied, could lead to only one end: Madness.

Note: All statements concerning Panzeran's reasoning and motives are purely theoretical on the part of the writer. The most he ever talked to Panzeran was to pass the time of day. But he did hear Panzeran talk to the guards who kept watch over him, for fourteen hours per day, every day, for almost a year, and having spent his entire adult and most of his youth in rather close association with criminals; he believes that he knows criminal psychology as well as any person who breathes, as well as he knows the palm of his own hand.

131

His conclusions are based upon his analyses of Panzeran's conversations with his guards in the light of almost half a century of study of the criminal mind, including his own.

Panzaran was not the type of man who goes off half cocked. All his life it had been his habit to think things through. He was serving what amounted in his eyes to a life sentence, so another life sentence would mean nothing to him. Kansas had no death sentence, and while three men had been sentenced to death, no one had ever been executed. If they would not execute a man who was sane, they surely would not execute a man who was insane, and only an insane man would seek his own execution. Only an insane man kill without reason. He was not the type of man who could or would play demented, but he could pattern his conduct in such a manner as to make anyone think that be must be demented.

He undoubtedly knew that the case or provocation amounting to justification that he could build in the case of Warnakey was so strong that no jury would ever hang him, but Warnakey was not the principal or only man that he wanted and intended to kill. The man that he really most wanted to kill was Zerbst, (note here by Lesser: "Fred Zerbst, Deputy Warden" and "as a substitute for Colonel Peak perhaps.") but by killing Warnakey, too, he would be doing a public service, ridding the world of a miserable sadist.

Of course, killing that monkey-faced baboon would be doing the world, and particularly his fellow inmates, a service, but he was not so sure that he would be able to convince the public of that. This would make him well liked within the prison; it would give him prestige with the younger generation of inmates; and if he did not come through alive and ever got out of isolation, it would be a long time before another Deputy Warden refused him a cellmate. If he did not come through, he would not have lost much, anyway. He would probably be better off dead than to be the way he was, since outside of the little joys to be found in prison, life had nothing in store for him. The writer having heard this line of reasoning from the lips of hundreds of hopeless men and on occasion having reasoned the same way himself, knows that it is the natural line of reasoning for a man in Panzaran's frame of mind to take. He was not the type of man who normally causes trouble in prison. Left alone, with a congenial cellmate, no one would ever know that be was in the institution, but he was not the type who can be pushed around with impunity, either.

He also planned to kill any stool pigeon who got in his way, too. That would boost his stock with his fellow inmates.

The Killing of Warnakey

Having made up his mind to kill, the next question was a choice of weapons, and it's right here that he made his first mistake. A knife was out. A man who amuck never uses a knife excepting by the accident of association. A butcher who blows his top, with knives all around him, never snatches up a knife. He always grabs the cleaver, for it is natural for the mad man to want to strike and chop. He did not have an ax or a clever, so he made up his mind to use a crow bar, although, in his case, using any weapon was foolish. As he had told the guard who struck him, he did not need any weapon but his hands, and they would not have attracted any attention.

There was a few days overlap between the taking over of the D. B, and the transfer for of the drug addicts, and it was at this time that Panzeran chose to make his move.

Freddy (note from Lesser: Fred Zerbst, Deputy Warden) usually came over to his office in the morning while the line was coming out of the dining room, about five minutes before the court call line came over. By stepping out of line while going into the dining room, Carl could manage to be at the head of the line when it came out. He could kill Warnakey before there were too many convicts around to spread the alarm, then he could go over to Freddy's office just ahead of the court call line and finish him.

On Wednesday morning, October 2, 1929, Panzeran made his play. He reached the laundry among the first half-dozen men, went over and picked up the crowbar that was used for opening boxes and crates, walked up to Warnakey and struck him over the head with it. He cracked Warnakey's skull like an eggshell, but hit him a couple more times to make sure. (note from Lesser: "Vogel said, I believe, crowbar was used as a lever for----washing machine."

Several convicts had witnessed the killing, but no one was sorry and no one gave an alarm. Panzeran, the bar held in his hand at his side, stepped calmly out of the laundry and walked over to the Isolation building, not over sixty feet away. He walked in the door and went on into Freddy's office just as if he owned the place, and no one paid a partical of attention to him.

Ballard, the only guard in the building at that moment, saw him, but he did not notice the crow bar, and he was too new at the institution to realize that Panzeran's actions were unusual. He had seen several other convicts come in and turn into the package room or the back office, and he did not realize that Panzeran did not belong there.

But right then is where Panzeran made his second big mistake. The office was empty. For some reason Zerbst had not arrived, and thinking that the alarm about the killing of Warnakey had surely gone out, he could not lay put. Had he just stepped over behind the door and stood there for a few minutes, Freddy would surely have walked in on him. But assuming that the alarm had gone out, he figured that anything that be intended to do had to be done fast. So instead of waiting, Panzeran charged into the back office where Freddy's clerks were just going to work. But a convict coming through a door where no convict was supposed to be was enough to put the clerks on their guard.

Panzeran swung at one of them, but they were all agile young men who played handball every day. The clerk easily sidestepped the blow, and he and his companions raced out of the door, out into the street and scattered. Panzeran then ran all the clerks out of the package room, and one, a known stool pigeon, he chased as far as the corner of the dining room, but could not catch him. Returning to the Deputy's office, he came upon a runner just about to enter the building and chased him as far as the corner of the powerhouse, but he was a heavy man; one of his legs had once been broken and was a little shorter than the other; and his short, thick, stubby legs had never been designed for running, anyway.

He came back to the Isolation, walked up to the door leading into the Isolation proper and, addressing Dale Ballard, announced: "I just killed Warnakey, and I came over here to kill Zerbst, but the monkey faced ___ ___ has not arrived yet, so you had just as well let me in." "Miller! Pearson!" cried Ballard, calling his two orderlies who were busy doing the breakfast dishes. To Panzeran he said: "Nothing doing! Not while you have that bar in your hands."

"Oh. hell! This must be my unlucky day." Panzeran threw down the bar. Ballard opened the door and let him in, and was in the act of dressing him in when Zerbst, his hands sunk deep in his pockets; his bullet-like head hanging between his heavy shoulders, as was his habit, came through the outer door and turned into his office, without glancing at anyone or even noticing the heavy crow bar lying on the floor.

By a quirk of fate and his own failure to realize the virtue of sitting tight, Panzeran had missed his principal quarry. Had he simply waited quietly, either in Freddy's office or the corridor in plain sight, no one would have paid the slightest attention to him, and Freddy would have walked right into his hands.

It had just happened that there was no one on court call that morning, and Freddy had stopped at the Captain's office to talk to someone. Had he reached his office at the usual time, the story would have been different. It is Indicative of how well Freddy was liked at that time that no one warned him against going into the office, even though all those clerks working in his office and the package were out in the street and could not have failed to have seen him.

When Freddy realized what a close call he had had, he had another attack of so-called indigestion and spent three day at home, sick. Had Panzeran caught him in the office, he probably would have died of fright before Panzeran reached him.

Panzeran was put in No. 13, right next to the orderlies cell, and was given only a tick on the floor. Ballard placed his chair right in front of Panzeran's door, and whenever he had to get up, he closed Panzeran's wooden door. About this time, Wren was sent to St. Elizabeth and the writer and Ono were the only ones left in Isolation. Ballard kept such close watch on them, that they had no chance to communicate with Panzeran, but when the writer, who has a good clear voice, had anything he wanted Panzeran to know, he would simply tell it to Ballard in a voice that he knew Panzeran would not fail to hear.

The killing of Warnakey was a very popular murder. At least ninety-nine percent of the inmates and forty per cent of the guards thoroughly approved of it. They felt that Panzeran had performed a public service, and at that time, just following the riot, percentages almost as large, if not larger would have been equally enthusiastic had he killed Freddy, too.

Had he chosen to make a defense of the contention that he had been driven to his act by persecution and mistreatment, he could have obtained a thousand witnesses who would have exposed just what had been going on in the institution, and there is hardly one chance in a hundred that he would have received a death sentence, but Panzeran chose the much more dangerous role of the homicidal maniac, who kills just to be killing.

All day long, day after day, he told Ballard murder stories of the most lurid and revolting variety. He told of sea murders by the score, all obviously based upon the crime for which he had been sent to prison, and in which he varied the number of victims from one to forty-eight. He told of box-car murders by the hundreds, of boys he had met on the road, induced to catch trains with him, raped, strangled, and thrown out along the right-of-way.
It was obvious to anyone listening who knew anything about such things that the stories were pure fiction, designed to convince Ballard that he was a homicidal maniac, and the details were so vague that Panzeran thought it would be impossible to check up on them.

Ballard, however, carried every one of the tales to Warden White, and White had everyone of them checked as carefully as possible, and railroad murders, being as common as they are, it was not surprising that in some cases, he hit the nail on the head by pure coincidence. When he told of a murder committed on such and such a railroad and such and such a division in 1921, or maybe it was 1922 or 1923, he was not sure, it was not surprising that in some case bodies had been found along the track during such a broad period of time and over such a long stretch of track. There are probably few railroad divisions in the United States along which at least one body has not been found in any three-year period.

The writer having listened to thousands of such stories is thoroughly convinced that practically all of Panzeran's murder stories were pure romances, told for the specific purpose of impressing Ballard. He has listened to the stories of many actual murders, too, but there is a vast difference between pseudo and the authentic variety. In telling of an actual killing, the killer dwells more upon the actions of the other party and his own subjective feelings roused by those actions, for he not only has to rationalize his conduct to himself, he has to rationalize it to his hearer. What he did is slurred over in the shortest possible sentences. A story that takes an hour in the telling, may be concluded with the simple words. So I let him have it. Then I did so and so.

Panzeran's stories lacked this quality. It was always a case of what he did, with the actions and reactions of the victim left very vague, and in no case was there any motive or any necessity for the killing, and people who really kill, never describe killings like that. The insane man, who really kills from pure lust, builds up the most complex systems of rationalization, and that is the one thing that Panzeran most carefully avoided, both in the case of Warnakey and mythical killings of which he told in such great number. Yet, he was very specific and emphatic in his reason for wanting to kill Zerbst.

By the time Panzeran went to trial, White and the United State Attorney had established a possible connection between his stories and eighteen unidentified bodies. There was not a bit of evidence that would actually connect him directly with any one of those bodies. Sometime there were months variation in time, several hundred miles variation in place, and totally different descriptions of the person killed, but taken in a group, they were altogether too convincing.

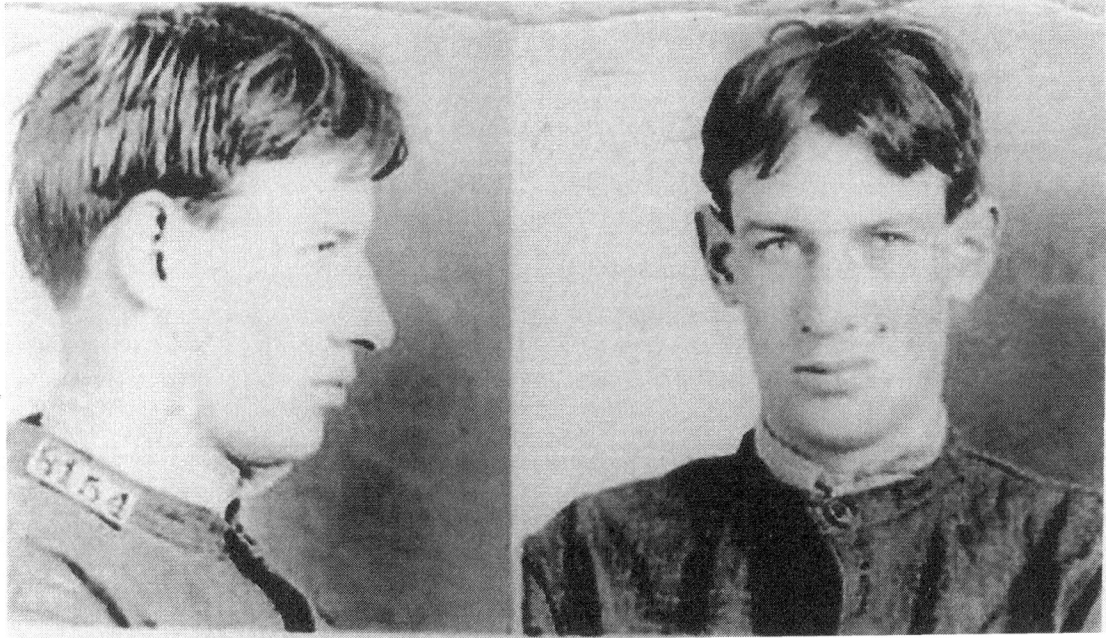

ROBERT STROUD - THE BIRDMAN OF LEAVENWORTH

DEPARTMENT OF JUSTICE
UNITED STATES PENITENTIARY
LEAVENWORTH, KANSAS

OFFICE OF THE PHYSICIAN

June 24, 1929.

Mr. T.B.White, Warden,
U.S.Penitentiary,
Leavenworth, Kansas.

Sir:

As soon as I entered the Institution, this morning, I was called to
Isolation.

When I arried there, I found
that Carl Panzran, Register Number 31614,
had gotten a hold of a safety razor blade
in some manner, and had cut the vein in his
elbow, anteriorily; losing a great deal of
blood. His pulse was quite rapid and feeble,
and Panzran was quite anemic and weak.

I sent Doctor Spence over to
clean the place up and put a sterilized dressing on his arm.

I left instructions with the
Attendant to give him plenty of coffee and
water.

This man stated to me that
the Government now had him and he might as
well end it the best way he could.

Respectfully,

C.A.Bennett,
Physician.

cc-FGZ

June 24 – 29

Deputy Warden
Institution

this Prisoner #31614 We are holding for
Investigation cut him self With a safty razor
blade Some time during the night While making
inspection of Cell this morning I found he was
cut on the Arm he told me he made a bad
Joh of it that he Would of made a good Joh
of it But he thought of one more he wanted to
take with him and decided to Wait And do bot
Jobs togeather

Sincerly Yours

H. Edmonds
Guard

137

31614

F. G. Zerbst,
Deputy Warden,
Institution.

Dear Sir;-

        In reference to the attempt of Carl Panzran
#31614 to take his life by cutting a vein in his elbow
what a safety razor blade that he got in some manner,
will state that I would like to have you issue all
necessary instructions to the Isolation Guards that all
precautions possible should be taken to prevent him
from taking his life.   If it is necessary to have a
Guard at his cell door for the entire twenty four hours
I want this done.

        I understand that since his wound was
dressed that he inflicted with a safety razor blade
that he pulled the dressings off and came very near
bleeding to death again and had to be admitted to the
Hospital for treatment.

        You can see that he is returned to Isolation
and carefully observed in order to prevent him from
destroying himself.

                    Very truly

                            T. B. White,
                            W A R D E N.

M

138

DEPARTMENT OF JUSTICE

UNITED STATES PENITENTIARY

LEAVENWORTH, KANSAS

OFFICE OF THE DEPUTY WARDEN

June 25, 1929.

I N S T R U C T I O N S

**TO GUARDS ON DUTY IN THE ISOLATION BUILDING IN
REFERENCE TO CARL PANZRAN, #31614.**

- - - - - - - -

This man has apparently twice made an effort to end
his life during the last few days, first by cutting a vein in
his arm and again by taking the bandage off of the injured
arm and re-opening the wound.

Every effort must be made to prevent this man from
taking his own life. During the day the guard on duty must
keep a constant watch to see that the prisoner does not
obtain anything with which he may destroy himself. Especially is there such danger while he is being shaved.
Have him shaved by a barber using a safety razor only. Be
careful to see that the dishes from which he eats or drinks
come out of the cell intact. No knife or fork are to be
allowed him. When he needs a hair cut, advise the undersigned in order that proper precautions may be taken.

Night guards must look into his cell frequently
and if not satisfied that all is right, call the Lieutenant
in charge of the shift.

Deputy Warden.

OFFICE OF THE DEPUTY WARDEN

June 26, 1929.

The Warden,
Institution.

Sir:-

Referring to your letter of yesterday in regard
to Carl Panzran #31614, I am enclosing for your information, a copy of instructions I have issued relative
to him. This should provide every reasonable safeguard.
However, if you wish to have an additional guard detailed
for the sole purpose of watching Panzran, please advise me
and such detail will, of course, be made.

We are so very short of guards that it will be necessary to draw such additional guards from places where they
are sorely needed. We have been extremely short of guards
for several weeks, due to sickness, transporting prisoners
on writs and the necessity of using guards for other special
duties, such as replacing absent officers other than guards,
on duty at the bridge, etc.

We should be operating the quarry and resume the re-
pairs of the Weston Bluff road as early as available guards
will permit. Repair of the Missouri River revetment also is
a necessity.

Respectfully,

F. G. Zerbst
Deputy Warden.

FGZ'W

140

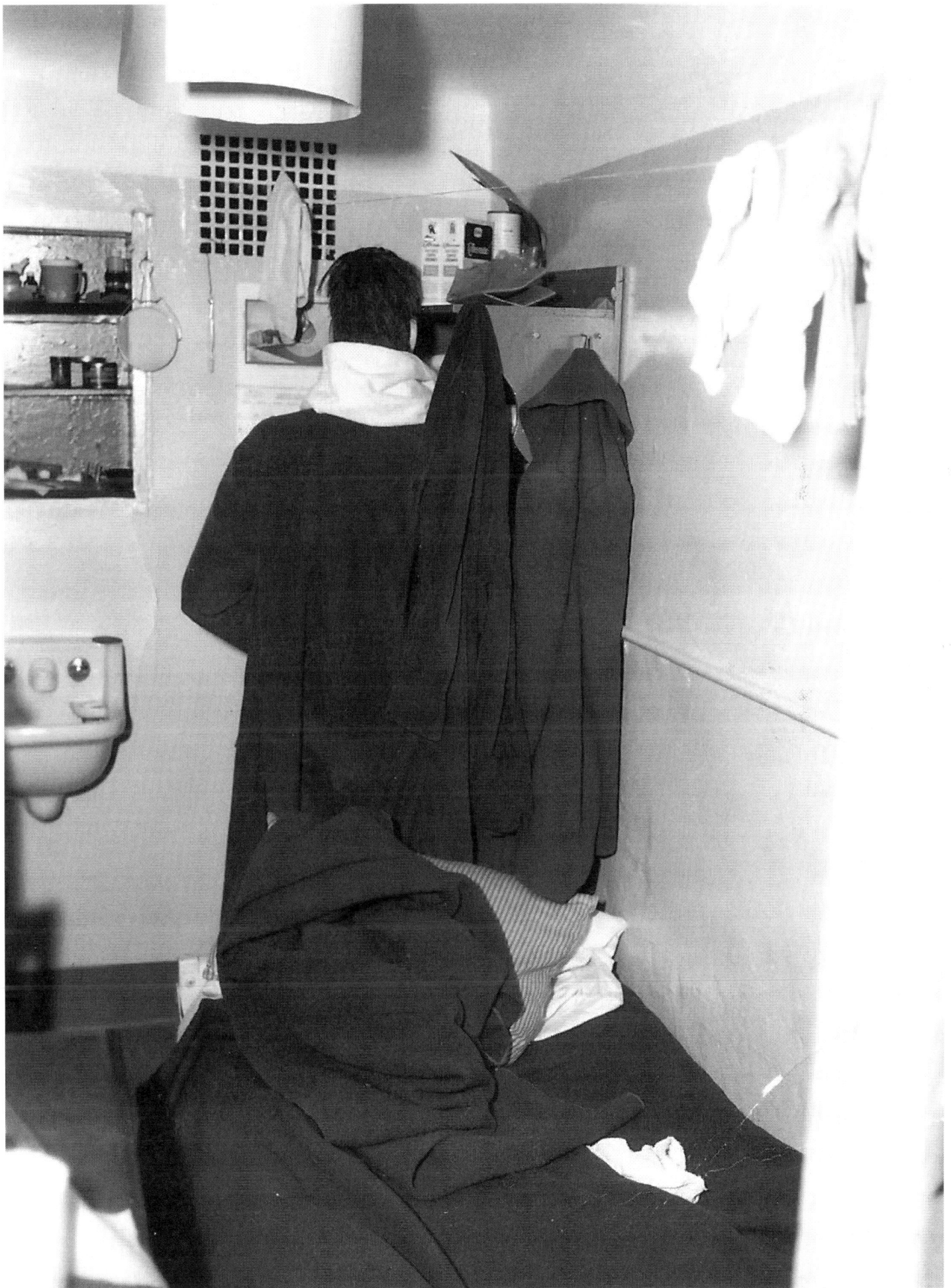

USP LEAVENWORTH PRISON CELL INTERIOR

31614.

Leavenworth, Kansas June 28 192 9.

Mr Henry James.
% Miss E. Trott.
The Linman Apts. 47.
No 2100 N. St. N.W.
Washington.
D.C.

This will be just a short letter, merely to let you know that I am all right, or at any rate as well as could be expected, considering all of the circumstances.

Should you read any thing very unusual in the papers about me, you mustn't take it for granted that it is all true.

I have no pen or ink at this time so you must excuse the pencil and my bum writing. I am a little bit nervous just now but I guess you can read what I write.

Later on I shall write to you and try to explain some things which are probably puzzling you just now. In the mean while I'll be wishing you good luck and waiting pailiently to hear from you.

I am.

Carl Panzram
No 31614. Box 7.
Leavenworth.
Kansas.

June 28, 1929

Letter from Carl Panzram to Henry Lesser.

This will be just a short letter, merely to let you know that I am all right, or at any rate as well as could be expected, considering all of the circumstances.

Should you read anything very unusual in the papers about, you mustn't take it for granted that it is all true.

I have no pen or ink at this time so you must excuse the pencil and my bum writing. I am a little bit nervous just now but I guess you can read what I write.

Later on I shall write to you and try to explain some-thing which are probably puzzling you just now. In the mean-while I'll be wishing you good luck and waiting patiently to hear from you.

I am.

Carl Panzram.
No. 31614.
Box 7. Leavenworth, Kansas.

July 1, 1929.

Superintendent of Prisons,
Department of Justice,
Washington, D. C.

Dear Sir;-

As I informed you in my report of June 23, 1929.
concerning the murder of our Laundry Foreman, R. G. Warnke
by prisoner Carl Panzram, No. 31614. I had our visiting
Psyciatrist, Dr. B. Landis Elliott, of Kanaas City, Mo.,
make an examination of Panzran in reference to his mental
condition, when he was at the Penitentiary on June 29th. Dr.
Elliott made this examination and submitted me a report of
the same, which is a very interesting one. I am enclosing
you his report in this connection for your full information.

I dont think there is any question about the truth
of the statements made by Panzran to Dr. Elliott concerning
the murder and his activities here in connection with his attempted
escapes etc., as the method of the murder was pretty well
described in the statements I sent you and correspond with his
statements. Then in the matter of his escape, we found ropes
and hooks some time last winter in back of the Laundry, that he
claims he had hidden there with the intention of escaping over
the wall back of the Laundry site.

You will note he states that the reason for the
murder was an accumulation of circumstances over a periodof
years that he has been confined in various institutions, in
most of which he claims to have been abused etc. Dr. Elliott
seems to think, as we all do, that the man is perfectly sane
but has a very vicious temper and disposition.

I may add in this connection that on June 24th
he attempted suicide by cutting an artery in his arm with a
safety razor blade. The safety razor blade had been smuggled
in to him, or else he carried it in his hair or some other
place of concealment when he was admitted to Isolation. When
it was discovered he had attempted suicide the Doctor was
called and the wound was dressed and he was left in Isolation,
but during the night sometime he tore the bandages off which
caused consideral loss of blood and he was admitted to the
Hospital on this occasion and was again given medical treatment. He responded to same and is now doing very well. I
am taking double precautions, having him watched day and night
to keep him from destroying himself. No knives nor forks are
given him. He is being made to eat with a spoon, what he can't

get with his fingers, and I am having him shaved with a safety razor and his hair cut with clippers and his room is bare, only what he has for bedding.

He gave as his reason for attempting suicide that the Government has him in the case of the murder of Mr. Warnke and he was going to kill himself before he was executed.

We will do all we can to care for him the best possible until he is brought to justice.

Very truly yours,

M.   Warden.

July 2, 1929.

Mr. T. B. White,
Warden, U. S. Penitentiary,
Leavenworth, Kansas.

Dear Warden:

I have had the opportunity to read over the statements which
you sent me relating to the attack on Laundry Foreman Warnke by inmate
Panzram.

I do not know how it really appears to you, but it does seem
as tho the guards did not show a great amount of bravery or resourcefulness in the handling of this inmate. It seems that they felt it was
more important for them to keep out of his way than to prevent him from
doing further damage. In fact, according to the statements, it was not
until he voluntarily threw down his weapon that he was eventually taken
into custody.

I do not think the testimony of guards and other inmates as
to whether this man was sane or insane is important—that is a matter for
psychiatrists or medical men to determine. It is quite obvious that
Panzram got Warnke in a defenseless position and finished him with one
blow. If your officers were fearless and on the alert it does not seem
that he could have been given a chance to assault anyone else.

Several of these statements say that Panzram was of a revengeful
nature but that he was sane. If he was perfectly sane then there must
have been some legitimate reason for his wanting his revenge. Was there
any adequate reason? Had Warnke done anything to this prisoner which
would have been legitimate cause for revenge such as Panzram eventually
carried out? If not, is there any evidence, taken together with history
of the man and his letters, which would indicate a certain mental abnormality, the results of which should have been foreseen and guarded against?
The law does not find it necessary to execute insane men, and, while
this case was a very terrible thing and if the man was in full possession
of his faculties he certainly should be punished, the institution should
not show too much anxiety to prove this inmate sane. If the alienists
decide that he was sane the law will take its course, but whether they
do or not, he should, of course, be kept in such close confinement that
he can do no further damage.

146

July 2, 1929

Mr. T. B. White
Warden, U.S. Penitentiary,
Leavenworth, Kansas

Dear Warden:

I have had the opportunity to read over the statements which you sent me relating to the attack on Laundry Foreman Warnke by inmate Panzran.

I do not know how it really appears to you, but it does seem as tho the guards did not show a great amount of bravery or resourcefulness in the handling of this inmate. It seems that they felt it was more imnportant for them to keep out of his way than to prevent him from doing further damage. In fact, according to the statements, it was not until he voluntarily threw down his weapon that he was eventually taken into custody.

I do not think the testimony of guards and other inmates as to whether this man was sane or insane is important-that is a matter for psychiatrists or medical men to determine. It is quite obvious that Panzran got Warnke in a defenseless position and finished him with one blow. If your officers were fearless and on the alert it does not seem that he could have been given a chance to assault anyone else.

Several of these statements say that Panzran was of a revengeful nature but that he was sane. If he was perfectly sane then there must have been some legitimate reason for his wanting revenge. Was there any adequate reason? Had Warnke done anything done anything to this prisoner which would have been legitimate cause for revenge such as Panzran eventually carried out? If not, is there any evidence taken, together with history of the men and his letters, which woudl indicate a certain mental abnormality, the results of which should have been foreseen and guarded against? The law does not find it necessary to seecute insane men, and, while this case was a very terrible thing and if the man was in full possession of his faculties he certainly shouldbe punished, the institution shoudl not show too much anxiety to prove this inmate sane. If the alienists decide that he was sane the law will take its course, but whether they do or not, he should, of course, be kept in such close confinement that he can do no further damage.

I realize that it is easy enough to sit here and criticize the action of your guards, and I want you to understand that I try to be in entire sympathy with the difficulties which constantly confront you and your assistants. It may be that your guards did all that could be expected of human beings, but it is not pleasant to contemplate the situation wherein one man with an iron bar is able to scattore inamtes and guards until, one statement says, one of the guards, by running in front of him, succeeded in bringing him in range of a machine gun.

I thank you for the prompt and frank way in which you kept us advised of this occurance, and I want to have the time to talk this over with you on your visit to Washington, as well as many other things.

Yours very truly,

SANFORD BATES,
Superintendent of Prisons

-2-

I realize that it is easy enough to sit here and criticize the action of your guards, and I want you to understand that I try to be in entire sympathy with the difficulties which constantly confront you and your assistants. It may be that your guards did all that could be expected of human beings, but it is not pleasant to contemplate the situation wherein one man with an iron bar is able to scatter inmates and guards until, one statement says, one of the guards, by running in front of him, succeeded in bringing him in range of a machine gun.

I thank you for the prompt and frank way in which you kept us advised of this occurrence, and I want to have the time to talk this over with you on your visit to Washington, as well as many other things.

Yours very truly,

SANFORD BATES,
Superintendent of Prisons.

BUNK CELLS USP LEAVENWORTH

PHILOSOPHY AND PESSIMISM

POST OFFICE BOX 7
31614.

Leavenworth, Kansas _July 12_ 192_8_

Mr. Henry James
⅟ Miss E. Trott.
No. 154 Quincy St.
Chevy Chase
Md.

I received your letter of July 9th this evening and am answering it at once. Your letter contained quite a bit of news. I was glad to get it. I have been puzzled a good bit about the general tone of your letters to me. Your superscriptions, especially have me wondering. The generally friendly tone all thru your letters. All of them. I cant help but believe your sincere in your profestation of friendship for me. But what gets me is, how in h--l any man of your intelligence and ability, knowing as much about me as you all, can still be friendly towards of a thing like me, when everime else are dead set against me. That is what puzzles me. Wonders will never cease! So Allen got himself reinstated in the good graces of the Law. How come that Right came out on top of Might. Doesn't seem reasonable to me. Even tho he is the Law and no friend of mine, I can and do respect him if I cant like him. Yes I read about the demise of one of my old companeross Frank Marlow of Silver Slipper fame. He isn't the first of that mob to be taken for a ride and if I know any thing of his crowd, he wont be the last. He is one of the push that hoisted the S.S. Mullhouse for a million it took, 8 or 9 years ago. If you keep on reading the miami papers you'll see some day, that some more of the black will be taken. 48 men pulled that Mullhouse trick and not a one of em ever done a day. Even the Everybody in New York, including the coppers knows it. They are too strong for the law but they are not strong enough. Keep on fighting among themselves and people at it. I dont wish any of em any bad luck but I hope they all go out like the Kid Kenzly pads did. Say I want to tell you something

to you I have been growing about
... I had to kill anybody to get at that ... I have time to crease. You can put ... story book, and if I keep on living ... some more to put in my grave yard ... I have been pretty well kept. Things ... have all shot to pieces. I thought ... either free or dead but I havent had any ... alive and locked up tighter then ... works wonders and time makes a ... out of love but I only know one that is a sure worker. Thats the Law of Compensation. That one never sure works. Say, About those things I was going to send you, the Bead necklace and the Bead Bracelet. Your out of luck for those I guess. I had em all right but when I went on the war path a couple of weeks ago, I lost them and every thing else I had and just now in for my life with em. To tell you the truth. But maybe I can lose it or throw it away yet I have hopes. Now I have another murder charge against me. Besides three in Massachusetts, Pennsylvania and Connecticut. I am bound to be tried some time for murder and then maybe the Law of Compensation will catch up with me and cook my goose. Maybe the Law will do my one favor in return for all the misery it has caused me. I look forward to a seat in the electric chair or a dance on the end of a rope just like some folks do for their wedding night. Well it's time to cut this thing short and for me to start walking up and down my cell floor, talking to myself and trying to figure out the quickest and easiest way out of this damn world. How are you making out with your dime novel. Dont lose it wont it. He did once at least his Slides, Brushes, did. Try Older, he'll take it. So Long.

Carl Panzram
31614 Box 7.
Leavenworth
Kansas.

July 12, 1929

Letter from Carl Panzram to Henry Lesser.

I received your letter of July 9th, this evening, and am answering it at once. Your letter contained quite a bit of news. I was glad to get it. I have been puzzled a good bit about the general tone of your letters to me. Your super-scription, especially has me wondering. The generally friendly tone all thru your letters. All of em. I can't help but believe your sincere in your protestations of friendship for me. But what gets me is, how the heck any man of your intelligence and ability, knowing as much about me as you do, can still be friendly towards a thing like me, when I even despise and detest my own self. That's what puzzles me. Wonders will never cease. So Allen got himself reinstated in the good graces of the law. How come that Right came out on top of Might. Doesn't seem reasonable to me. Even though he is the Law and no friend of mine, I can and do respect him if I can't like him. Yes, I read about the demise of one of my old companeeroes Frank Marlow of Silver Slipper Fame. He isn't the first of that mob to be taken for a ride and if I know anything of his crowd, he won't be the last. He is one of the push that hoisted the S.S. Mullhouse for a million in boose, 8 or 9 years ago. If you keep on reading the newspapers you'll see some day where some more of his click will be taken. 18 men pulled that Mullhouse trick and not a one of 'em ever done a day even though Everybody in New York, including the coppers knows it. They are too strong for the law but they are not strong enough to keep on fighting among themselves and prosper at it. I don't wish any of 'em any bad luck but I hope they all go out like the Killkenmy Cats did. Say I want to tell you something you know in my letters to you I have been grousing about my job here. I didn't like it and wanted a change. Well I got a change all right but I had to kill my boss to get it. That makes either 22 or 23 that I have to my credit. You can put that down in your little story-book, and if I keep on living much longer I may have some more to put in my grave-yard. For the past two or 3 weeks I have been pretty well upset, things all went wrong for me. My plans have been all shot to pieces. I thought for a while I would soon be either free or dead but I haven't had any luck either way. I am still alive and locked up tighter than before. But patience works wonders and time makes all things equal. I know a lot of laws but I know one thing is a sure worker. That's the Law of Compensation. That one will sure work. Say, about those things I was going to send you the Bead necklace and the Bead hand-bag. Your out of luck for those I guess. I had 'em all right but when I went on the war-path a couple of weeks ago, I lost them and everything else I had and damn near lost my life with them. Too bad I didn't. But maybe I can lose it or throw it away yet. I have hopes. Now I have another murder charge against me besides those in Massachusetts, Pennsylvania, and Connecticut. I am bound to be tried some where for murder and then maybe the Law of Compensation will catch up with me and cook my goose. Maybe the Law will do me one favor in return for all the misery it has caused me. I look forward to a seat in the electric chair or dance on the end of a rope just like some folks do for their wedding night. Well it's time to cut this thing short and for me to start walking up and down my cell floor talking to myself and trying to figure out the quickest and easiest way out of this damn world. How are you making out with your dime novel. Don't Hearst want it? He did once, at least his Editor, Bushbane did. Try Older, he'll take it.

So Long.
Carl Panzram
31614 box 7
Leavenworth, Kansas

July 27, 1929

Letter from Carl Panzram to Henry Lesser.

On July 9th you wrote me a letter. That's the last one I received from you. This is my third letter to you sine then. I have been wondering if you get all the letters that I write to you. I don't think that I have written anything in any of my letters that isn't permitted here. If you don't get my letters then there isn't much use in my writing them. I write them for your benefit and my own and not for the benefit of some third party. I should like to continue to correspond with you, but only so long as I am assured that you get the letters I write to you. I don't mind having my letters read by anyone else but I do expect to have you get them eventually. That's, That.

I see by the papers that another one of the predictions which I made to you in Washington, has some true. I am referring to the Riot which occurred lately at Dannemora. But I suppose you forgot what I told you about that. The news is old now. Have you spoken to Allen lately? How about Sinclair and Day? Have either of them even talked to you about me? Have you heard anything more from Dr. Carl Murchism of Macs? So your girl pal is living at Chevy Chase now. I lived near there for awhile. At St. Elmo Ave. Bethesda, Md. Just up the line a few blocks from where she lives now. How is she making out in The Poetry Racket. Is there any profit in poetry? Some kinds maybe. Do you think you could manage to scare up a few nickels and dimes for me. I would like to have enough to buy some matches and cigarettes papers. I have plenty of tobacco but I have no way of getting around to rustle the balance of what I need to complete a smoke. Just a single dollar will keep me going. Probably as long as I'll need it. 6 months more ought to see me thru. Have you quit that job yet? If not, why not? Don't forget what I told you. If you stay too long in that racket you won't be fit to go to Hoboken or anywhere else. Try some-thing else before it's too late. Well this is a warm day and my thinking machinery is not in any to good running order today as I'll just run out on you now.

So long and good luck
I am
Carl Panzram

Mr. Henry James:
% Miss E.V. Trott.
No 151 Quincy St.
Chevy Chase
Md.

On July 9th you wrote me a letter. That's the last
one I received from you. This is my third letter to you
since then. I have been wondering if you get all the
letters that I wrote to you. I don't think that I have
written anything in any of my letters that isn't
permitted here. If you don't get my letters then there
isn't much use in my writing them. I write them
for your benefit and my own and not for the benefit
of some third party. I should like to continue to correspond with you, but only so long as I am assured
that you get the letters I write to you. I don't mind
having my letters read by anyone else but I do expect to
have you get them eventualy. That's That.

I see by the papers that another of the predictions
which I made to you in Washington [...]
referring to the Riot which occured [...]
But I suppose you forgot what I [...]
is old now. Have you spoken to [...]
about Sinclair and Day? [...]
talked to you about me? Have y[...]
more from Dr. Carl Murchison or [...]
Pal is living at Chevy Chase [...]
while. At St. Elmo Ave? Bethesda [...]
line a few blocks from whe[...]
How is she making out in [...]

Is there any profit in Poetry? Some kind maybe
Do you think you could manage to scare up a few
nickles and dimes for me. I would like to have enough
to buy some matches and cigarett papers.
I had plenty of tobacco but I have no way of getting
around to roll the balance of what I need to enjoy
a smoke. Just a single dollar will keep me going.
Probably as long as I'll need it. 6 months more ought
to see me thru. Have you sent that [$] yet? If not, then
Don't forget what I told you. If you stay too long in that
racket you won't be fit to do the thackian or any other else.
Try something else before its too late. Well this is a
warm day and my thinking machinery is not in any
too good running order today so I'll just run out on
you now.

So Long and Good Luck
I am,
Carl Panzram.
31614. Box 7.
Leavenworth
Kansas.

Department of Justice
Office of the Superintendent of Prisons
Washington

ADDRESS ALL COMMUNICATIONS TO
SUPERINTENDENT OF PRISONS

July 18, 1929.

31614

Mr. T.B. White,
Warden, United States Penitentiary,
Leavenworth, Kansas.

Dear Sir:

I thank you for sending us the extra copy
of the psychiatrist's report on Carl Panzran.

We have yet been unable to find the original.

Very truly yours,

Sanford Bates

Sanford Bates
Superintendent of Prisons.

Panzram's psychiatrist's report is one of the few documents which has not been located.

HMC:JG
62-21811

July 30, 1929.

Mr. T. F. Cullen,
Harley-Wright Bldg.,
Washington, D. C.

62-21811

Dear Sir:-

The Kansas City Office, as the office of origin, is conducting an investigation relating to the case entitled: - CARL PANZRAM, Prisoner, Reg. No. 31614. Murder of Civilian R. G. Warnke at Federal Penitentiary, Leavenworth, Kansas, on June 20, 1929. Information has recently been received by the Bureau from Warden T. B. White of the Leavenworth Penitentiary to the effect that subject Panzran is corresponding with one Harry or Harvey James, c/o Miss E. Trott, 151 Quincy Street, Chevy Chase, Maryland.

Warden White suggests that an inquiry be made in connection with the investigation now pending in order to ascertain the identity of James and such other information as you may be able to obtain concerning him in order to ascertain definitely his connections with the subject of the above investigation.

Copies of your reports relating to this matter should be furnished to the Kansas City Office and an additional copy should be submitted for the information of Warden White.

Very truly yours,

Director.

RECORDED & INDEXED

62-21811-2
BUREAU OF INVESTIGATION
JUL 31 1929 A. M.

JUL 30 1929

The FBI conducted an investigation into the murder of Warnke and discovered Lesser's true identity.

~ORT MADE AT:	DATE WHEN MADE:	PERIOD FOR WHICH MADE:	REPORT MADE BY:
Washington, D. C.	9/9/29	8/8, 14 & 21/29	F. J. Lackey ES

TITLE:	CHARACTER OF CASE:
CARL PANZRAN, Prisoner, Reg. No. 31614	MURDER OF CIVILIAN H. G. WARNKE AT FEDERAL PENITEN- TIARY, LEAVENWORTH, KANS.

SYNOPSIS OF FACTS:

Miss Eleanor Trott advises that Harry James is a pseudonym used by Henry Lesser, a guard in the District Jail, who has been corresponding with subject Panzran for the alleged purpose of studying Panzran's psy- chology. UNDEVELOPED LEAD WASHINGTON FIELD OFFICE.

P.

REFERENCE: Bureau letter dated 7-30-29.

DETAILS:

    Agent made investigation at 151 Quincy Street, Chevy Chase, Md., which address is occupied by DAVID C. TROTT, an inspector in the U. S. Health Service, CLARA TROTT, wife of David C. Trott, was discreetly interviewed, and stated that she had never heard of either a Harry or Harvey James. Mrs. Trott stated that no E. Trott was residing at 151 Quincy St., Chevy Chase, Md., but that her husband had a niece by the name of Eleanor Trott, address unknown.

    Agent located Miss Eleanor Trott, who is a typist in the Internal Revenue Division of the Treasury Department. She stated that she formerly resided at 153 Quincy St., Chevy Chase, Md., and that she had received some mail at 151 Quincy St., Chevy Chase, Md., which mail was directed to Harry James; that the name Harry James is a pseudonym or alias affected by a boy friend of hers - Henry Les- ser, who resides at 1343 Clifton Street, N. W., Lincoln 1302, and has been employed for the past two years as a guard at the District of Columbia Jail; that Lesser became acquainted with Panzran while Panzran was a prisoner in this jail and that Lesser had become interested in Panzran's psychology and in his pursuance of his study of psychology had continued to correspond with Panzran after Panzran's incarceration in the Federal Penitentiary at Leavenworth, Kansas; that she had

DO NOT WRITE IN THESE SPACES

APPROVED AND FORWARDED:		RECORDED AND INDEXED:
[signature]	SPECIAL AGENT IN CHARGE	SEP 10 1929
	62-21811-4	CHECKED OFF: SEP 17 1929
COPIES OF THIS REPORT FURNISHED TO:	BUREAU OF INVESTIGATION SEP 9 1929 P. M.	
2-Bureau 2-Washington Field 3-Kansas City (1 for Warden White)	DEPARTMENT OF JUSTICE ROUTED TO FILE	JACKETED:

received several letters from Panzran addressed to Harry James and that she had read these letters, and that these letters did not contain anything that would lead her to believe Lesser had anything whatever to do with Panzran's recent murder of Civilian R. G. Warnke. Miss Trott further stated that these letters showed what Panzran had been doing and requested Lesser to send him money with which to purchase cigarettes and candy. Miss Eleanor Trott is at the present time residing at 625 Jefferson St., N. W., Washington, D. C.

Agent ascertained from the District of Columbia Jail & Asylum that Lesser has been employed as a guard there for about two years and that during the month of August he worked from 12 midnight until 8 A. M., and that commencing September 1, 1929, Lesser would start working in the daytime hours as yet undetermined.

UNDEVELOPED LEADS:

WASHINGTON FIELD OFFICE will make suitable investigation at the Washington Asylum & Jail and ascertain Lesser's record at that institution; also, interview Lesser in regard to his correspondence with Panzran.

PENDING.

POST OFFICE BOX 7

31614.

Leavenworth, Kansas Aug. 4, 1929

Mr. Henry James.
℅ Miss E. Trott.
No. 625 Jefferson St. N.W.
Washington.
D.C.

I recieved your letter of July 29th all O.K. I wrote you three other since the 4th July. I write once every week now. I hope you get them all. I believe that I get all of yours all right. Your last letter had quite a lot of news and as usual all of it good. Too bad that all of mine can't be that way also. But you know enough about me by this time that wherever I go there is sure to be bad luck and hard times for some body and some times for every body. I am old man bad luck, himself. The last time I stopped anywhere long enough for the people to know me very well was in Pennsylvania. There I had a lot of different people ask me at different times who I was and what good I was. My answers were always the same. "I am the fellow who goes around doing people good." Asked what good I had ever done any one. Again my answers were the same to all. "I put people out of their misery." They didn't know that I was telling them the truth. I have put a lot of people out of their misery and now I am looking for some one to put me out of mine. I am too damned mean to live. If your friends the Glueck Bros from Harvard should ever express their real opinions to you about the causes of my mean disposition, then I wish you would let me know their versions. So Mr. Baker is still interested in Lucky Baldwins autobiography. More power to him at it.

_____

—m afraid your out of luck first place, so it is again — thing like that could also — when I wrote it I was — then I am now then I — many people, now I see — as than that. Then I had — and paper. Now I have — a flush. The one I am — d and must return it — I had no money to buy any thing with. On the other hand if I still have every thing I needed including permition from the officials here, then I would gladly spend a month or two in putting down on paper the things I know and also the things that I think I know. But I cant do anything myself. Perhaps you can, tho. Thats up to you. If you care to write to the Supt, Warden or Deputy Warden here, those are the only ones who can give me this permition. You must use your own judgement. Any way I couldn't do anything about it just now because I expect to go up for trial next month and I would have to wait until I see if I get my wish then. Well so long and Good Luck. From
Carl Panzram.
31614 Box 7.
Leavenworth
Kansas.

Aug. 4, 1929

Letter from Carl Panzram to Henry Lesser.

I received your letter of July 29th all. OK. I wrote you three others since the 12th of July. I write one every week now. I hope you get all of em. I believe that I get all of your all right. Your last letter had quite a lot of news and as usual all of it good. Too bad that all of mine can't be that way also but you know enough about me by this time that where ever I go there is sure to be bad luck and hard times for somebody and some-times for every-body. I am old man bad-luck, himself. The last time I stopped any where long enough for the people to know me very well was in Dannemora. There I had a lot of different people ask me at different times who I was and what good I was. My answers were always the same. "I am the fellow who goes around doing people good." Asked what good I had ever done any one. Again my answers were the same to all. "I put people out of their misery." They didn't know that I was telling them the truth. I have put a lot of people out of their misery and now I am looking for some-one to put me out of mine. I am too damned mean to live. If your Friends the Gleuck Bros from Harvard should ever express their real opinions to you about the causes of my mean disposition, then I wish you would let me know their versions of it. So Menckin is still interested in Lucky Baldwins Autobiography. More Power to him at it. You Remember, I once told you that I wrote out another 75,000 words along that line. Well in your last letter to me you expressed the desire that you would like to have that else. The truth of the matter is that I am afraid your out of luck for these reasons. In the first place it is against the rules to write any thing like that and also against sending it out. When I wrote it I was in a different position than I am now. Then I could see and talk to many people, now I see very few and talk to less than that. Then I had plenty of time, pens, ink and paper. Now I have only time. I haven't even a pencil. The one I am writing with now, I borrowed and must return it. I have no money to buy any thing with. On the other hand, if I did have every thing I needed including permission from the officials here, then I would gladly spend a month or two in putting down on paper the things I know and also the things that I think I know. But I can't do anything about it just now because I expect to go up for trial next month and I would have to wait until I see if I get my wish then. Well So Long and

Good Luck. From
Carl Panzram.

Aug. 20, 1929

Letter from Carl Panzram to Henry Lesser.

I received your last letter July 29th. This is my third letter since then.
Whats the matter? Don't you get all of my letters or don't you care to answer them. If you don't want to write to me. Just say so and I'll not bother you any more. I believe that you would write to me all right if you got my letters but it looks to me as though you don't get 'em all. But why you should get some of 'em and not all is what I can't understand. All of my letters are alike. I write just exactly what I think and believe that I obey all of the rules in regards to letter writing. Of course there are a lot of things I would like to write about that is verbotten here so I write only what I think will pass the censor here. Maybe the fault is that I don't know what's all right and what's all wrong. I always believed, "I do yet too," that I knew right from I wrong. It looks to me as the others do not agree with me. There are some folks who actually believe I am just a little bit nutty. But I don't worry about I that because they don't know me like I know myself. I know myself far better than any one else knows me and I am firmly convinced that I am not crazy. What got me started along this line of thinking today is an article I read in the New Era, The Prison paper published here. The Issue of August '29. I am sending it to you in a separate cover along with this envelope. The article to which I refer is on Page 14. Paragraph No 1 in Column 2 is what steamed me up. This does not mention me by name but I am the one that is meant all right. I don't know who wrote it and don't care but I do care when he or any one else thinks or says I am insane. I wish you could get a publisher for that story of mine. I would like to have a copy of it when I go to trial. I expect to go up for trial next month or maybe Oct. I don't care what they do to me just so they don't try to prove I am crazy. I don't want no part of that. Let 'em hang me, burn me or anything they want but I am going to see that they don't bug me. I am not very good on trying to explain things by talking especially in a court room. I get mad and fly off the handle too easy but if I can get a copy of what I wrote in Washington D.C. and then produce it in Court, I am sure I can convince any one who is even half way open to reason that if the Law is right then so is

Carl Panzram

Sept. 20, 1929

Letter from Carl Panzram to Henry Lesser.

I see no reason why you shouldn't get this letter. I received your short letter of August 19th with the one dollar enclosed. Many thinks for both. I did not answer that letter until now, because in one of your previous letters, you asked me to write more often and at greater lengths. At that time, during July and August I did as you requested, I wrote you about 6 or 8 long letters. But I don't think you ever received them so, I figured that if you didn't get the letters I wrote, then why should I write. That's why I waited so long in answering yours of Aug. 19. But now I have some hopes that you will receive my letters as there have been some big changes here lately. I won't write a great deal at this time because I want to wait and see if you get this letter and my next 2 or 3. If I don't hear from you in answer to this letter and my next 2 or 3 then I can only conclude that someone other than myself has put a stop to my correspondence. But if I hear from you I shall be very glad to continue our correspondence as long as we are permitted to do so. So Long and Good Luck From

Carl Panzram

Leavenworth, Kansas. Aug. 20. 1929.

K

Mr Henry James.
% Miss E. Trott.
No 625 Jefferson St. N.W.
Washington
D.C.

I recieved your last letter July 29th. This is my third letter since then. What's the matter? Don't you get all of my letters or don't you care to answer them. If you don't want to write to me just say so and I shan't bother you any more. I believe that you would write to me all right if you got my letters but it looks to me as tho you don't get them all. But why you should get some of them and not all is what I can't understand. All of my letters are alike. I write just exactly what I think and I believe that I obey all of the rules in regard to letter writing. Of course there are a lot of things I would like to write about that is verboten here so I write only what I think will pass the censor here. Maybe the fault is that I don't know what's all right and what's all wrong. "I do yd too" that I knew as well to me as the others do. No doubt there are some folks who actually are a little bit nutty. But I don't [...] They don't know me like I [...] myself far better than any one [...] and I am firmly convinced [...] crazy. What got me started [...] thinking today is an article [...] New Era, the Prison paper pu[...] Issue of August. 29. I [...]

to you in a separate cover along with this envelope. The article to which I refer is on Page 14. Paragraph no 1 in Column 2 is what steamed me up. This does not mention my by name but I am the one that is meant all right. I don't know who wrote it and don't care but I do care when he or any one else thinks or says I am insane. He don't know me and probably never even saw me and yet he has crust enough to say that I am a bug. I defy any body to prove that I am crazy. I have been examined at least a dozen times by bug doctors at different times and different places and I don't believe that a single one of them ever said that I was insane. I wish you could get a publisher for that story of mine. I would like to have a copy of it when I go to trial. I expect to go up for trial this month or maybe Oct. I don't care what they do to me just so they don't try to prove I am crazy. I don't want no plea of that. Let em hang me, burn me or any thing they want but I am going to see that they don't bug me. I am not very good on trying to explain things by talking especialy in a court room. I get mad and fly off the handel too easy but if I can get a copy of what I wrote in Washington D.C. and then produce it in Court, I am sure I can convince any one who is even half way open to reason that if the Law is right then so is

Carl Panzram.
No 31614 Box 7.
Leavenworth
Kansas.

POST OFFICE BOX 7
31614.

Leavenworth, Kansas Sept 28. 1929

Mr. Henry James.
% Mr. Headon Lesser
The Melrose Apt. 22.
No 1343 Clifton St. NW.
Washington.
D.C

Yesterday evening I recieved your letter
of Sept 25th. In it you asked me 8 questions.
It would take 10 or 14 pages of paper like this form
to fully answer all of your questions. That can't be done.
You should allready know the answer to most
of em. Read your manuscript over again and you
will understand. You surely know the facts if
any one does besides myself. If you don't now
you probably never will understand. I wrote out
plainly and distinctly enough for any one to
understand. All except 2 of your questions.
The last one about the murder which I
committed here, you might not understand. You
asked me why I done it and if I got a kick out of
doing it. I had not one reason for doing it, but
about 47 reasons and each one of them was
a good reason. Good enough for me any way. You
know the deal I got in Wa. D.C. can for. Or peaks.
Did you think I would forget and forgive that.
I told you all then while in my cell, again in the
open court room, again when I came here, I told
every one I came into contact with that I would
sure knock off the first guy who ever bothered me.
I even told that to the deputy warden here and

I warned em all to leave
me alone. They didn't leave me
and tried to kill a dozen others.
puts out is this way. If it was
now to do the things to me that
[i]t right for me to do the same
K was the one, I waited 5
[h]e didn't come here so I stopped
one just like him. You asked
[i]f killing people. Sure I do.
If you don't think so, you do as I had done to me
and as I done myself then you'll know. You just let
5 or 6 big huskys walk in on you and let em
hammer you unconcious, then drag you down
in a cellar and chain you up to a post and
work you over some more and then if you feel like
forgiving and forgetting all about it write and
tell me about it will you. I have had 22 years
of this kind of stuff dont you know it and yet
your chump enough to wonder why I am what I
am. Dont be so dumb. Judging by the tone of your
letter you now figure I am a big of sorry king. a
fire bug or a homicidal maniac. Thats where
your wrong. I am no bug even if I do get a kick
out things which would have the direct opposite
effect on you. Another thing, You ask of about sending
me say cigars. Now you know better than
that. Thats high treason. If your going to send me
money thats got OK. At the same time you can
have the Haldeman Julius Co send me their
Catalog as I can buy some of their books.

Carl Panzram
31614
B7. Leavenworth Kansas.

Sept 28, 1929

Letter from Carl Panzram to Henry Lesser.

Yesterday evening I received your letter of Sept 25th. In it you asked me 8 questions. It would take 10 or 15 pages of paper like this for me to fully answer all of your questions. That can't be done. You should already know the answer to most of 'em. Read your manuscript over again and you will understand. You surely know the facts if any one does besides myself. If you don't know you probably never will understand. I wrote it plainly and distinctly enough for any one to understand. All except 2 of our questions. The last one about the murder I committed here, you might not understand. You asked me why I done it and if I got a kick out of it. I had not one reason for doing it, but about 47 reasons and each of them was a good reason. Good enough for me anyway. You know the deal I got in the D.C. can from Peake. Did you think I would forget and forgive that. I told you all then while in my cell, again in the open court room, again when I came here, I told every one I came into contact with that I would surely knock off the first guy who ever bothered me. I even told that to the Deputy Warden here and the man I killed. I warned 'em all to lay off me and leave me alone. They didn't leave me alone and I killed one and tried to kill a dozen others. The way I figure things out is this way. If it was all right for the law to do the things to me that it has then it's all right for me to do the same thing to the law. Peake was the one I waited 5 months to get but he didn't come here so I stepped out and got another one just like him. You asked if I get a kick out of killing people. Sure I do. If you don't think so, you do as I had done to me 5 or 6 big huskeys walk in on you and let 'em, hammer you unconscious, then drag you down in a cellar and chain you up to a post and work you over some more, and then if you feel like forgiving and forgetting all about it write and tell me about it you will. I have had 22 years of this kind of stuff and you know it and yet your chump enough to wonder why I am what I am. Don't be so dumb. Judging by the tone of your letter you figure I am a bug of some kind. A fire bug or a homicidal maniac. That's where your wrong. I am no bug even if I do get a kick out of things which would have the direct opposite effect on you. Another thing, you asked about sending me some cigars. Now you know better than that. That's high treason. If your going to send me money that all ok. At the same time you can have the Haldeman Julius Co send me their catalog so I can buy some of their books.

Carl Panzram

Oct. 6, 1929

Letter from Carl Panzram to Henry Lesser.

I received your letter of Sept 25. I answered it at once but was unable to fully answer some of questions which you asked me. I'll try to answer some of 'em in this letter. As for my next trial, I don't know when its due. Sometime soon I believe. But probably Nov. or Dec. in the Federal Court at K.C.K.

You seldom answer any of my questions but that's all right as it doesn't make much difference either way. But I wish you would always let me know if or when you get all of my letters. You asked me as to my motives in doing some of the things I have done. Surely you know that I am very impulsive, very vindictive and absolutely unscrupulous. Those are reasons enough to explain my actions. You also know why I feel and am that way. As for the kick I get out of it. I mean figuratively and not literally. What ever possessed you to think that me or anyone else ever had a sexual like feeling when we commit a crime like murder or arson. That's the bunk. I myself have intelligence enough to know the feeling but I haven't knowledge enough to explain it so that you could understand it. The only way I know of for you to find out just what sort of a kick I get out of it is for you to do as I done.
Experiment; go buy yourself a box of matches, or go get an ax and bop some guy on the back of the neck. It's easy when you know how. Besides you put 'em out of all their misery when you knock 'em off. Now then for your question about my ideas of any dreams I have had and their effects on me. Sure I have dreams but they have no effects whatever on my actions during my waking moments. What started you thinking about that was probably my questions about Bill Pellys article in the American Mag for March '29. Just forget it, you probably have already; because you never answered my question. Since I read that I have read some more of his writings and I have come to the conclusion that he is some kind of a bug or more probably a hop-head. I am neither. I can reason things out just as logically and clear as anybody. I can see the truth and I can admit it where a great many other people are unable to see the truth and are unwilling to admit it even if they do see it. Well that's about enough of my philosophy for this time. Now about you. I would like to know when if ever your going to quit that lousy job and get a real one. That job is doing you no good. Its doing you harm. If you stay with it long enough you'll be as bad as that great criminologist who studied his subject for 28 years and then thought "he still does" that he knows it all. If you don't believe it ask him you know who I mean. That great Christian and Military hero. The Major. Now then as for the money and cigars which you promised me, just forget it or wait until you peddle your manuscript and then if you get a real bankroll, "Donate", to

Carl Panzram

Leavenworth, Kansas Oct. 6. 1929.

Mr. Henry James.
℅ Mr. Isador Lesser.
The Melrose Apt. 22.
No. 1343. Clifton St. N.W.
Washington
D.C.

I recieved your letter of Sept 25. I answered
it at once but was unable to fully answer all of the
questions which you asked me. I'll try to answer some of
em in this letter. As for my next trial, I don't
know when its due. Sometime soon I believe. But
Probably Nov. or Dec. in the Federal Court at K.C. Mo.

You seldom answer any of my questions,
but that's all right as it doesn't make much diff.
either way. But I wish you would allways let me
know if or when you get all of my letters. You ask
me as to my motives in doing some of the things I have
done. Surely you know that I am very impulsive,
very vindictive and absolutely unscrupulous.
Those are reasons enough to do most anything.
You also know why I feel that way.
Its for the kick I get out of it. I
am not literaly. Whatever pleasure
me or any one else ever had a sense
when we comitt a crime like, no
the bunk, I myself have inteligence enough to
know the feeling but I havent the words to
explain it so that you could understand
why I know of for you to find out just what
kick I get out of it is for you to
Experiment. go try your self and

or go get an ax and bop some guy on the back
of the neck. Its easy when you know how. Beside you
put em out of all their misery when you knock em off.
Now then for your question about my ideas of any
dreams I have had and their effects on me. Sure I have
dreams but they have no effects whatever on my
actions during my waking moments. What started
you thinking about that was probably my question
about Bill Pelly, article in the American Mag
for March 28. Just forget it, you probably have allready, because you never answered my question. Since
I read that I have read some more of his writings
and I have come to the conclusion that he is some
kind of a bug or more probably a hop-head. I am
neither. I can reason things out just as logicaly
and clearly as any body. I can see the truth and
I can admit it where a great many other people
are unable to see the truth and are unwilling
to admit it even if they do see it. Well thats about
enough of my philosophy for this time. Now about you
I would like to know when if ever your going to quit
that lousey job and get a real one. That job is doing
you no good. Its doing you harm. If you stay with
it long enough you'll be as bad a that great criminologist
who studied his subject for 28 years and then thought he
"he still does" that he knows it all. If you don't believe
it ask him. You know who I mean. That great
Christian and Military hero, The Major. Now then
as far the money and cigars which you promised me, just
forget it or wait until you peddle your manuscript
and then if you get a real bank-roll, Donate to

Carl Panzram
31614 Box. 7.
Leavenworth. Kansas.

Leavenworth, Kansas Oct. 11. 1929.

Mr Henry James
℅ Mr. Isador Lesser.
the Milross Apt 22.
No 1343 Clifton St. N.W.
Washington.
D.C.

I wrote two letters in answer to yours of Sept 20th.
this is my third and yet I haven't had room to answer
half of the questions which you asked me in your
letter of that date. But before I do that I want to ask
you something. Do you remember what I told you
and the predictions I made to you in regards to the
conditions and the probable results and the consequences of it in New York State. Especialy in Dannemora
and Auburn. Now you know that what I said would
happen has happened. You know why too. But thats
merely the beginning and not the end. The worst is yet
to come. Colorado was no surprise to me. Neither would
it have been to any one else who has kept track of that place
since and during the regime of Warden Tynan. Here is
another little tip for you. History repeats itself. Just
keep your eye on Texas, Rusk and Huntsville. They are
both due for the blow off. The same for Eastern and
Western in Pa. Baltimore is due for a jam and so are a
good many others. When Jeff City and Lansing turn
loose there will noise and smell enough so that
the people must see and hear the truth. whether they like
it or not. The powers that be are beginning to get it in the
neck the same as any other crooks. The prisons all over
the country are beginning to close their gates on
officers, Chiefs of Police, Sheriffs, Lawyers, Judges

& many others who make the laws
afraid to enforce them. People who
a generation or more are now
to the fact that laws are made to
ot by all except those who made them
hers. I sure used to get a good kick
to my last jaunt, when I could sit
it there, right beside some soft-
handed, smooth tongued blizzard who bragged that he
had been a Sheriff or a Chief of Police or some other kind of
a copper. Believe me, I never missed an opportunity
to tell em what I thought. thats one privilag I sure
enjoyed and took full advantage of. But I can't do
it any more. Now I have no one to talk to except
myself. But I like that fine. I can say just what I
want to myself with out any fear of being contradict
or having my block knocked off. I figure everything
has its advantages, even solitary confinement. I am
as contented now as I have ever been or even expect to
be. I have a large, clean airy cell, plenty to eat
and pretty good eats too, far better than I have
ever had in any hoose-gow before, I have a bed to
sleep on, magazine and news papers to read, twice
a week a good barber gives me a good shave, a good
hot and cold shower bath every week with a clean
change of linnen, plenty of tobbacco to chew and smoke
No work to do, and no one to bother about and no
one bothers me in any way, not yet any way. But still
I am not satisfied. There is one thing I still lack
and thats a nice comfortabl grave to be dumped
into. When I get that I'll be fully contented.
Carl Panzram
31614 Box 7.
Leavenworth Kansas.

Oct. 11, 1929

Letter from Carl Panzram to Henry Lesser.

I wrote two letters in answer to yours of Sept 20th. This is my third and yet I haven't had room to answer half of the questions which you asked me in your letter of that date. But before I do that I want to ask you something. Do you remember what I told you and the predictions I made to you in regards to the conditions and the probable results and the consequences of it in New York State. Especially in Dannemora and Auburn. Now you know that what I said would happen, has happened. You know why too. But thats merely the beginning and not the end. The worst is yet to come. Colorado was no surprise to me. Neither would it have been to any one else who has kept watch of that place since and during the regime of Warden Tynar. Here is another little tip for you. History repeats itself. Just keep your eye on Texas, Rusk and Huntsville. They are both due for the blow off. The same for Eastern and Western in Pa. Baltimore is due for a jamb and so are a good many others. When Jeff City and Lansing tear Ioose where will noise and smell enough so that the people must see and hear the truth whether they like it or not. The powers that be are beginning to get it in the neck the same as any other crooks. The prisons all over the country are beginning to close their gates on officers, Chiefs of Police, Sheriffs, Lawyers, Judges, Governors and a good many others who make the laws and those who are supposed to enforce them. People who have been asleep for a generation or more are now beginning to wake up to the fact that laws are made to be obeyed by all and not by all except those who made them or enforce them on others. I sure used to get a kick out of it, "before I got into my last Jamb," when I could sit down in the mess-hall here, right besides some other kind of a copper. Believe me, I never missed an opportunity to tell 'em what I thought. That's one privilege I sure enjoyed and full advantage of. But I can't do it anymore. Now I have no one to talk to except myself. But I like that fine. I can say just what I want to myself with out any fear of being contradicted or having my block knocked off. So you see everything has its advantages. Even solitary confinement. I am as contented now as I ever have been or expect to be. I have a large, clean, airy cell plenty to eat and pretty good eats too, far better than I have ever had in any hoosegow before. I have a bed to sleep on, magazines and newspapers to read. Twice a week a good barber gives me a good shave, a good hot and cold shower bath every week with a clean of linens, plenty of tobacco to chew and smoke. No work to do, and no one for me to bother about and no one bothers me in any way, not yet anyway. But still I am not satisfied. There is one thing I still lack and that's a nice comfortable grave to be dumped into. When I get that I'll be fully contented.

Carl Panzram

Oct. 20, 1929

Letter from Carl Panzram to Henry Lesser.

I received your letter of Oct. 9th Glad to hear that you got both of mine of the 25th of Sept. and the 6th of Oct. I wrote you another on Oct. 11th. I am glad that you didn't take any offense at my cranky letters. your a pretty level headed sort of a fellow and you know I am always in a bad humor just like a mad dog. Still for a little while after I got your last letter I felt pretty good. Almost human. Yes I have read in the papers about Allen and his stirring up a row there. He is a pretty clever guy for a youngster but he is battling a bunch that is not only clever but very unscrupulous as well. They have the edge on him in that way. Allen has principles and scruples where his opponents are without either. So he had better watch his step or some skunk like me, "there are plenty" more who can be hired for a C note or less to bump him off. Now then about your sending me money. That's OK by me but I am not in need of anything so don't put yourself out. I didn't get the Little blue book catalog yet but I have an advertisement out of a mag and I am going to try to send an order for 40 little blue books. I may not be permitted to have 'em but I'll try anyway. No harm in trying. If I can't have 'em I'll get myself some Royal Bergals and have a smoke of good weed on you.

You asked me about my school days. I'll try and explain briefly. I started to school at the age of 5 years and attended regularly until I was 11 years old. In that time I finished the 6th grade. I did not like school. I was pretty dumb but I kept up with the others in my classes. When I was 11 years old I was sent ot the Reform School. There I stayed nearly 2 years. During all of my time there I went to school but never learned a damn thing. In fact I was in the 5th grade of school when I left there. So you see that after 2 years in the Reform School I was farther back than when I started there. From that day to this I have never advanced any farther in school than I was before I went to my first R.S. I may not have accomplished much in a scholarly way while there but I learned to become a first class liar and hypocrite and the beginnings of degeneracy. I also learned how to sing hymns, say prayers and read the bible. I learned so much about the Christian religion that I finally came to detest, despise and hate everything and everybody connected with it. I still do. You asked me about my parents and my early upbringing. I had little of either. My father was no good and mother was very little better. Father pulled his freight when I was 7 or 8 years old so you see I know little about him and none of that good. Mother was too dumb to know anything good to teach me. There was little love lost. I first liked her and respected her. My feelings gradually turned from that to distrust, dislike, disgust and from there it was very simple for my feelings to turn into positive hatred towards her.

Carl Panzram

Mr. Henry James.
% Mr. Isador Leiser
The Melrose Apt. 2 2.
No 1343. Clifton St. N.W.
Washington
D.C.

I recieved your letter of Oct. 9th. Glad to hear that you got both of mine, of the 25th of Sept. and the 6th. that I wrote. You another on Oct 11th. I an glad that you didn't tak any offence at my cranky letter. You a pretty livethbodied sort of a fellow and you know I'm allway in a bad humor just like a mad dog. Still for a little while after I got your last letter I felt pretty good. Almost human. — Yes I have read in the papers about Allen and him stirring up a row there. He is a pretty clever guy for a youngster but he is battling a bunch that is not only slow, but very unscrupulous as well. They have the edge on him in that way. Allen has principle and — — while his opponents are without. — — watch his step or some other more who can be hired for a C— him off. Nother about your... OK. by me but I am not in need put yourself out. I didn't get th... yet but I have an advantage... an going to try to send an o... folks. I may not be permitted... by any way. No harm in try... I'll get myself a Royal Bargain of good will or you.

You asked me about my school days. I'll try and explain briefly. I started to school at the age of 5 years and attended regularly until I was 11 years old. In that time I finished the 6th grade. I did not like school. I was pretty dumb but I kept up with the others in my classes. When I was 11 years old I was sent to the Reform School. There I stayed nearly 3 years. During all of my time there I went to school but never learned anything. In fact I was in the 5th grade of school when I left there. So you see that after 2 years in the Reform school I was farther back than when I started there. From that day to this, I have never advanced any farther in school than I was before I went to my first R.S. I may not have accomplished much in a scholarly way while there but I learned to become a first class liar and hypocrit and the beginning of degeneracy. I also learned how to sing hymns, say players and read the bible. I learned so much about the Christ, religion that I finealy came to detest, despise and hate everything and everybody connected with it. I still do. You also asked about my parents and my early up bringing. I had little of either. My father was no good and mother was very little better. Father killed his freiss when I was 7 or 8 years old so you see I know little about him and none of that good. Mother was too dumb to know anything good to teach me. There was little love lost. I first liked her and believed her and respected her. My feelings gradualy turned from that to distrust, dislike, disgust and from there it was very simple for my feelings to turn into positive hatred towards her.

Carl Panzram.
31614 Box 7.

THIS CASE ORIGINATED AT	KANSAS CITY, MO.			
REPORT MADE AT:	DATE WHEN MADE:	PERIOD FOR WHICH MADE:	REPORT MADE BY:	
WASHINGTON, D. C.	10/25/29	10/19/29	F. J. FITZGERALD	MH
TITLE: CARL PANZRAN, Prisoner, Reg. No. 31614			CHARACTER OF CASE: MURDER OF CIVILIAN R. G. WARNKE AT FEDERAL PENITENTIARY, LEAVENWORTH, KANSAS.	

SYNOPSIS OF FACTS:

FILE #62-1564

Henry Lesser interviewed at his place of employment, District Jail, who advised that he corresponded with subject because he was interested in criminology and considered subject an ideal person to study in order to further his research in criminology.

R. U. C.

REFERENCE: Report of Agent F. J. Lackey, Washington, D. C., September 9, 1929.

DETAILS: At the District Jail, Agent was advised that Henry Lesser was appointed a guard at the jail March 1, 1928, at a salary of $1500 a year and is still employed there.

Agent interviewed Mr. Lesser, who stated that he has been corresponding with subject for some time and that they exchange an average of three or four letters a month, and gave as his reason for such correspondence, the fact that he is interested in criminology and in his opinion subject is an ideal person to study. He further advised that he used the alias Henry James because he feared that his corresponding with a prisoner might prevent his appointment as a guard in a Federal Prison, he having made application for such position. He further stated that the reason for not having the mail directed to his own home was identical with the reason for not using his own name.

Mr. Lesser's reputation record at the District Jail is very good and he stated that he had never known subject until he was a prisoner at the District Jail some time ago. Lesser is described as

DO NOT WRITE IN THESE SPACES

APPROVED AND FORWARDED:	R. E. Vetterli SPECIAL AGENT IN CHARGE	62-21841-7 BUREAU OF INVESTIGATION	RECORDED AND INDEXED: OCT 28 1929
COPIES OF THIS REPORT FURNISHED TO:			CHECKED OFF: NOV 5 1929
2 - Bureau		DEPARTMENT OF JUSTICE	JACKETED:
2 - Washington Field			
3 - Kansas City (1 for Warden White)		ROUTED TO: FILE	

U. S. GOVERNMENT PRINTING OFFICE 1929

7—1323

follows:

> Age - 27 years
> Height - 5 ft. 7 in.
> Weight - 155 lbs.
> Eyes - blue
> Complexion - fair
> Build - medium
> Teeth - slightly dark and uneven.

There being no further investigation here, the case is

REFERRED UPON COMPLETION TO OFFICE OF ORIGIN.

Reg. No. 31674

UNITED STATES PENITENTIARY

LEAVENWORTH, KANSAS

Oct 21, 1929

Mail Dept.:

Please charge my stamp account with
.... cents.

Purpose: *Purchase Books*

To: *Haldeman-Julius*

Street: *Dept. A-291*

City: *Girard*

State: *Kansas*

Carl Panzram

Prisoner's Signature

Form 104-L

Panzram's requests to purchase books.

Cell *Isolation*

Request to See Warden or Deputy

UNITED STATES PENITENTARY

LEAVENWORTH, KANSAS

Oct 1st 1929

Undersigned Prisoner requests audience with the

Warden

for the following reason:

*To order Books
from Haldeman
Julius co*

Name *Panzram*

Reg. No. 31674

Audience held _____ 192

DISPOSITION OF CASE

_____

_____

_____

_____

Form 63-L _____

THE LEAVENWORTH USP LIBRARY

Leavenworth, Kansas Oct 31. 1929

Mr Henry James
℅ Mr Zachton Fesser.
The Melrose Apt. 22.
No 1343. Clifton St. N.W.
Washington
D.C.

I recieved your Letter of Oct 9. I wrote twice since then. Last Sunday I ordered 4 little Blue books with the 2 ¢ which you sent me, but I have since then found out that if I cant be done. they are not permitted here. So I still have the money. Now I'll try to figure out some other way to spend it. . . . . Letters today because I feel pretty mean. . . . . . . here as a few. I . . . . or kicked around, cha . . . . I most forgotten how . . . I have just finished . . . . I started with bacon . . . bread and butter, ste . . . sample of the meals . . . After I finished this . . . down to smoke a . . . . . and comfort. Now, ... is a bit different fro . . you. This is sure a co . . . after roaming all ov . . in jails and in so . . . very little, I a one of . . I was sloughed up . . . then treated worse . . .

would treat a mad dog. That treatment I received, not for what I had done but for what others thought I might do. There I done nothing to deserve all of the abuse I got. Now notice the contrast. I come here expecting to get more of the same kind of treatment, but determined that this time I wont get it for nothing. This time I am hostile and dont care what the consequences may be. This time I figure I'll beat em to it. I make one attempt to escape, I fail but I dont get caught, immediatly I begin getting all readyed up to try again in another place. But before I can get properly organized I get into a small fracce, this causes some to figure, "judging by past performances in other prisons," that I am due to get another kicking around, So to fore stall all that, I grab myself a 10 pound iron bar and go on the war-path. Before I have finished I kill one man and try to kill a dozen more. After doing all these things I walk into a cell fully expecting to be chained up and beaten to death. But what happens, the exact reverse of that. No one lays a hand on me. No one abuses me in any way. This is how things have been with me up to now. I have been for the past 3 or 4 months trying to figure it out and I have come to the conclusion that, if in the begining I had been treated as I am now, then there wouldn't have been quite so many people in this world that have been robbed, raped and killed and perhaps also very probably I wouldn't be where I am today. Maybe I am wrong tho. I am too dumb to know what myself have been but I am not so dumb that I cant see a little way into the future. Not very far but far enough to see the end of

Carl Panzram -
31614. Box 7.
Leavenworth
Kansas.

One of, if not THE, most important letters written by Carl Panzram where he discusses his past tortures at the hands of his captors and the fact that if he would have been treated in a humane way in the past, maybe he would not have became the hate filled person who he is. Panzram may have thought about his lot in life as he moved from institution to institution, but he became very introspective just before his death.

Oct. 31, 1929

Letter from Carl Panzram to Henry Lesser.

I received your letter of Oct 9. I wrote twice since then. Last Sunday I ordered 40 little blue books with the $2.00 which you sent me but I have since then found out that it can't be done. They are not permitted here so I still have the money. Now I'll try to figure out some other way to spend it. I thought I would write you a letter today because I feel pretty good just now. In fact I feel pretty near human. For several different reasons here are a few. It's so long since I have been beaten or kicked around, chained up or knocked down that I have almost forgotten how it feels but not quite. I still remember. Another reason is that I have just finished my supper and man what a feed. I started with bacon and eggs, candied sweet potatoes, bread and butter, stewed prunes and 4 fresh pears. That's a sample of the meals we gather every day, lately. After I finished throwing this feed into myself, I sat down to smoke and read the daily paper. In peace, quiet and comfort. Now perhaps you will know why this letter is a bit different from some of the others I have written to you. This is sure a queer old world. Here I am getting old after roaming all over the world, after serving over 20 years in jails and in some of 'em I got plenty abuse for very little. In one of which, that's the last one in N.Y. I was sloughed up in the Isolation for over 2 years and there treated worse than you and many other people would treat a mad dog. That treatment I received, not for what I had done but for what others thought I might do. There I done nothing to deserve all of the abuse I got. Now notice the contrast. I come here expecting to get more of the same kind of treatment, but determined that this time I won't get it for nothing. This time I am hostile and don't care what the consequences may be. This time I figure I'll beat 'em, to it. I make one attempt to escape. I fail but I don't get caught, immediately I begin getting all readied up to try again in an other place. But before I can get properly organized I get into a small jam, this causes one to figure, judging on past performances in other prisons, that I am due to get another kicking around. So to forestall all that, I grab myself a 10 pond iron bar and go on a war path. Before I have finished I kill one man and try to kill a dozen more. After doing all these things I walk into a cell fully expecting to be chained up and beaten to death. But what happens. The exact reverse of that. No one lays a hand on me. No one abuses me in any way. This is how things have been for the past 3 or 4 months trying to figure it out and I have come to the conclusions that, if in the beginning I had been treated as I am now, then there wouldn't have been quite so many people in this world that have been robbed, raped and killed and perhaps also very probably I wouldn't be where I am today. Maybe I am wrong though. I am too dumb to know what might have been but I am not so dumb that I can't see a little way into the future. Not very far but far enough to see the end of

Carl Panzram

> **"I haven't the least desire to reform."**
> -Carl Panzram

Nov. 13, 1929

Letter from Carl Panzram to Henry Lesser.

Your letter of Nov. 7 reached me this Eve. What a kick I got out of reading it. You have it all doped out, Eh. You have it all figured out that if I was given my freedom today, financial independence, moral support and a helping hand from powerful people and everything necessary that would help me to reform and lead a good clean Christian life, that's all that would be required. You figure that I would jump at it and be all reformed up to the minute I hit the front gate. What a dream. your all wet. Wake up kid your having a nightmare. I can dream better dreams than that myself. If there was even the faintest possibility of your idea ever becoming a fact, then I would be right on he job. I would be the best little yes man you ever saw. You may not believe me, but if I cared to, I could be just as smooth a liar and hypocrite as any would be Christian you ever saw or heard tell of and they are all experts. But it just so happens that I don't care to lie just now. I am not going to try to deceive you and neither am I going to kid myself. I know myself and my own state of mind far better than you or anyone else knows me and the more I look deep into my own self, the less good I can see. You seem to think that all that is necessary for a person to do when he wants to change his mode of living is to just change and that's the end of it. All reformed up just like that. That's how easy it is in theory. But the reality is far different when you take into consideration all of the facts. The real truth of the matter is that I haven't the least desire to reform. Very much the reverse of that is the truth. I would not reform if the front gate was opened right now and if I was given a million dollars when I stepped out. I have no desire to do good or to be good. I am just as mean now as I can possibly be, and the only reason I am no worse is because I lack the power and the proper opportunities for meanness. If I had the power and the opportunities, then I would soon show you what real meanness was. You overlook the fact that the law and a great many people have been trying their damnedest for 25 years to reform me. I am tired of having people try to reform me. What I want to do is reform them and I think the best way to reform 'em is to put 'em out of their misery. It took me 38 years to be like I am now, then how do you figure that I could if I wanted to, change from black to white in the twinkling of an eye. Have you some kind of a secret formula, some mumbo jumbo, or hocus-pocus that could cause this great change. If you know something like that let me have it and I'll try it out on someone to see how it works. I have a good subject here that I would like to try it on. He is nearly a bad skunk as I am. Not quite though. Now then to answer some more of your questions. The little Blue books are not allowed to anyone here but books from any other Publishing Co. are permitted here why that is I don't know. It's a rule here, that's all I know about it. I have never read Jack Black's book, "You Can't Win." Harpers or Scribners mags seem to be popular here. There are lots of good magazines here but I don't get many good ones. But I guess that's because I don't love Jesus or maybe they want to lead me into paths of uprighteousness by handing me such mags as The Argosy and Western thrillers. No there is nothing you can do for me unless your rich uncle should open his heart and his pocket-book. In that case you could if you would, have sent these two books, direct from the publisher to

Carl Panzram

POST OFFICE BOX 7
31614

Leavenworth, Kansas Nov. 13. 1929.

Mr Henry James.
% Mr Isador Lesser.
The Melrose Apt. 22.
No.1343 Clifton St. N.W.
Washington
D.C.

Your letter of Nov. 7 reached me this eve. What a kick I got out of reading it. You have it all doped out Eh." You have it all figured out that if I was given my freedom today, financial independence, moral support and a helping hand from powerfull people and every thing neccessary that would help me to reform and lead a good clean Christian life, thats all that would be required. You figure that I would jump at it and be all reformed up the minute I hit the front gate. What a dream. Your all wet. Wake up Kid your having a night-mare. I can dream better dreams than that, myself. If there was ever the faintest possibility of your idea ever becoming a fact, then I would be right on the job. I would be the best little yes man you ever saw. You may not believe me, but if I cared to, I could be just as smooth a liar and hypocrit as any would be Christian you ever saw or heard tell of and they are all experts. But it just so happens that I don't care to lie just now. I am not going to try to decieve you and neither am I going to kid myself. I know myself and my own state of mind far better than you or any one else knows me and the more I look deep into my own self, the less good I can see. You seem to think that all that is neccessary for a person to do when he wants to change his mode of living is to just change and thats the end of it. All reformed up just like that. Thats how easy it is in Theory. But the reality is far different when you take into consideration all of the facts. The real truth of the matter is that I havent the least desire to reform, very much the reverse of that is the truth. I would not reform if the front gate was opened right now and if I was given

a million dollars when I
good. I am just as mean
I am no worse is because
for meanness. If I had the f
show you what real mean
The law and a great m
for 25 years to reform
reform me. What I wa
the best way to reform
It took me 38 years to
that I could if I wanted t
twinkling of an eye. Tha
some mumbo-jumbo
great change. If you kn
it and they try it out on
suiged here that I would
skunk as I am. Not you
your questions. The little
here but Books from any other Publishing Co. are permitted here.
Why that is I don't know. Its a rule here, thats all I know about
it. I have never read Jack Black's Boook, "You Cant Win."
Harpers or Scrifners mags seem to be unpopular here. I
havent seen one of either since I've been here. There are lots of
good magazines here but I don't get many good ones. But I
guess thats because I don't love Jesus or maybe they want to
lead me into paths of uprighteousness by handing me such mags.
as the Argosy and Western Thrillers. Neither is nothing you can
do for me unless your rich uncle should open his head and his
pocket book. In that case you could if you would, have sent
~~the books I asked for if you will, to~~
Carl Panzram
No 31614. Box 7.
Leavenworth
Kansas

POST OFFICE BOX 7
31614.

Leavenworth, Kansas Nov. 19, 1929.

Mr Henry James
% Mr Meador Lease,
The Melrose Apt. 22.
No 1343 Clifton St. N.W.
Washington.—
D.C.

I recieved your letter of Nov. 7th. which I answered the same day I got it. I had to cross out the last 2 or 3 lines of that letter because I wanted to enclose a small clipping of a magazine advertisement. But after writing the letter I found out a new rule here, which I knew nothing about. Clippings are not permitted to be sent either in or out of here. It doesn't make any diff any way so just forget it. The books I wanted to get were Schopenhours Essays and Kants Critique of Pure Reason. They were a buck each in the add I saw in the mag. I have the two bucks which you sent to me and I think I'll use them to get these two books later on. not now. because I expect to go out for my trial very shortly. I figure it will be some-time in Dec. Then I'll see about it. I also def...

that I have been wanting for a long time to read. But now, that, that possibility is out of order I may as well forget about it. Besides its very unlikely that I'll live long enough to be able to do very much reading of any kind. That will be about all for this time. Perhaps I'll feel more like a human being by this time next week, if so I'll write then but just now I feel more like a mad dog than—

Carl Panzram
No 31614. Box 7.
Leavenworth
Kansas.

Nov. 19, 1929

Letter from Carl Panzram to Henry Lesser.

     I received your letter of Nov. 7th. which I answered the same day I got it. I had to cross out the last 2 or 3 lines of that letter because I wanted to enclose a small clipping of a magazine advertisement. But after writing the letter I found out a new rule here which I knew nothing about. Clippings are not permitted to be sent either in or out of here. It doesn't make any diff any way so just forget it. The books I wanted to get were Schopenhauer's Essays and Kant's Critique of Pure Reason. They were a buck each in the ad I saw in the mag. I have the two bucks which you sent to me and I think I'll use them to get these two books later on. Not now because I expect to go out for my trial very shortly. I figure it will be sometime in Dec. Then I'll see about it. It all depends how I make out at my trial then. Now then about that Autobiography. I have no further interest in it. It's yours and whatever you do with it will make no difference to me. My only motive in writing it was to express myself and to state my beliefs fully and truthfully. I don't care what you or anybody else, thinks, says or does about it. The question of what the outcome of it might be, held my interest only so long as there was some little hope that I might profit by it to the extent that I might benefit by getting myself some good books that I have been wanting for a long time to read. But now, that, that possibility is out of order I may as well forget about it. Besides it's very unlikely that I'll LIVE long enough to be able to do very much reading of any kind. That will be about all for this time. Perhaps I'll feel more like a human being by this time next week, if so I'll write then but just now I feel more like a mad dog then

Carl Panzram

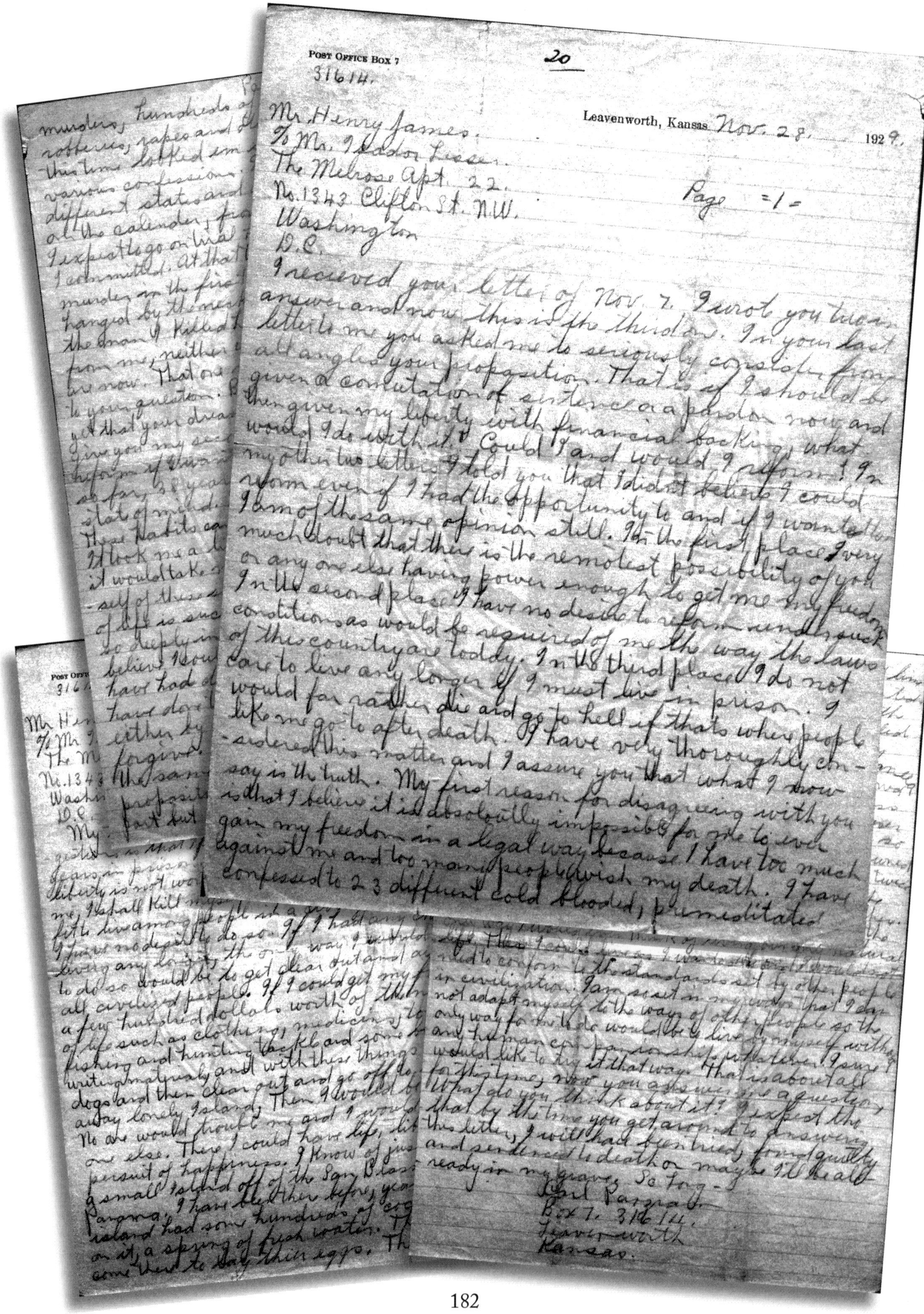

POST OFFICE BOX 7
31614.

Mr. Henry James.
% Mr. 9 Eddor Lesser.
The Melrose Apt. 22.
No. 1343 Clifton St. N.W.
Washington
D.C.

Leavenworth, Kansas Nov. 28.   1929.

Page =1=

I received your letter of Nov. 7. I wrote you two answers and now this is the third one. In your last letter to me you asked me to seriously consider your proposition. That is if I should be given a commutation of sentence or a pardon now and then given my liberty with financial backing, what would I do with it? Could I and would I reform? In my other two letters I told you that I didn't believe I could reform even if I had the opportunity to, and if I wanted to. I am of the same opinion still. In the first place I very much doubt that there is the remotest possibility of you or any one else having power enough to get me my freedom. In the second place I have no desire to reform, in as much as the laws and constitution as would be required of me the way the laws of this country are to-day. In the third place I do not care to live any longer if I must live in prison. I would far rather die and go to hell if that's where people like me go to after death. I have very thoroughly considered this matter and I assure you that what I now say is the truth. My first reason for disagreeing with you is that I believe it is absolutely impossible for me to ever gain my freedom in a legal way because I have too much against me and too many people wish my death. I have confessed to 2 3 different cold blooded, premeditated

[overlapping page - partially visible:]
murders, hundreds of robberies, rapes and ... this time I robbed em ... various confessions ... different states and ... all the calender, ... I expect to go on tria ... I committed. At that ... murder in the first ... hanged by the ne... the man I killed th... from me, neither ... tis now. That on... to your question. ...

[lower right page:]
...They say ... had to conform to the standards set by other people in civilization. I am set in my ways so that I can not adapt myself to the ways of other people so the only way for me to do would be to live my own way with any human cry & passion which I believe I am, I would like to try it that way. That is about all for this time, now you are in possession of a question. What do you think about it? I expect that by the time you get around to answering this letter, I will have been tried found guilty and sentenced to death or maybe I'll be all ready in my grave. So long -

Carl Panzram.
Box 7. 31614.
Leavenworth
Kansas.

[lower left page:]
POST OFFICE BOX 7
31614
Mr. Hen...
% Mr. J...
The M...
No. 134...
Washing...
D.C.
My ...
guilty ... of ...
years in prison ...
liberty is not wor...
me, I still kill my...
 little time amon...
I have no desire to do so. If I ha...
living any longer the only way I c...
to do so would be to get clean out and a...
all civilized people. If I could get my...
a few hundred dollars worth of the...
of life such as clothing, medicines, fo...
fishing and hunting tackle and some...
writing material and with these things...
dogs and then clear out and go off to...
away lonely island. Then I would b...
no one would trouble me and I would...
one else. There I could have life, lib...
pursuit of happiness. I know of jus...
a small island off of the San Blas...
Panama. I have been there before, years...
island had some hundreds of coc...
on it, a spring of fresh water. Th...
come there to lay their eggs. Th...

I received your letter of Nov. 7. I wrote you two in answer and now this is the third one. In your last letter to me you asked me to seriously consider from all angles your proposition. That is if I should be given a commutation of sentence or a pardon now and then given my liberty with financial backing, what would I do with it. Could I and would I reform. In my other two letters I told you that I didn't believe I could reform even if I had the opportunity to and if I wanted to. I am of the same opinion still. In the first place I very much doubt that there is the remotest possibility of you or any one else having power enough to get me my freedom. In the second place I have no desire to reform under such conditions as would be required of me the way the laws of this country are today. In the third place I do not care to live any longer if I must live in prison. I would far rather die and go to hell if that's where people like me go to after death. I have very thoroughly considered this matter and I assure you that what I say now is the truth.

My first reason for disagreeing with you is that I believe it is absolutely impossible for me to ever gain my freedom in a legal way because I have too much against me and too many people wish my death. I have confessed 23 different cold blooded, pre-meditated murders, hundreds of cases of arson, burglaries, robberies, rapes and other crimes. The law has by this time looked 'em up and verified the truth of my various confessions. I am wanted in dozens of different states and other countries for every crime on the calendar, from petty larceny to murders. I expect to go on trial here next month for the last murder I committed. At that time I expect to be found guilty of murder in the first degree and then sentenced to be hanged by the neck until I am as dead as a dodo for the man I killed here last June. And you can take it from me, neither will ever be any deader, than they are now. That one reason should be sufficient answer to your question. But just in case your not convinced yet that your dream is impossible of fulfillment I'll give you my second reason and that is that I could not reform if I wanted to. It has taken me all my life so far, 38 years of it for me to reach my present state of mind. In that time I have acquired some habits. It took me a lifetime to form these habits and I believe it would take more than another lifetime to break myself of these same habits even if I wanted to. My philosophy of life is such that very few people ever get and it is so deeply engrained and burned into me that I don't believe I could ever change my beliefs. The things I have had done to me by others and the things I have done to them, can never be forgotten or forgiven either by me or others. I can't forget and I won't forgive. I couldn't if I wanted to. The law is in the same fix. Those are two very good reasons why your proposition is not feasible. It's only a dream on your part but I have no illusions as to it's practicability.

My third reason for not agreeing with your suggestions is that I prefer death before spending more years in prison. My belief is that life without liberty is not worth having. If the law won't kill me, I shall kill myself. I fully realize that I am not fit to live among people in a civilized community. I have no desire to do so. If I had any choice in living any longer, the only way I would consent to do so would be to get clear out and away from all civilized people. If I could get my freedom and a few hundred dollars worth of the necessaries of life such as clothing, medicines, tools, seeds, fishing and hunting tackle and some books and writing materials, and with these things a couple of dogs and then clear out and go off to some far away lonely island. Then I would be contented. No one would trouble me and I would trouble no one else. There I could have life, liberty and the pursuit of happiness. I know of just such a place a small island off of the San Blass Coast of Panama. I have been there before, years ago. The island had some hundreds of coconut trees on it, a spring of fresh water. The sea tortoises come there to lay their eggs. There are plenty of fish, some banana trees some mango and lime trees. The soil will grow anything that's planted. This island is about 40 or 50 miles off the reefs directly East by north from a place called Peters Island which is east of Chucumbally which is on the main land and south of Povamella where the Panamanian Government has stationed their Port of Entry for traders on the San Blass Coast. I was a trader and skipper, and owner of a small sloop down there in 1919 and 20 so I know what I am talking about. This island is owned by the San Blass Indians and they visit it once or twice to harvest the coconuts and gather in the eggs of the sea turtles, other wise no one ever goes there. That's what I would like to do and that's about the only way I would even think of living out my natural life. There I could live as I wanted to and I would not need comfort to the standards set by other people in civilization. I am so set in my ways that I can not adapt myself to the ways of other people so the only way for me to do would be to live by myself without any human companionship whatever. I sure would like to try it that way. That is about all for this time. Now you answer me a question. What do you think about it? I expect though that by the time you get around to answering this letter, I will have been tried, found guilty and sentenced to death or maybe I'll be already in my grave. So Long- Carl Panzram

Dec. 20, 1929

Letter from Carl Panzram to Henry Lesser.

      I received your letter of Dec. 7, several days ago but I delayed in answering it until now, because I wished to think matters over quite well before I reached the decision I have come to. I have been thinking for some time that our correspondence isn't worth while continuing. It does no one any harm but neither, on the other hand does it do me any good. I have been writing to you for a year or more and now after making a check up I find that from you I receive more promises than anything else. I can't spend your promises, so don't waste your and my time sending any more of them. You have written me several times that you enjoyed and may sometime in the future derive some benefit from my letters. Please bear in mind that I have no future. I may be brought to trial any day, just a few days ago I read in the K.C. Paper that The Federal Grand Jury has indicted me for first degree murder and that the rider had declared that he will demand the death penalty for me. OK by me. In any case have the means at my disposal and the determination to use them to wind things up. I am all thru and ready to check out. Either one way or another. In the mean time there is very little that you or any one else can do for me. All I want and that you could get for me if you wanted to is some more reading matter. If you have been and still are sincere in the promises which you have made me then I believe it's about time for you to fulfill them. If your unable or unwilling to do the little I ask of you then don't waste your time and my time in politeness and diplomacy. The address of the publishing Co. that publishes the two books I referred to namely, Kants Critique of Pure Reason and Schopenhauers Essays for one buck each is

    Schultes Bookstore
    No 80 Fourth Ave and 10th St.
    New York City

I should also like to have a subscription for 6 months to the Saturday Evening Post. Also if you could possibly manage it I would like to have a three "3" months subscription to a New York Paper. Either the Evening Journal or the Graphic.
I believe that will keep me going as long as I'll be able to read. I do not know Pat Crowe. I only know of him.
You have been saying and thinking of changing your line of work for a long time. I think it's about time you done it instead of merely thinking about it.
      I am not in a very good humor for the past week or so for reasons other than I have mentioned here but they wouldn't interest you even if I told you. Otherwise everything is lovely. I am getting fat and greasy, lousy and lazy and I don't think it will be long now. I mean time not my neck. I believe that my time is getting shorter but my neck will soon be longer. More truth than poetry perhaps but any way my address is still

Carl Panzram

Leavenworth, Kansas Dec. 20. 1924,

Mr Henry James.
% Mr. H. P. Lesser
No 1466 Chapin St. N.W.
Washington
D.C.

I received your letter of Dec 7, several days ago but I delayed in answering it until now, because I wished to think matters off, quite well before I reached the decision I have come to. I have been thinking for some time that our corresponding isn't worth while continuing. It does no one any harm but neither on the other hand does it do us any good. I have been writing to you for a year or more and now after making a check up I find that from you I recieve more promises than my love anything else. I can't spend your promises, & don't want your promises the times that you engaged and may some time in the future derive some benefit from my letters. Please bear in mind that I have no future. You may be thought to trial any day, just a few days ago I read in the K.C. Paper that The Federal Grand Jury has indicted me for first degree murder and that the reason has declared that he will demand the death penalty for me. Of, by no means have I the means at my disposal and the elimination to see them to it and things and the de-and ready to check out. Either one way or another. I am all through. There is any little that you or any one else can do for me, all I want and that you could get for me if you wanted to is some more reading matter. If you have been and still are sincere in the promises which you told me then I believe it's about time for you to fulfill them if you are able or unwilling to do the little I ask of you then I don't want your and my time in politeness and all of this...

I am most in a...
week or so for reasons other than I told you. I am
otherwise, every-thing is lovely. I am
they wouldn't interest you even if I told you
fat and greasy, lousy and lazy and I don't think it will be
long now. I mean time not my neck. I believe that my
time in getting shorter but my neck will soon be longer
More truth than poetry perhaps but any way my address
is still
Carl Panzram.
Box 7. 31614.
Leavenworth.
Kansas.

The address of the jail
I referred to normally 12
Essays for one half
Schultie
No 80 to
New

I should also
4 th Saturday
Also if you at
have a three
Paper. Eith

I believe th
to read.
I do not
You have
writ for a long
of newly-thinking at

But before I leave this world entirely there is a few things that I can do for you. I can give you a few ideas things that may some day prove to be of great value to you. I am not asking you for any thing in return for what I will give you. I would have given these inventions or ideas long before now but I have been waiting to see if you realy meant just what you said and if you could keep the promises that you have made to me. Now that I see that you are sincere and realy mean what you say I will try to re- ciprocat by doing some favors for you. You know that when I last saw you I told you that I had some ideas for new inventions. Some I showed you, others I held back. Those I am now going to tell you about. You can do as you like about them. You can be smart and make yourself a bundle of jack or you can be a boob and throw them away or give them away or let some one else run them. I know that these ideas of mine are very valuable if they are handled by the right man in the right way. One of my inventions which I told you of and which you made no use of. I have since told to another man here. He gave me 5.00 for it. He in turn has drawn up the plans of the 5, 6 and 7 compartment cases, he has sent them out to his folks, and they in turn have invested a little money in having a number of models made and they have applied for a patent on it. They will make money on it. You and I will make nothing. This simply because you havent the imagination to see the possibilities and notions I havent the opportunities. Now then in these next letters of mine to you. I want you to get one permanant address and keep all of my letters for future reference. Let me know of each and every letter you receive here-after, from

Carl Panzram.
31614. Box 7.
Leavenworth, Kansas.

Leavenworth, Kansas Jan 14, 19__ 30

...Dec. 7th I answered it ...vent written until now. I have ...tead of your writing me a letter ...paper The N. Y. Evening Journal which I asked you for. Now I shall explain a few things to you that have been in my mind for some time but which I havent said any thing about. You know how suspicious I am of every one. I never believe any thing that any one ever tells me. I allways think the worst of every one. Even when any one does me a favor I allways impute the worst motives for his doing so. I hate to believe any thing good of any one. It is very hard for me to believe in such things as altruistic friendships. I cant believe in it myself and its practicly impossible for me to believe that any one else can.

But I have known you for some time now and I havent ever yet known of you to be two-faced or selfish. You have allways been quite frank with me in every way. You never have tried to fill me full of bull, you never flattered me or tried to gain any thing in any way from me. You have been pretty decent to me and show I am begining to believe that your only motive in writing to me is to be a friend to me and to do for me whatever good your able to. I realize that your not in a position to do a great lot for me. I dont expect it of you. Time is getting very short and soon I'll be where I wont need any thing from any one. My trouble will soon be over.   over

Jan. 14, 1930

Letter from Carl Panzram to Henry Lesser.

I received your last letter of Dec. 7th. I answered it on Dec. 20th. Since then I haven't written until now. I have been waiting for you to write. Instead of you writing me a letter I have received a daily newspaper. The N.Y. Evening Journal which I asked you for. Now I shall explain a few things to you that have been in my mind for some time but which I haven't said anything about. You know how suspicious I am of everyone. I never believe anything that anyone ever tells me. I always think the worst of everyone. Even when anyone does me a favor I always impute the worst motives for his doing so. I hate to believe anything good of anyone. It is very hard for me to believe in such things as altruistic friendship. I can't believe in it myself and it's practically impossible for me to believe that anyone else can.

But I have known you for sometime now and I haven't ever yet known of you to be two-faced or selfish. You have always been quite frank with me in every way. You never have tried to fill me full of bull. You never flattered me or tried to gain anything in any way from me. YOU have been pretty decent to me and now I am beginning to believe that your only motive in writing to me is to be a friend to me and to do for me whatever good your able to. I realize that your not in a position to do a great lot for me. I don't expect it of you. Time is getting very short and soon I'll be where I wont need anything from any one. My troubles will soon be over. But before I leave this world entirely there are a few things that I can do for you. I can give you a few ideas on things that I can do for you. I can give you a few ideas on things that someday may prove to be of great value to you. I am not asking you for anything in return for what I will give you. I would have given these inventions or ideas long before now but I have been waiting to see if you would keep the promises that you have made to me. Now that I see that you are sincere and really mean what you say I will try to reciprocate by doing some favors for you. You know that when I last saw you I told you that I had some ideas for new inventions. Some I showed you, others I held back. Those I am now going to tell you about. You can do as you like about them. You can be smart and make yourself a bundle of jack or you can be a boob and throw them away or give them away or let some one steal them from you. I know that these ideas off mine are very valuable if they are handled by the right man in the right way. One of my inventions which I told you of and which you made no use of, I have since told to another man here. He gave me $5.00. He in turn has drawn up the plans of the 5, 6 and 7 compartment cases. He has sent them out to his folks, and they in turn have invested a little money in having a number of models made and they have applied for a patent on it. They will make money on it. You and I will make nothing. This is simply because you haven't the imagination to see the possibilities and me because I haven't the opportunities. Now then in these next letters of mine to you. I want you to get one permanent address and keep all of my letters for future reference. Let me know each and every letter you receive hereafter from

Carl Panzram

Jan. 26, 1930

Letter from Carl Panzram to Henry Lesser.

I received your letter of Jan. 15th. I have been getting the Evening Journal of New York every day since the 11th of January. The book Critique of Pure Reason by Kant also reached me. So you see everything is all right. I am pretty well fixed for reading matter now. This is my third letter to you so far this month. I hope that you got the other two. In my last letter to you I explained an idea for an invention. It was nothing to get excited about. It wouldn't make you a millionaire if it should be successful. That one was only an idea which I have never worked out to a final conclusion. But in this letter I'll give you an idea that is not only plausible but possible as well. Because I have experimented and proved conclusively that it can be and has been done and what has been done before can be done again. I know that this idea is very valuable, but how, who, when or where, money can be made out of it, is more than I know. That's up to you, But I do know it can be done. I have done it. I have discovered a new kind of food, or rather it is an extremely old kind of food but just a new way of utilizing it. This food is now in common use by all the people in the world. But it is used in only one way. That is it is eaten raw in its natural state. The way it is eaten now it can only be eaten in that way while it is fresh and ripe. I have found out a way in which this food can be preserved indefinitely without impairing its value. The value would be enhanced because it could be prepared, at its sources and at very little cost. It grows only within the tropics where labor and land is cheap. Nowadays the food can be transported in any kind of a vessel. It needs very little advertising because it is already known all over the world. To be eaten it need not be cooked. It can be eaten by itself or it can be aided to any or all of the breakfast foods, that are now on the market, such as oatmeal, cornflakes, rice, hot-cakes or it can be added to the flour in the baking of cakes or put in nearly any kind of a pudding or dessert.

Now I hope that you are able to see the large possibilities in this new idea of mine. I believe that you can sell the idea alone but if you take my advise you will get busy and experiment until you have by positive proven tests got a good result, take that result and get a patent out in your own name. If you do this then you have something that should make you a millionaire many times over. Now you will want to know what its all about. If you have done as I told you to do, to get from the Dept. of Agriculture some treatises and papers of the subject of Dehydration of fruits and vegetables, then all you will need to do is to go to the nearest grocery store and buy a quarters worth of ripe bananas. That's all you need. Dehydrate them until they are thoroughly dry and then grind the result into fine flour. Then eat it. You will find that it is very good. I have done this myself and I know. Did you ever eat oatmeal with chopped up bananas in it? That's something pretty good to eat but it is much better when it is fixed up as suggested by

Carl Panzram

POST OFFICE BOX 7
31614

Leavenworth, Kansas. Jan. 26. 1930.

Mr. Henry James.
% Mr. H. R. Lesser.
No. 1466 Chapin St. N.W.
Washington
D.C.

I recieved your letter of Jan. 15.th I have been getting the Evening Journal of New York every day since the 11th of Jan The Book Critique of Pure Reason By Kant also reached me. So you see every thing is all right. I am pretty well-fixed for reading matter now. This is my third letter to you so far this month. I hope that you got the other two. In my last letter to you I explained an idea for an invention. It was nothing to get excited about. It wouldn't make you a millionaire if it should be unsuccessful. That one was only an idea which I have never worked out to a final conclusion. But in this letter I give you an idea that is not only plausable but possible as well Because I have experimented and proved conclusively that it can be and has been done and what has been done before can be done again. I know that this idea is very valuable, but how, who, when or where, money can be made out of it, is more than I know. Thats up to you. But I do know it can be done, I have done it. I have discovered a new kind of food. or rather it is an extremely old kind of food but just a new way of utilizing it This food is now in common use by all the people in the world. But it is used in only one way. That is it is eaten raw in its natural state. The way it is eaten now it can only be eaten in that way while it is fresh and ripe. I have found out a way in which this food can be preserved indefinately without impairing its value The value would be enhanced because if could be prepared, at its source and at very little cost. It grows only in the tropics where labor and land is cheap

Nowdays this food can be [...] constructed refrigerators [...] preserving it at it can be [...] It needs very little advert[...] over the world. To be eaten [...] by itself or it can be ad[...] that are now on the market [...] rice, hot-cakes or it can [...] of cakes or put into bread [...] Now I hope that you are [...] this new idea of mine [...] idea alone but if you take [...] experiment until you have [...] result, take that result a[...] If you do this then you [...] you a millionaire many time over. Now you will want to know what its all about. If you have done as I told you to do to get from the Dept. of Agriculture some treatises and papers of the subject of the dehydration of fruit and vegetables, then all you will need to do is to go to the nearest grocery store and buy a quarters worth of ripe bananas, Thats all you need. Dehydrate them until they are thoroughly dry and then grind the result into fine flour. Then eat it. You will find it very good. I have done this myself and I know. Did you ever eat oat-meal with chopped up bananas in it. Thats something pretty good to eat but it is much better when it is prep[...] up as suggested by
Carl Panzram
31614. Box 7.
Leaven-worth
Kansas

In your letter to me you say that at the first available opp-
-ortunity you intend to have sent to me the Book. Schopen-
houses Essays. Please dont trouble about that and also dont
bother to send me any money because now I am doing pretty
well as far as reading matter is concerned, and as for money
althoe I have none, I need none. I have every thing that I need
now. But you can if you will. have sent to me The Saturday
Evening Post for 6 months. With that I'll be well fixed
for reading matter, at least up until the 11th of April
and by that time I expect my trial will be all over.
At least I hope so any way. When my trial is all
thru, I expect I'll be thru too. At any rate I am sure that
it wont be long after. In the mean time I shall, from time
to time give you some other ideas, for you to work out if you care
to bother with them. But first I want to make sure that
you get them and not some one else. Even if you dont fully
understand now, you will later on so please have patience.
Kants Critique is pretty hard for me to read and understand but I am digging away at it and I enjoy and believe
all that I am able to understand of it. In the letter that
was lost I explained an alltogether different invention
to you but now there is no use in repeating it to you. But
perhaps later on I'll be able to explain that one and some
others that I have in mind. In the mean while you
can concentrate on the Food Product. that one is easy for
you to work out and it is a very good one if you can handle it. I have
others just as good or better. But first I want to make sure that you
get all the letters that I write to you. Should you recieve an unfavorable opinion of the Food Product, from the Chemist of the Dept of Agriculture
dont give up hope because neither he nor you know all that I have in my
mind. So Long and Luck to you from
Carl Panzram.
No 31614 Box 7.
Leavenworth. Kansas.

...Jan. 29th I recieved
...that you recieved but two
...thru hasn't been a mistake
...it wasn't made by either you
...in fact Therefore one of my
...were this mistake occurred I
...I do know that the same
...Hereafter I shall take more
precautions. I shall not write anything that the censor can take
objection to. I hope that you will understand without going more fully
into explanations. just remember that others as well as you or I can
see a dollar as far a d as quick as any one else. I am realy glad that
even if you did lose one of my letters that you got my last one of
Jan. 21st. In sending that one you got a very good idea, but
wether or no you can do any thing with it, still remains to be seen.
It's yours to do with as you like or are able. You owe me nothing
Of course I gave you only the bare outline of the idea, but
if you handle it right, that's all you need. I am glad to hear
that you have a powerfull and intelligent friend in the
Dept of Agriculture who you believe to be honest. But you
take my advise and dont put too much faith in some-
-one-elses honesty without first protecting your own interests
I also advise you that in your future letters to me you
say nothing that might benefit some one else and to your
own disadvantage. It is not necessary that I should
know all that you have done or are doing.

Feb. 2, 1930

Letter from Carl Panzram to Henry Lesser.

The letter which you wrote on Jan. 29th I received yesterday. In your letter you say that you received but two letters from me in Jan. You see if there hasn't been a mistake. Yes there has been a mistake, but it wasn't made by either you or me. I wrote you three "3" letters in Jan. Therefore one of my letters never reached you. How or where this mistake occurred I don't know. I can only suspicion. But I do know that the same mistake won't be made by me again. Hereafter, I shall take more precautions. I shall not write anything that the censor can take objection to. I hope that you will understand without going more fully into explanations. Just remember that others as well as you or I can see a dollar as far and as quick as anyone else. I am really glad that even if you did lose one of my letters that you got my last one of Jan. 26th. In sending that one you got a very good idea, but whether or not you can do anything with it, still remains to be seen. It's yours to do with as you like or are able. You owe me nothing. Of course I gave you only the bare outline of the idea but if you handle it right, that's all you need. I am glad to hear that you have a powerful and intelligent friend in the Dept. of Agriculture who you believe to be honest. But you take my advice and don't put too much faith in someone else's without first protecting your own interests. I also advise you that your future letters to me you say nothing that might benefit some one else and to your own disadvantage. It is not necessary that I should know all that you have done or are doing.

In your letter to me you say that at the first available opportunity you intend to have sent to me the book, Schopenhauer's Essays. Please don't trouble about that and also about bothering to send me any money because now I am doing pretty well as far as reading matter. At least up until the 11th of April, and by that time I expect my trial will be all over. At least I hope so anyway. When my trial is all thru, I expect I'll be thru too. At any rate I am sure that it won't be long after. In the meantime I shall from time to time give you some other ideas for you to work out if you care to bother with them. But first I want to make sure that you get them and not someone else. Even if you don't fully understand now, you will later on, so please have patience. Kant's Critique is pretty hard for me to read and understand but I am digging away at it and I enjoy and believe all that I am able to understand of it. In the letter that was lost I explained an altogether different invention to you but now there is no use in repeating it to you. But perhaps later on I'll be able to explain that one and some others that I have in mind. In the meanwhile you can concentrate on the food product. That one is easy for you to work out and it is a very good one if you can handle it, I have others just as good or better. But first I want to make sure that you get all the letters that I write to you. Should you receive an unfavorable opinion of the food product, from the chemist of the Dept. of Agriculture, don't give up hope because neither he nor you know all that I have in my mind. So long and luck to you from

Carl Panzram

Feb. 9, 1930

Letter from Carl Panzram to Henry Lesser.

I received your last letter of Jan 29th which I answered last Sunday Feb. 2nd. Yesterday I received a package of literature from you which deals with patents. I wrote you three,"3" letters in January. One of 'em you didn't get. Why I don't know. I can only guess. It's useless to make any complaint about it. Just forget about it. The letter that was lost was a good one and I wanted you to get it. I wrote 2 double pages and I did not think when I wrote it that I put anything in it that was contrary to the rules there. But maybe I did. Anyway I won't write anything more like it or anything that some wise egg thinks can make a dollar out of. Several times since I have been here I have tried to explain about my mail privileges. I don't believe you have ever understood me. Surely if you stop and think a bit you will understand that, me in the position I am now in as a convict, I have no rights whatever except those that are given to me, or that I am able to take. And I assure you that I can take very, very little and anything I take I'll have to pay for and pay a hell of a big price for it too. So I don't take any chances. I expect to have my trial sometime the latter part of this month or the first of the next. Then we will see what we will see. Either one way or another, I'll be wound up and all thru. In the meantime I'll just slide along the easiest way I can. I won't write anything that I think would do any one else any good or me any harm. You, from your experience in the work you are doing should surely know the inside workings of these kind of places. There is no use in me trying to explain any further to you. The papers which you sent from the U.S. Patent Office were interesting reading, but I know all of that before. I knew that there were such machines and patents in existence, but none that you sent me has my idea. I done the same as I have told you and I had no complication or expensive machinery to do it with. The only machinery I had was a small coffee grinder to grind the dried product into flour.

The only other things I used was sunshine and a few little odds and ends such as some pieces of wire, wooden boxes with glass covers and fresh air. You know I told you that I once worked in the United Fruit Co. at their Costa Rica Division. In that part of the world there are only 2 seasons, the rainy and the dry season. You know I am no chemist and I have no technical ability, so I know nothing whatever about the finer points as they are explained in the papers you sent me. All that I do know is that I dried the Food product, ground it into flour and eat it and found it good. What I done anyone else can do. I have no doubt but what other people have had the same idea in mind. Some have developed the idea much farther than I have, but none have done anything worth while with it. The finished product is not on the market. That's where it belongs and not simply stored away in someone's mind on a shelf in a store-room. Whether or not you can do this I don't know. That's up to you. I don't much like to write letters and I like it less when I take the trouble and time to write to you and then you have someone else have the benefit of what I write to you and thereby depriving you who I am writing it for. It won't be long now when it will be the end of

Carl Panzram

POST OFFICE BOX 7
31614.

Leavenworth, Kansas Feb. 9, 30
19—

Mr. Henry James,
℅ Mr. H. R. Gisser.
No. 1466 Chapin St. N.W.
Washington
D.C.

I recieved your last letter of Jan. 29th which I answered last Sunday Feb 2d. Yesterday I recieved a package of literature from you which deals with Patents. I wrote you three, 3 letters in January. One of them you didn't get. Why I don't know. I can only guess. Its useless to make any complaint about it. Just forget about it. The letter that was lost was a good one and I wanted you to get it. I wrote 2 double pages and I did not think when I wrote it that I put anything in it that was contrary to the rules here. But maybe I did. Anyway I wont write anything more like it or anything that some wise-egg thinks he can make a dollar out of. Several times since I have been here I have tried to explain to you about my mail privileges. I don't believe you have ever understood this. Surely if you stop and think a bit you will understand that, me in the position I am now in as a convict I have no rights whatever except those that are given to me or that I am able to take. And I assure you that I can take very little and anything I take I'll have to pay for and pay a hell of a big price for it too so I don't take any chances. I expect to have my trial sometime the latter part of this month or the first of the next. Then we will see what we will see. Either one way or another I'll be wound up and all thru. In the mean time I'll just slide along the easiest way I can. I wont write any thing that I think would do any one else any good or me any harm. You from your experience in the work you are doing should surely know the inside workings of these kind of places. There is no use in me trying to explain any

[second page]

further to you. The ... office were interested ... knew that there ... but now that yo... I have told you ... machinery to d... a small coffee ... The only other ... odds and ends ... with glass o... over stocked f... In that part ... and the dry ... did in the ... no technical ... finer form ... me, little that ... beyond its to flow ... any one else could ... What I do or anyone else ... other people have had the same idea in mind, but am ... the idea much further than I am but now I am on the interior ... worth while with it. The finished product is not on the ... Thats where it belongs and not simply stored away in some ... one mind or on a shelf in a store room. Althro my boy ... can do this I don't know. Thats up to you. I don't much like to write letters and I like it less when I take the trouble and time to write to you and then have some one else have the knife of what I write and thereby depriving you who I am writing it for. It wont be long now when it will be the end of

Carl Panzram
31614. Box 7.
Leavenworth
Kansas

Feb. 16, 1930

Letter from Carl Panzram to Henry Lesser.

I won't waste much time in writing this letter because I don't know if you will get it or not. Some of my others that I took considerable time and trouble to write to you, you never got at all. I wrote you three, "3" letters in January and this is my third one this month, the other two I wrote on Feb.2 and Feb 9th. The last letter I got from you on Jan. 29th. But I did receive a package of literature in regards to patents from you.

My trial is soon coming up and in the meantime I am trying not to do anything, say or write anything which could be used as evidence to convict me of insanity. I know that there are some who would like nothing better than to send me to the madhouse. This I don't want because I would rather be dead. There are people here as there are elsewhere who are sincere in their belief that I am a lunatic, but there are others who know I am not insane but who want to have me declared mad. I don't want to give these people any more reasons to believe I am a bug. You know that one of the many different kinds of insanity is the invention bug. There are people in this world who are too stupid to invent anything new themselves and when they see someone else who has intelligence and ingenuity enough to discover a new idea, they at once say he is crazy but they themselves are not unwilling to steal the same idea and profit by it. I have other reasons also, why at this time and place I don't care to write a great deal. First I shall wait until my trial is over with. Whatever the outcome may be, then in time enough to continue explaining some of my other ideas to you. In the meantime continue to have patience as I do.

Carl Panzram.

March 2, 1930

Letter from Carl Panzram to Henry Lesser.

Your last letter was recieved by me on Jan. 29th. In January I wrote you three letters.
In February I wrote you four letters.
In this letter I am sending you three small watch-chains which I made out of some string. They are no good as they are. I only send them to you so you can see what they look like.
If I had a half a dozen spools of silk thread different colors, I would up a dozen or two of these trinkets and send 'em to you.

Just to pass the time away.
This will be all until I hear from you.
I am
Carl Panzram

POST OFFICE BOX 7
31614.

Leavenworth, Kansas Feb. 16, 1930

Mr. Henry James
% Mr. H. P. Besser.
No. 1466 Chapin St. N.W.
Washington
D.C.

I wont waste much time in writing this letter because I don't know if you will get it or not. Some of my others that I took considerable time and trouble to write to you, you never got at all. I wrote you three "3" letters in January and this is my third one this month, the other two I wrote on Feb. 2, and Feb 9th. The last letter I got from you on Jan 29th, But I did recive a package of literature in regards to Patents from you.

My trial is soon coming up and in the mean time I am trying not to do any thing, say or write any thing which could be used as evidence to convict me of insanity. I know that there are some people who would like nothing better than to send me to the mad-house. This I don't want because I would rather be dead. There are people too as there are also-where who are sincere in their belief that I am a lunatic but there are also others who know I am not insane but who want to have me declared mad. I dont want to give these people any more reasons to believe I am a bug. You know that one of the many different kinds of insanity is the invention bug. There are people in this world who are too stupid to invent any thing new themselves and when they see someone else who has intelligence and ingenuity enough to discover a new idea, they at once say he is crazy but they themselves are not unwilling to steal the same idea and profit

by it. I have other reasons also, why, at this time and place I dont care to write a great deal. First I shall wait until my trial is over with. What ever the out-come maybe, then is time enough to continue explaining some of my other ideas to you. In the meantime, continue to have paitence as I do.

Carl Panzram
31614. Box 7.
Leavenworth.
Kansas.

but I finaly broke off diplomatic relations with him and I agree
to disagree. Then lately there has been another man here who has
tried to be diplomatic and civil to me for the past week or 10 days
From all outward appearances he seems to be not only willing
but anxious to talk to me and to have me speak to him. But you
know how I am, I dont believe any one means right by me. I think
bad of every one and good of no one. A man must be a real man
or a man and a half before I'll believe any good of him and
even then he must convince me that he means well by me
before I'll believe any good of him. And believe me this takes
some proving before I am convinced.

I understand now that I will not be tried in K.C. this
this month; I'll be put on trial here in the town of Leaven
Kansas City next month. That is providing that I
consent to wait that long. I have waited for 8 months now
and I am pretty tired of waiting. The longer I have waited
the madder I have got untill now I am so hot that I am
liable to explode and blow myself completely out of
not only this prison but out of this world also.

During this past week I have done some writing. So far
I have written about 25,000 words. Along the same lines
of the subject which your interested in. I would ask
it to you if I was permited to but I dont think it wou
be allowed. So I consider trying to send it to Mr. Mac
Cormick the Assistant Supt of Prisons. I dont even
know if I'll be able to do even that. I believe you know
him, dont you? If you don't you ought to. He is a good
man for you to know.

So Long
Carl Panzram
No. 31614, Box 7,
Leavenworth
Kansas.

letter of March 6. Also a
cards to the string watch chain
spect I'll get the Sat. Eve. Post
lik to read and all that I have
ea which you had sent me
s you sent to me. I dont get any
getting both for a while but
the kind I wanted so I refused
to accept the ones that was offered to me so now I got none at al.
The Book which you sent me Kants Critique, I read for about a
month but it is too deep for me to understand, the most of it
went over my head. Finaly I got so disgusted and discouraged
that I went into a tantrum and in a mad rage, I tore it
up into 10,000 pieces and fired it out of my door. That left me
with my two papers only and those I havent been reading very
much because for the past month I have been pretty hostile. I am
allways mad any way like a mad dog but sometime, I get a
little more peeved than at other times and those are the times when
most anything is liable to happen to me or any one else who may
be near me. As you know I am confined in the Isolation here
but its all right so far, no one has bothered me or abused me.
There are men here who would talk to me if I would listen to
them and if I cared to speak to them but I wont do either one. There
is no one here that I care to talk to or to have talk to me. For a while
here there was one man that I used to talk to and to listen to occaisionaly

March 9, 1930

Letter from Carl Panzram to Henry Lesser.

This evening I received your letter of March 6. Also a return receipt from the P.O. in regards to the string watch chain which I made and sent to you. I expect I'll get the Sat. Eve. Post soon. I'll be glad to get it. Because I like to read and all that I have to read now days is the newspaper which you had sent to me and the one I ordered with the 2 bucks you sent to me. I don't get any books or magazines anymore. I was getting both for a while but then towards the last I couldn't get the kind I wanted so I refused to accept the ones that was offered to me so now I get none at all. The book which you sent me Kants Critique, I read for about a month but it is too deep for me to understand. The most of it went over my head. Finally I got so disgusted and discouraged that I went into a tantrum and in a mad rage, I tore it up into 10,000 pieces and fired it out of my door. That left me with my tow papers only and those I haven't been reading very much because for the past month I have been pretty hostile. I am always mad anyway like a mad dog but sometimes I get a little more peeved than at other times, and those are the times when most anything is liable to happen to me or anyone else who may be near me. As you know I am confined to the isolation here, but it's all right so far, no one has bothered me or abused me. There are men here who would talk to me if I would listen to them and if I cared to speak to them, but I won't do either one. There is no one here that I care to talk to or to have talk to me. For awhile here there was one man that I used to talk to and listen to occasionally but I finally broke off diplomatic relations with him and I agreed to disagree. Then lately there has been another man here who has tried to be diplomatic and civil to me for the past week or 10 days. From all outward appearances he seems to be not only willing but anxious to talk to me and to have me speak to him. But you know how I am, I don't believe anyone means right by me. I believe bad of every one and good of no one. A man must be a real man or a man and half before I'll believe any good of him and even then he must convince me that he means well by me before I'll believe any good of him. And believe me this takes some proving before I am convinced.

I understand now that I will not be tried in K.C. Kansas this month. I'll be put on trial here in the town of Leavenworth, Kansas early next month. That is providing that I consent to wait that long. I have waited for 8 months now and I am pretty tired of waiting. The longer I have waited the madder I have got until now I am so hot that I am liable to explode and blow myself completely out of, not only the prison, but out of this world also.

During this past week I have done some writing. So far I have written about 25,000 words. Along the same lines of the subject which your interested in. I would sent it to you if I was permited to but I don't think it would be allowed. So I consider trying to send it to Mr. MacCormick the Assistant Supt of Prisons. I don't even know if I'll be able to do even that. I believe you know him, don't you? If you don't you ought to. He is a good man for you to know.

So Long
Carl Panzram

THE TRIAL

The Trail

Panzeran tried to enter a plea of guilty and refused the services of an attorney, but, while it is perfectly legal for a Federal Judge to inflict a death sentence upon a plea of guilty to murder in the First Degree, the practice is illegal in many states and is usually considered very bad form, and in many states, even where such a plea may be accepted, the corpus delicti must be proved by witnesses. At that time, State practice in such matters was controllable in Federal Courts.

So the Judge refused to accept Panzeran's plea and appointed attorneys to defend him. Panzeran refused to cooperate with his appointed attorneys. Stated in open court that he had killed Warnakey without any motive or reason, and asked both the Jury and the court to hang him.

The attorney put up a good defense of insanity. Carl Menninger offered his services without charge, appeared as a witness for the defense, and swore that Panzeran was a homicide maniac and totally irresponsible for his conduct, but he accepted the authenticity of all of Panzeran's stories to Ballard.

Note: Menninger discusses this case in Man Against Himself, a work dealing with the suicide complex, but the writer is convinced that he completely missed the motivation behind Panzeran's conduct.
The picture that the United States Attorney was able to draw was so revolting, however, that the question as to whether Panzeran was actually insane or sane was never really considered by the jury. It took them only a few minutes to find Panzeran guilty and fix the death sentence.

Panzeran never departed from the pose that he wanted to be hanged. He refused to sign a petition for clemency; he continued to tell Ballard his vile and harrowing murder stories, but as the days and weeks slipped by and the day of his execution came nearer and nearer, remarks about the execution of insane persons slipped more and more into his conversation. Of course, these took the form of expressions of fear that they would not execute him, but it became obvious that he had never believed that they would, that he had staked his life upon a false premise and lost, though it must be said of him that he did not turn crybaby, as so many men have done. As he realized that he was going to the gallows, he began talking more and more of self-destruction. If he just had the means and knew a sure way of doing it, he would cheat them out of the satisfaction of hanging him.

That was the talk that the writer had been waiting many months to hear. He and Ono had fought long and hard to prevent the precedent of no hangings in Kansas from being broken. They had both been prepared to destroy themselves, if necessary, to keep from breaking it, and the writer had come within three days of the limit that he had set for himself. They did not want it broken now.

The writer began talking about suicide in a voice that he knew Panzeran could not help but hear. He could not talk to Panzeran, but he could talk to Ono, to Ballard, to the orderlies, and with death hanging over the house, they were all good listeners.

Time after time the writer explained how simple and painless it really is to do a good job: just press two fingers down into the groin until the throb of the big femur artery can be felt; work the fingers back and forth until the artery is brought against the skin; then cut it. Just a little nick, which does not have to be more than a quarter of an inch long and no deeper than that. A determined man could tear that thick skin and pinch the artery in two with his thumb nail. He could scratch through the skin with a lead pencil, a pen point, a needle, almost anything. If a man had just a little chip of razor blade, it would be so simple; cut one side and he would be dead in ten minutes; cut both sides and he would be dead in five minutes.

The writer explained in detail how it is that the femur artery is the only one in the body that can be reached easily, yet cannot be tied off. Cut a man's throat, and if only one carotid is severed, it can be tied off, and the man will live. Cut a femur, and the end slips back into the abdomen, where it cannot be reached with a hemostat. Yet, even if this did not occur, the femur would not be tied, for the leg has no colateral circulation, and the man would die, anyway.

The writer went over these simple facts time and again, until he was sure that Panzeran must understand them. He mentioned an alternate method that is equally effective, which is to make a small paper quil, then open a large vein in the arm, insert the quil, then either blow in the quil or stick it in a bowl of water, and run plain hydrant water into the blood stream.

Everytime the writer went to bathe, he carried a razor blade in his hand, and one Friday, about three weeks before Panzeran was due to hang, the writer got a chance to throw the blade into Panzeran's cell. Someone else, probably Ono, working independently, had done the same thing.

Panzeran, too, had his own idea. He had saved a bowl of beans until they were very rotten. Then he made his try. He ate those rotten beans and he cut a gash about six inches long in the fleshy part of his leg, nowheres near the artery. He probably did not lose more than two ounces of blood, but the beans made him sick, and in vomiting, he exposed his leg. The guard saw blood, called the doctor, and had the wound closed and Panzeran's stomach pumped. Naturally, they searched Pan's cell and found the two razor blades.

The writer as fit to be tied. The next morning he asked Ballard what had happened, although he already knew, and when Ballard told him, he blew his top.

"Why, the God damn stupid c___s___, the moronic___ ___" the writer shouted. "Why didn't the damn fool cut the artery in his groin? Didn't he know that no doctor could patch that. Why didn't he pour some mineral oil on top of those beans to keep the air out, then watch for gas bubbles. If he'd got gas under that oil then one teaspoon would be enough, but the groin was the safest bet. No doctor could fix that'

"Those were Gillette blades. Maybe you gave them to him." Ballard said. "You use a Gillette."

"So what? I didn't give them to him only because I've had no chance but If I thought the stupid c___s___ had sense enough to do it right, I'd sure as hell see that he gets one."

The writer knew that he would get one more chance, but he still had one good bet. He wrote the full instructions on a slip of paper, broke a new Gillette blade in two and wrapped the paper around the top halves of the broken blade, dug up an old tube of water-color black and painted the package the same color as the concrete floor. The radio (Part III Chapter XXII) had been installed, but inmates had to buy their own earphones. There was a new fellow, a mulatto kid only serving a short sentence, who had recently been made orderly in Isolation, and who had no earphones.

The writer called him.

"How would you like to use a pair of earphones?"

"Gosh! I'd appreciate it!" said the boy eagerly.

"O.K.! I know how you can get a set, but you will have to do something for me, and you will have to keep your mouth shut. I have the phones right here and I will loan them to you now, but if you want to keep him or keep a whole hide, you will throw this into Pan's cell the first time Ballard turns his head. If you do it, he will give me a signal by saying a certain thing to Ballard. As soon as I hear that signal, the phones will be yours."

"I'll do it when I feed him this noon."

"Fine!"

It was not more than half past twelve when Pan started telling Ballard the story of the guy he dropped off the bridge at Budapest. That was the signal. Pan had been in most seaport cities, but he had never been in Budapest and did not know that there are any bridges.

About four o'clock, the writer heard Panzeran say to Ballard:

"I guess that they are going to have to hang me after all. I can kill others, but I haven't got the guts to kill myself, so I had just as well give you these."

"Where did you get them?" Ballard demanded upon seeing the pieces of blade. "None of your damn business."

IN THE DISTRICT COURT OF THE UNITED STATES

FOR THE DISTRICT OF KANSAS,FIRST DIVISION.

The United States

      vs.   No.5465.

Carl Panzran

The President of the United States of America to the Warden of
the United States Penitentiary at Leavenworth,Kansas,Greeting:

    You are hereby commanded that you have the body of Carl
Panzran,now detained in the United States Penitentiary at Leaven
worth,Kansas,under your custody and control as a prisoner,under
safe and secure conduct before the United States District Court
within and for the First Division of the District of Kansas
sitting in regular session at Topeka,Kansas,on the 15th day of
April,A.D.1930,at the hour of ten o'clock a.m.of said day and
thereafter during said term of court as the court may order or
require and that you shall have him then and there before said
court to abide any and all orders,judgments and decrees therein
as may be rendered by the Court.

    And that he,the said Carl Panzran immediately after the
trial or other disposition of his case is ended,be returned to
the aforesaid United States Penitentiary at Leavenworth,Kansas,
and there held by you in custody to complete serving out his
sentence on the commitment to said institution under which he
is now held,and have you then and there this writ.

    Witness the Hon.RICHARD J.HOPKINS,Judge of the United States
      District Court for the First Division of the District of
      Kansas.

    Given under seal of said court this 26th day of March,A.D.
      1930.

                    F.L.Campbell,Clerk,

    (SEAL)

               By   Adaline White
                       Deputy Clerk.

A true copy:

ATTEST: F.L.Campbell,Clerk,

    By *Adaline White* Deputy Clerk.

March 16, 1930

Letter from Carl Panzram to Henry Lesser.

I am writing you this short letter to try to let you know that I have received the first issue of the Saturday Evening Post.

Also that I received a letter from you dated Jan. 29th and one dated March 6th. Those are all.

I wrote you three letters in January, 4 in February and this is my third to you so far this month.

I don't know if you will get this or not so I'll not waste any more time in writing. I would write a good deal more if I had the assurance that you would receive all of my letters. But for some mysterious reason or other, when I do take the time and trouble to write you long letters, you never get 'em. There are a good many things I would like to write and tell you because I am sure they would be interesting to you and very possibly some might prove to be valuable also. But under the present circumstances it is useless for me to write all of what I have in my mind,

Well So Long for this time

I am still

Carl Panzram

March 23, 1930

Letter from Carl Panzram to Henry Lesser.

I received your letters of March 6th and 15th. I wrote you on March 16th, 18th, and today the 23rd. The only news that I have which might interest you is that the date of April 20th, 1930 has been set aside as the time I'll be tried and the place set as Topeka, Kansas in the U.S. Federal Court under the jurisdiction of Judge Hopkins and Judge Pollock.

Why there should be 2 judges I don't know or why the place chosen for the trial should be Topeka, I don't know either and care less. The only part that interests me is what the result will be and I already know what that will be.

It might pay you to get a subscription for your own use of a Topeka or a Leavenworth paper for the month of April next. In that way you'll learn more about my case than I could tell you in my letters. But in reading the papers you must remember to use your own judgement about what is printed about me because the papers are only interested in printing what they think their subscribers would like to read. The truth has very little appeal to them.

Both of my papers will run out on the 11th of April, but I don't want the subscriptions renewed, neither of them. What little time I'll have left after the 11th of next month. I won't care to spend in reading a lot of lies and hot air that the papers will publish about me.

I don't feel much like scribbling any more today so I'll cut this short here.

I am

Carl Panzram.

UNITED STATES ATTORNEY

DISTRICT OF KANSAS

Topeka, Kansas.
March 26, 1930.

Mr. T. B. White,
Warden, U.S. Penitentiary,
Leavenworth, Kansas.

Dear Mr. White:

I have received a letter from Mr. Timmons,
Acting Administrative Assistant, relative to the
appointment of Attorneys for various defendants to be
tried in Topeka April 14th.

Judge Hopkins has also called my attention to the
letter written him by Carl Panzran. Of course an attorney
will be appointed for Panzran whether he wants it or not.
However, the Judge is interested in this man's mental
condition and desires to know whether or not you have a
commission of doctors who could pass upon his mentality
at the present time.

What the Court desires to know is, is the man of
sound enough mind that he knows he is being tried for murder
and is he of sound enough mind to defend himself, or advise
an Attorney of any defense he may have, at the trial. Was
he, at the time of the murder, sane enough to know that he
was committing a murder? It is difficult for me to express
what is wanted by the commission of doctors. I suppose that
what I am trying to say is this, that any person who commits
a murder, any other ordinary person would really regard him
as unsound mentally or he would not have committed it, but
that is not excusable if he was possessed of his ordinary
faculties.

With the above in mind, will you kindly advise me
if you have a commission of doctors there that could make
some findings that I could furnish to the Court.

Yours very truly,

L. E. Wyman
Assistant U.S. Attorney.

W:L

204

March 30, 1930

Letter from Carl Panzram to Henry Lesser.

I received your last two letters of March 6th and 15th. I wrote to you on March 16th, 18th, and 23rd and now the 30th. You asked me in your last letter to continue to write down my ideas because you would like to get them. I am not doing any writing nowadays, simply because I don't care to. There are a good many things I would like to write down, some of which I believe to be of considerable value, and all of which I believe to be truthful and interesting, but at the present time under the existing conditions it would be worse than useless for me to do any writing. Should conditions be changed in such a way that what I write wouldn't harm me but do me good and harm my enemies, then I would be only too glad to express myself in writing.

You also asked me if there was anything you could do for me. Yes there is. You can, if you will, subscribe for the Christian Science Monitor, a Boston newspaper, for me by the month. One month at a time as long as I am alive to read it, which I believe will be not over 3 months at most and probably 2 months but possibly only one month.

At the present time I am getting 2 newspapers daily, but they both run out in a week or 10 days and I don't want either one of those subscriptions renewed. Soon the papers will be writing me up and putting me on the pan. They will be publishing a lot of hot air about me and I don't care much about reading things from some one else's point of view. The Monitor is a pretty good paper because it does not print a lot of bull or lies and no criminal news.

What it does print can be depended on to pretty near true and the most of what it does print is on subjects which interests me, world affairs. This paper doesn't interest most people but it does me. I know your bank roll isn't very fat, but this won't break you I guess. How about that silk thread you were going to send me. When you do send it be sure that it is the rayon or imitation kind, like the bit I sent to you.

I don't know if you got all my other letters or not, but I believe not, but I think you'll get this one all right because no one can take exception to anything I have written here. Now I'll ring off in this one before I do write something that's not according to the laws of John L Sullivan or some other all powerful God.
So Long

Carl Panzram

March 29, 1930

31614

Honorable L. E. Wyman,
Assistant United States Attorney,
Topeka, Kansas

Dear Sir:

I just have your letter of March 26th in which you
ask to be advised for the benefit of the Court as to the
mental state of our Carl Panzran, Register No. 31614.

Will state in this connection that shortly after
Panzran committed the murder here of our Laundry Foreman,
R. G. Warnke, I had a Visiting Psychiatrist, Dr. B. Landis
Elliott of Kansas City examine him and make me a report.
I am herewith submitting to you a copy of his report which
is dated June 29, 1929.

It is my opinion that this man knows he is to be
tried for murder. He is probably of sound enough mind to
defend himself, but I doubt the advisability of this course
on account of his ungovernable temper. I do not know whether
he would consult with an attorney or not. He makes a claim
that he is tired of this life and wants a death penalty put
upon him. Of course, I believe that he was sane enough to
know that he was committing murder and doing the wrong thing.
I do not think that he is normal mentally, but I do not
think he is so abnormal that I would class him as insane.
I believe, though, that what the Psychiatrist had to say
about his examination is much more conclusive than anything
I might say.

If there are any further examinations you would
like made, I will be glad to bring this about. We have with
us a very noted Psychiatrist, Dr. J. K. Fuller, who is
connected with the United States Public Health Service and
is in charge of the Psychiatric Division of the Medical Force
of the USP Annex at Fort Leavenworth. I will have him
examine this man if you think the Court would want it done.

Very truly yours,

TBW-L   Warden

1 encl-

April 1, 1930.

31614

Mr. Carl Panzram,
(#31614)

Dear Sir:

I am today passing to Mr. McCormack, Assistant
Superintendent of Prisons the article you wrote for him
in connection with your present experiences.

Very truly yours,

Warden

Place   Work Isolation
Cell 13

Request to See Warden or Deputy

UNITED STATES PENITENTIARY
LEAVENWORTH, KANSAS

April 8.   192 30

Undersigned Prisoner requests audience with the

for the following reason:

I wish to get 6 spoo
of silk thread that
is now held for m
the storeroom

Name Carl Panzram   Reg. No. 31614

                              192

Audience held

DISPOSITION OF CASE

Form 83-L

207

31614.

Leavenworth, Kansas. April. 2. 19 30

Mr. H. P. Lesser
No. 1466 Chapin St. NW.
Washington
D.C.

I recieved your letter of April 2. in which
you state that you have not recieved all of the letters
that I wrote to you.

I suspected that all along.

The officials here know who and what you are
and knowing that they also know that you are not the
type of man to do any thing wrong in corresponding
with me.

will be sometime this month, probably about
the 14th at Topeka Kansas. In the U.S.
Court under the jurisdiction of Judge
Hopkins.

I am in receipt of a letter from him in
which he states that he has already
appointed an attorney to defend me.
His name is Capt. Ralph O'Neil of Topeka

So Long

Carl Panzram
31614. Box 7.
Leavenworth
Kansas.

April 2, 1930

Letter from Carl Panzram to Henry Lesser.

I received your last 2 letters or March 6th and 15th.
I wrote you four letters since then. Mar. 16th, 18th, 23rd. and 30th.
The only thing new that I can tell you is that the date of my trial has been definitely set for sometime this month, probably about the 14th at Topeka, Kansas in the U.S. Court under the Jurisdiction of Judge Hopkins.
I am in receipt of a letter from him in which he states that he has already appointed an attorney to defend me. His name is Capt. Ralph O'Neil of Topeka.
So Long

Carl Panzram

April 5, 1930

Letter from Carl Panzram to Henry Lesser.

I received your letter of April 2, in which you state that you have not received all of the letters that I wrote to you.
I suspected that all along.
The officials here know who and what you are and knowing that they also know that you are not the type of man to do anything wrong in correspondence with me.
As for me I couldn't if I wanted to. Still my letters are stopped and no reason given me. I never know when a letter of mine will be held up by the censor here. The censor in this case is the warden here. He has the power to do just as he pleases with my mail and it seems to please him to stop some of my letters occasionally.
I can't stop him from doing this but what I can do and will do is to stop writing letters.
I won't write to you any more under the circumstances as they are now.
When if ever a change is made, then I will consider renewing our correspondence.

I am Carl Panzram

UNITED STATES OF AMERICA   )
DISTRICT OF KANSAS.   ) SS.

      At a term of the District Court of the United States
of America for the District of Kansas, begun and held at the
City of Topeka, in said District, on Monday, the 14th day of
April, 1930, proceedings were had and appeared of record, in
words and figures following, to-wit:

                Wednesday, April 16, 1930.

"The United States

      vs.   No. 5465. Vio. Sections 273 and 275 P. C.

Carl Panzran

      Now on this 16th day of April, 1930 come the parties
hereto same as on yesterday, the defendant Carl Panzran being
present in his own proper person; thereupon comes the jury into
open court and through its Foreman presents the following
Verdict to-wit:

"IN THE DISTRICT COURT OF THE UNITED STATES FOR THE DISTRICT
OF KANSAS, FIRST DIVISION. The United States vs. Carl Panzran,
No. 5465. We, the jury in the above entitled cause, duly impaneled
and sworn, upon our oaths, find the defendant Carl Panzran
guilty as charged in the indictment herein. O.A. Kirkendall,
Foreman."

      Thereupon the defendant through his attorney re-
quested that the jury be polled and thereupon each juror is
specially called and answers that the Verdict as read is
his Verdict. Thereupon, it is by the court ordered that the
Jury be and is hereby discharged from further consideration of
this case.

      Thereupon the United States Attorney moves the
court for judgment and sentence upon the Verdict of the Jury
returned herein; and thereupon the court inquired of said
defendant Carl Panzran, if he had anything to say why the
judgment of the court and sentence of the law should not be
pronounced against him at this time to which interrogatory of
the court the defendant Carl Panzran replied he had nothing
to say.

THIS CASE ORIGINATED AT

REPORT MADE AT:	DATE WHEN MADE:	PERIOD FOR WHICH MADE:	REPORT MADE BY:
KANSAS CITY, MO.	4-23-30	4-14-15-30	J. R. BURGER MJ

TITLE:

CARL PANZRAM, Prisoner, Reg. No. 31614

CHARACTER OF CASE:

MURDER OF CIVILIAN R. G. WARNKE AT FEDERAL PENITENTIARY, LEAVENWORTH, KAS., JUNE 20, 1929

K.C. 70-47

SYNOPSIS OF FACTS:

Subject convicted by jury at Topeka, Kansas, 4-16-30, and the death penalty was imposed following the verdict of the jury in Federal Court. Federal Judge Hopkins on the same date and place sentenced Subject to be hanged between six and nine o'clock on the morning of 9-5-30 at the U. S. Penitentiary, Leavenworth, Kansas, ninety days being allowed by the Court for filing a bill of exceptions. Case to be carried inactive until date of execution 9-5-30.

P.

REFERENCE: Report of Special Agent J. R. Burger, Kansas City, 1-22-30.

DETAILS: Subject was convicted of murdering R. G. Warnke, civilian, at the U. S. Penitentiary, Leavenworth, Kansas, on 6-11-29, by a Federal Jury at Topeka, Kansas, on 4-16-30 and the death penalty was imposed following the verdict of this jury by Federal Judge Richard J. Hopkins, who presided, and sentenced by said Court to be hanged between six and nine o'clock on the morning of 9-5-30 at the U. S. Penitentiary at Leavenworth, Kansas.

Counsel for defense, Barton Griffith, requested the Court to set a time for filing a bill of exceptions at which time Subject stated that he, Subject, refused to file any bill of exceptions. However, the Court stated that he had seen fit to provide an attorney to protect Subject and ninety days were allowed to file bill of exceptions by defense counsel which proceedings amount to a motion for a new trial for the case and provides for an appeal if one is

DO NOT WRITE IN THESE SPACES

APPROVED AND FORWARDED: C. D. White   Acting   SPECIAL AGENT IN CHARGE

COPIES OF THIS REPORT FURNISHED TO:

3-Bureau
1-U.S.Atty., Topeka, Kas.
1-U.S.Penitentiary,Leavenworth, Kas.
2-Kansas City

62-21811-14

BUREAU OF INVESTIGATION

DEPARTMENT OF JUSTICE

ROUTED TO: FILE

RECORDED AND INDEXED:
APR 26 1930
CHECKED OFF:
MAY 1. 1930
JACKETED:

desired. Therefore, case will be carried inactive until date set for execution of Subject, 9-5-30.

PENDING

FEDERAL JURY VOTES HANGING IN KANSAS

Execution of Convict Made Mandatory, Although the State Bars the Death Penalty.

TOPEKA, Kan., April 16 (AP).—A verdict which makes mandatory a sentence of death on the gallows for Carl Panzran, prisoner at Leavenworth Federal penitentiary, for the slaying of R. G. Warnke, civilian laundry foreman of the prison, was returned in Federal court today by a jury of Kansans whose State long ago abolished capital punishment.

Judge Richard J. Hopkins sentenced Panzran to be hanged Sept. 5, between 6 and 9 A. M., at the penitentiary.

The convict objected to any move for a new trial, but Judge Hopkins granted the defense ninety days in which to file.

The jury received the case late yesterday after a sanity commission appointed by the court reported its belief that the defendant was of unsound mind, but knew the difference between right and wrong.

THE GALLOWS

POST OFFICE BOX 7
31614,

Leavenworth, Kansas. April 17. 1930.

Mr. H.P. Less
No 1466 Chap.
Washingt.

POST OFFICE BOX 7
31614.

venworth, Kansas April 17 1930

I believe that the intentions of the people who tried me was to perpetrate a travesty of justice, not to give me a fair and impartial trial but to give me a legal trial. The actual results accomplished are that I was not only given what the people wanted to give me but what I also wanted. Then to give me, they gave me justice. This is the one and only case that I actualy know of where law and justice were synonomous. I believe that I got justice for the first and only time in my whole life of dealing with the law.

I believe that I know what justice is and justice is what I have been wanting and trying to get all of my life but what I have never got until now and I wont get that until the fifth of next Sept.

That is what I wanted to tell you first but there are a number of other things that I also want to tell you.

During my time in this prison I have received very fair treatment in every way. I have been treated far better than I have treated others and far better than I deserved to be and also better than I would mete out to others if I had the power which they have, if I was in their place and they were in my position.

I don't deserve very many of the good things of this world. I expect very little and I ask for very little. Among the things that I think I am entitled to and that I would like to have is enough reading matter to occupy my mind and my time for the balance of my life which is very short. At the present time all of the reading matter I have is only one magazine and that one is the Saturday Evening Post which you were good enough to have sent to me. This isn't enough for me. I want more. I realize that I cant have every thing I want but I want very little and that little ____ again. ____ taken away from me when I

I do not want to read
Now this is what I want
ou to choose from the
magazine and on paper
tho which I would
pages of it and the
paper I think is all
Health only news-
magazines I would
dum, Time
kly, Liberty
Review. I dont
read them all or not
to go to. I wish you
months for me.
that you will
nt you to accept
want you to do it
rather send
ow and not
bread which
am not permit
deputy,
__ which __
you nearly great

and it is my opinion that you deserve ____ a bit of good luck. That is all that I can tell you Now this will be the end of this letter and in 89 days from today will be the end of Me.

Copper John II.

Carl Panzram

April 17, 1930 - *Letter from Carl Panzram to Henry Lesser.*

I have known you for nearly 2 years. During that time we have been in correspondence with each other continuously with only a few brief interruptions. But now, circumstances are such that I believe the time has come for our correspondence to end.

Therefore, I am writing this letter which I now believe will be the last letter I shall ever write to you or anyone else. I shall endeavor to explain to you a number of things that I believe you would like to know, and these explanations are the last I intend to make to you or anyone else. Ten months ago I killed a man here in this prison, yesterday I was taken into court, given a legal trial, found guilty of the crime charged against me and then sentenced to death. This execution to take place here at this prison on Sept. 5th, 1930 between the hours of 5 A.M. and 9 A.M.

With my trial and the sentence of the court I am perfectly contented although I have believed all along and I still believe that it was the intention of the court and the majority of those connected with it to give me the full benefit of the law, but not a fair and impartial trial. They succeeded in giving me a legal trial and between these two there is some difference, but this difference is in my favor. I prefer to have things just as they are now. I believe that the intentions of the people who tried me was to perpetrate a travesty of justice, not to give me a fair and impartial trial but to give me a legal trial. The actual results accomplished are that I was not only given what the people wanted to give me, but what I also wanted them to give me. They gave me justice. This is the one and only case that I actually know of where law and justice were synonymous. I believe that I know what justice is and justice is what I have been wanting and trying to get all of my life but what I have never got until now, and I don't get that until the 5th of next September.

That is what I wanted to tell you first, but there are a number of other things that I also wanted to tell you. During my time in this prison I have received very fair treatment in every way. I have been treated far better than I have treated others and far better than I deserved to be and also better than I would mete out to others if I had the power which they have, if I was in their place and they were in my position. I don't deserve very many of the good things of this world. I expect very little and I ask for very little. Among the things that I think that I am entitled to and that I would like to have is enough reading matter to occupy my mind and my time for the balance of my life which is very short. At the present time all of the reading matter I have is only one magazine, and that one is the Saturday Evening Post which you were good enough to have sent to me. This isn't enough for me. I want more. I realize that I can't have everything I want but I want very little and that little I want to choose my own self. I do not want to read what others want me to read. Now this is what I want you to do if you will. I want you to choose from the following list a number of magazines and one paper. The daily Christian Science Monitor which I would enjoy reading, that is the first 4 pages of it and the editorial page. The balance of the paper I think is all rubbish and not worth reading. That's the only newspaper I care to read. About the magazines I would like to read are the Mercury, The Forum, Time, The Atlantic Monthly, Colliers Weekly, Liberty, The Pathfinder, and the Psychiatrists Review. I don't want all of these because I couldn't read them all and it would be too much expense for you to go to. I wish you would subscribe for a few of these for 3 months for me. That's all I want from you. I believe that you will receive this letter and if you do I want you to accede to this, my last request of you, and I want you to do it now and not wait until I am dead and then send me reading matter. I want to read now and not sometime next year.

I also wish to tell you that the silk thread which you sent me came here all right but I am not permitted to have it. Today I am going to ask the deputy warden here to return it to you. Also I am going to ask him to send to you the bead necklaces which I made and promised to send to you nearly a year ago, but which was taken away from me when I got into this jamb. If you get this letter you need not answer it, except by subscribing for some reading matter for me. That will be sufficient.

You are one of the very few men in this world that I know and who I do not wish to harm, and do not wish you any bad luck but I do wish you all the good luck that you are entitled to, and it is my opinion that you deserve quite a bit of good luck. That is all that I care to tell you now. This will be the end of this letter and in 89 days from today will be the end of me.

Copper John II
Carl Panzram.

May 23rd, 1930

Letters from Carl Panzram to Society for the Abolishment of Capitol Punishment. (Never mailed.)

National Headquarters
Washington D.C.

I, Carl Panzram, No. 31614 of the U.S. Penitentiary at Leavenworth, Kansas, am writing this statement of my own will without any advice or suggestions from anyone.

In the year 1928 at Washington, D.C., I was charged with and tried for the crimes of burglary and grand larceny. Although I was guilty of both of these crimes, I stood trial and pleaded not guilty, but the jury found me guilty on both charges and the judge at once sentenced me to the term of 25 years.

On February 1st, 1929 I began serving this sentence at the U.S. Penitentiary at Leavenworth, Kansas.

On June 25, 1929, I murdered one man, a civilian employee of the prison, by the name of Warneke and at the same time and place I also attempted to murder a dozen other men, both guards and convicts. The only reason I did not kill them also was because I couldn't catch them.

For this crime I was indicted by a U.S. Grand Jury and on April 15th and 16th I was tried in the U.S. Court at Topeka Kansas. This court was called and sat under the jurisdiction of Judge Hopkins.

At this trial I pleaded not guilty and was at once put on trial for the crime of murder in the first degree. So far as I know, I was given a legal trial and was not deprived of any of my constitutional rights. The jury found me guilty as charged in the indictment. The judge thereupon pronounced sentence on me and the sentence was that I should be hanged by the neck until I am dead. This sentence to take effect between the hours of 6 A.M. and 9 A.M. at the Penitentiary at Leavenworth, Kansas on the date of September 5, 1930.

The findings of the Court and the sentence of the judge meet my approval and I am perfectly satisfied to have the sentence carried out without any further interference from anyone. I do not wish to have another trial and I do not wish to have that sentence changed in any way.

If I am given another trial or if the death sentence should be commuted to life imprisonment either in a penitentiary or an insane asylum, it will be against my will.

Now then I come to the reason why I have written this letter.

I have been informed that your organization, or at any rate some of the members of it, have made or are making an attempt to change my sentence to life imprisonment in solitary confinement in a prison or in an insane asylum.

This you are doing without my consent and absolutely against my will.

I shall never willingly grant you my permission to have this done for me.

For your information and guidance, I am going to inform you of some facts which I believe you are unaware of at this time.

May 24, 1930

I believe that your reasons for trying to set aside the sentence of death in my case are that you think that this penalty is not a humane form of justice. You are sincere in your beliefs that this is a barbaric and inhuman form of punishment.

Another one of your reasons is that you are laboring under the delusion that I am insane and therefore not responsible for my acts.

Now, I am going to attempt to show you that this sentence of death is absolutely just and also that it will be carried out in a very humane manner and I will also try to convince you that I am in full possession of my faculties and that I am now and always have been perfectly sane and I am therefore fully responsible for everything I have ever done.

First, I shall try to convince you that I am quite sane at this time. I believe that any person who is sober and sane and who is not blind and who is able to read and understand the English language as I am here writing, he or she should be convinced without any further argument that I am perfectly sane in every way and therefore responsi-

216

POST OFFICE BOX 7
31614.

Abolishment
Society for the ~~Promotion of~~
Capital Punishment.
National Headquarters
Washington
D. C.

Leavenworth, Kansas May 23 1930

I, Carl Panzram No. 31614. of the U. S.
Penitentiary at Leavenworth, Kansas, am writing
this statement of my own free will without any advice
or suggestions from any one.

On the year 1920 at Washington D.C. I was
charged with ...
and Grand ...
these crimes ...
The jury found ...
at once sen...

On Feb...
at the U. S. P...

On June...
employ of ...
the same ...
a dozen othe...
reason I did ...
catch them...

To the ...
jury and on...
at Topeka ...
The jurisdi...

At this ...
once put on...
degree.

POST OFFICE BOX 7
31614

Page 4.

Abolishment
Society for the ~~Promotion of~~
Capital Punishment.
Washington
D. C.

Leavenworth, Kansas May 24 1930

I believe that your reasons for trying first
and the sentence of death in my case are that you
think that this penalty is not a humane form
of justice. You are sincere in your belief that this
is a barbarous and inhuman form of punishment.

Another one of your reasons is that you are
laboring under the delusion that I am insane and
therefore not responsible for my acts.

Now I am going to attempt to show you that
this sentence of death is absolutely just and also
that it will be carried out in a very humane
manner, and I shall also try to convince you that I
am in full possession of all of my faculties and that
I am now and always have been perfectly sane and that
I am therefore fully responsible for everything I have
ever done.

First I shall try to convince you that I am quite sane
at this time. I believe that any person who is others and can
and who is not blind and who is able to read and understand the English language as I am here writing the
argument that I am perfectly sane in every way
and therefore responsible for my acts.

I am at this time 38 years old. A big powerful
man strong in both body and mind. My physical
fitness is not as good as it once was but my mental
faculties are unimpaired in any way.

ble for my acts.

I am at this time 38 years old, a big, powerful man, strong in both body and mind. My physical fitness is not good, as it once was, but my mental faculties are unimpaired in any way. I have never used drugs of any kind at any time. I am and always have been a very moderate drinker of liquor. Practically a total abstainer. I have never had any disease of any kind which would have a tendency to weaken my intellect. I have never been addicted to any habits of sexual excesses of any kind over which I didn't have complete control over myself.

So far as I know, none of my relatives or ancestors have ever been in any kind of an institution for mental defectives.

I, for my own part, have been examined on numerous occasions for various duly qualified, capable, and impartial doctors as to my sanity, and so far as I know, I have never been pronounced to be insane or incapable or irresponsible for my acts.

I have never spent one single day of my life in any institution for the insane.

But I have spent 22 years of my lifetime in various penal institutions.

I started doing time when I was 11 years old and have been doing practically nothing else since then. What time I haven't been in jail I have spent either getting out or getting in again.

During this time I have been into every kind of a penal institution there is in this country and some in other countries.

Therefore I consider myself pretty well qualified to know what the conditions of prisoners, prisons, police, courts, prison guards, prison officials and the existing conditions of penal institutions are today, here and now. Knowing the real facts as I do from practical experience, and also knowing that there is only one chance in a thousand of my ever getting my freedom and also knowing that I, like all other men, must some day die, I have deliberately and intentionally made my choice.

I choose to die here and now by being hanged by the neck until I am dead.

I prefer that I die that way, and if I have a soul and if that soul should burn in hell for a million years, still I prefer that to a lingering, agonizing death in some prison dungeon or a padded cell in a mad house.

Now, I want to know, if this isn't good logic and reason, then what the hell is it?

Now then, I shall give you my second reason why this sentence should be carried out. I do not believe that being hanged by the neck until dead is a barbaric or inhuman punishment. I look forward to that as a real pleasure and a big relief to me. I do not feel bad or unhappy about it in any way. Every day since I received that sentence I have felt pretty good. I feel good right now and I believe that when my last hour comes that I will dance out of my dungeon and on to the scaffold with a smile on my face and happiness in my heart.

Another reason why I believe that this sentence should be carried out is because I believe it is justice and I am quite sincere when I say that this is the first and only time in all my life of battling with the law that I ever did get justice from the law.

Now, you who do not know me or my wishes, you decide without consulting me in any way; you start to try to revoke the judgement of a legally constituted court and the sentence that was pronounced on me.

One other thing I am going to tell you before I stop this letter and that is this;. the only thanks you or your kind will ever get from me for your efforts in my behalf is that I wish you all had one neck and that I had my hands on it, I would sure put you out of your misery, just the same as I have done with numbers of other people.

I have no desire whatever to reform myself. My only desire is to reform people who try to reform me. And I believe that the only way to reform people is to kill 'em.

My motto is: "Rob 'em all, rape 'em all and kill 'em all."

I am very truly yours
Signed
Copper John II
Carl Panzram
No. 31614, Box 7
Leavenworth,
Kansas

Another reason why I believe that this sentence
should be carried out is because I believe it is justice
and I am quite sincere when I say that this is the
first and only time in all my life of battling with
the law that I ever did get justice from the law.

Now, you who do not know me or my wishes, you
decide, without consulting me in any way, you start out
to try to revoke the judgement of a legaly constituted
court and the sentence that was pronounced on me.

One other thing I am going to tell you before I stop
this letter, and that is this, The only thanks you
or your kind will ever get from me for your efforts
in my behalf is that I wish you all had one
neck and that I had my hands on it, I would
sure put you out of your misery just the same as I
have done with a number of other people.

I have no desire whatever to reform myself. My
only desire is to reform people who try to reform me.
And I believe that the only way to reform people is
to kill em.

My motto is, Rob em all, Rape em all and
Kill em all.

    I am very truly yours

      Signed

    Copper John II.

Carl Panzram.

No 31614. Box 7.

Leavenworth.

Kansas.

May 30, 1930

Letter from Carl Panzram to President Herbert Hoover. (Never mailed.)

c/o Attorney General Mitchell,
Washington, D.C.

I am writing this letter to notify you that I have been tried in the U.S. Court for the crime of murder in the first degree; I was found guilty and sentenced to be hanged by the neck until I am dead.

I hereby notify you that I am perfectly satisfied with my trial and the sentence. I do not want another trial. Neither do I want to have that sentence changed in any way.

The only way this sentence can be changed is by the direct action of the President of the United States. I believe that I am within my constitutional rights when I refuse to accept a pardon or a commutation from the death penalty to a sentence of life imprisonment, either in a prison or an insane asylum.

I absolutely refuse to accept either a pardon or a commutation should either one or the other be offered to me.

      Signed
Carl Panzram

POST OFFICE BOX.
31614.

Leavenworth, Kansas ...May 20...... 193_

President Herbert Hoover.
Attorney General Mitchell.
        Washington.
            D.C.

    I am writing this letter, to notify you that
I have been tried in the U.S. Court for the crime
of Murder in the first degree; I was found guilty
and sentenced to be hanged by the neck until
I am dead.

    I hereby notify you that I am perfectly
satisfied with my trial and the sentence.

    I do not want another trial.

    Neither do I want to have that sentence changed
in any way.

    The only way the sentence can be changed is
by the direct action of the President of the U.S.

    I believe that I am within my constitutional
rights when I refuse to accept a pardon or a
commutation from the death penalty to a sentence
of life imprisonment, either in a prison or an
into an asylum.

    I absolutely refuse to accept either a pardon or a
commutation should either one or the other be offered
to me.

                    Signed

                Carl Panzram.
                No. 31614, Box 7.
                Leavenworth,
                Kansas.

221

June 5th, 1930

Letter from Carl Panzram to Henry Lesser.

Enclosed in this letter I am sending you a number of different letters and articles that I have written since my trial April 15th and 16th. You can do as you please with them all. Within the legal papers, journal entries and the certified copy of my indictment, you will find the names and addresses of all of nearly all of the men who had anything to do with my trial. Among them you will find the names of the doctors who were appointed and sat as a commission to inquire as to my sanity and who pronounced me to be insane, or of unsound mind, as you will see. According to the Clerk of the U.S. Courts, Certified copy of the journal entries. I believe this verdict was unfair and I also believe that if you would send each or all of them a copy of the book of my life story, which I wrote and gave to you, they would be quite convinced that their verdict of insanity against me was and is unsound and not my mind that is unsound.

By the time you or they get this letter I'll be very very dead, so it won't make any difference to me, but it may to someone else sometime.

(Signed)

Carl Panzram, 31614

P.S. The other two letters, one to the president of the U.S. and the other to the Society for the Abolishment of Capitol Punishment, I wrote but did not mail, because after I wrote 'em I found that it was unnecessary to mail them to those I wrote them to, so I am sending 'em along to you to do with as you like. Probably heave 'em into your waste basket, but anyway, they will help you to make up your mind as to my state of mind and my reasons therefore.

C.P.

June 5th, 1930

Letter from Carl Panzram to Henry Lesser.

I am writing this letter today, June 5th, but I don't except to have it mailed to you until September 6, 1939, because on that day I will be dead and buried.

There are a good many things I would like to say or write to you, but because I don't know whether or not you'll ever get this letter, I cut it kind of short.

First, I want to tell you that up to now, I have been getting the reading matter which you were good enough to subscribe to for me, these including
The Saturday Evening Post
The Christian Science Monitor
The Forum
Time
The Pathfinder
And also the American Mercury, just now received.

I also want to tell you that I have enjoyed reading them all. There is nothing I can do for you to repay you for the many favors you have done for me, excepting to thank you and wish you good luck. I would like to be able to truthfully tell you that I do thank you, but this I cannot do, simply because there is no such thing as gratitude left in me.
There was at one time, but that time is long gone. Gratitude is one of the many things that have been kicked out of me. I can and do truthfully wish you good luck, all that you deserve and I am of the opinion that you are one of the very few men I have ever known that really deserve good luck in this world. You deserve what I have missed in life- happiness, peace and contentment.
As for me, I'll soon be at peace. I have never had the good fortune to find it in life, so I expect to find it in death. I hope so and believe so.
To some people my death will seem to come in a horrible form, but to me it seems a very easy way to die. I look forward to it as a pleasure and relief.
It is a far easier death than I have dealt out to some of the people I have killed. I couldn't and don't ask for any easier way to die.
This will probably be the last I'll ever write to anyone, because in just 90 days more I'll be hanged by the neck until I am dead. But I feel fine and am feeling better every day as the time grows shorter.

I intend to leave this world as I have lived in it. I expect to be a rebel right up to my last moment on earth. With my last breath I intend to curse the world and all mankind. I intend to spit in the warden's eyes or whoever places the rope around my neck when I am standing on the scaffold. I always did want to spit in a copper's eye and also a preacher or priest. That will be all the thanks they'll get from me. I don't know which I despise and detest the most, a copper or a buck. I guess the soul-saver takes the palm. I have met only one priest that I felt I could respect, but I have known quite a number of coppers I could, did, and still do respect. You are one of them. I never have liked any of them, but I did respect 'em, when they have deserved it – and some do – not many, but some anyway.

June 20, 1930

Letter from Carl Panzram to Henry Lesser.

       The other half of this letter I wrote 20 days ago. Since then conditions here have been changed a bit. Not very much, but just enough for me to commit suicide tonight instead of waiting until September 5th to be legally hung.
So if I succeed in my effort at suicide tonight, then this will sure be the last I'll ever say or write on this earth.
The choice is mine and I fully realize just what I am doing.
I would like to have it known just why I do this. I had no choice about coming into this world and nearly all of my 38 years in it have had very little to say and do about how I should live my life. People have driven me into doing everything I have ever done. Now the time has come when I refuse to be driven any farther.
Tonight I die and tomorrow I go to a grave farther than that no man can drive me I am sure glad to leave this lousy world and the lousier people in this world; but of all the lousy people in this world I believe that I am the lousiest of 'em all.

Today I am dirty, but tomorrow I'll be just

Dirt.

Mr. H. P. Lesser,   Page (2)

No 1466 Chapin St. N.W.

Washington

D.C.

The other half of this letter I wrote 2 days ago. Since then conditions here have changed a bit.

Not very much but just enough for me to still suicide tonight instead of waiting until Sept 6 to be legally executed.

So if I succeed in my effort at suicide tonight then this will sure be the last letter I'll ever say or write on this earth.

The choice is mine and I fully realize just what I am doing.

I would like to have it known just why not all I had no choice about coming into this world, and nearly all of my 38 years is it I have had very little to say or do about how I should live my life people have driven me into doing every thing I have ever done. Now that I'm old, this is when I refuse to be driven any farther.

Tonight I die and tomorrow I go to a grave, farther than that no man can drive me.

I am sure glad to leave this lousy world and the lousier people that live in it.

But of all the lousy people in this world, I believe that I am the lousiest of 'em all.

Today I am dirty but tomorrow I'll be just

Dirt.

Captain Night Watch

June 20th 1930.   193

MEMORANDUM FOR:

The Deputy Warden,

Sir;

At 11:50 this dateGuard S.Q.
Alexander called me to the Isolation
I hastened to answer his call and on
arriving I found Panzran # 31614. Had
tried to sever the arteries in both
legs near the ankels. And was dancing
around the room and was bleeding very
bad, I also found he had plugged the
key hole in the door and we could not
open   it. I called Dr Smith and
proceeded to cut the lock off the door.
After some persuading he passed the
peice of brass button out to me that he
cut his self with. By the time the Dr
arrived with his instruments we had the
door open and was ready for him to
administer first aid.
You will find enclosed the peice of
the brass button he cut his self with.

Respectfully.

J.C. Brummett

June 21st, 1930.

Mr. T. B. White, Warden,
U. S. Penitentiary,
Leavenworth, Kan.

31614

Dear Sir:-

Dr. Conklin and the writer were
called to the Institution last night shortly
after midnight, to Isolation to see Panzram,
Register Number 31614, and found he had cut the
large veins on both lower legs above the ankles.
He was bleeding quite freely and lost aboutna
quart of blood, or more.   He was still bleeding
some when we arrived.

The incisions were cleaned out
well with iodine. The bleeders were tied off
and the incisions closed with sutures requiring
four stitches to each cut. Sterile dressings
were applied.

He also has a small cut on the
left arm, which was painted with iodine, but did
not require dressing.

He was left in Isolation and seemed
to be in good condition. His pulse was only 86,
and seemed fairly strong. He was conscious and
co-operative.

He was seen by Dr. Conklin this-
morning, and reported to be in relatively good
condition.

Respectfully,

T. H. Smith,
Asst. Physician.

THS:I:Z.

IN THE DISTRICT COURT OF THE UNITED STATES FOR THE DISTRICT OF KANSAS, FIRST DIVISION.

The United States

    vs.   No. 5465.

Carl Panzran

       Now on this 16th day of July, 1930, it appearing from the record that no Bill of Exceptions has been filed herein within the time heretofore allowed and no application having been presented to the court for an extension of time in which to file said Bill of Exceptions and that no Petition for Appeal has been filed herein, and the time allowed by Statute for filing Petition for Appeal having expired, it is by the court ordered that the United States Marshal for this District, cause the judgment and sentence of this court entered herein on the 16th day of April, 1930, to be carried into effect.

       The clerk of this court is hereby directed to deliver to said Marshal, a certified copy of the judgment and sentence herein, and of this order, and the said Marshal is directed to return the same, with a full and true account of the execution of the same.

                    RICHARD J. HOPKINS, JUDGE.

Thereupon, it is now here by the court considered, ordered and adjudged that the said Carl Panzran be remanded to the custody of the Warden of the United States Penitentiary at Leavenworth, Kansas, and by said Warden kept in solitary confinement in said Penitentiary until Friday, September 5th, 1930, and that on that date between the hours of 6 a.m. and 9 a.m. the said Carl Panzran be by the United States Marshal for the District of Kansas, taken to some suitable place within the walls of said United States Penitentiary and be then and there hanged by the neck until he is dead.

Thereupon said defendant Carl Panzran, through his attorney moves the court for time within which to prepare and present herein his Bill of Exceptions, and it is thereupon by the court ordered that said defendant be and he is hereby granted ninety days from this date within which to prepare and present his Bill of Exceptions herein."

c/o Atlanta Pententiary,
Atlanta, Georgia,
August 4th, 1930.

Mr. Carl Panzram, #31614,
P. Ol Box #7,
Leavenworth, Kan.

Dear Carl:-

I want to thank you very sincerely for the letters
which you asked Austin McCormick, Assistant Director of
Bureau of Prisons to hand over to me. He informed me of your
attempt at suicide. I believe that you are under the impression that Mr. McCormick did not receive the material which you
sent him some time back dealing with your views on crime, and
criminals. I know for a fact that he received it, and I am
sure that he must have acknowledged it, although you may not
have received the acknowledgement.

You asked me to submit a copy of your autobiography
to the psychiatrists who declared you to be of unsound mind
although aware of the difference between right and wrong,
which made you legally responsible for your act.

I have already sent Dr. Carl Menninger, whom you
already have met, a copy of your story. You say that you
would like to write me about certain things. If you still
care to, I will be more than glad to hear from you. I see no reason
why your letters will not reach me, even though you send them
directly to me. It seems that your life story will be published shortly just as it was written, so that society will
know your side of it. I am telling you this because you always seemed to be anxious to have your version of things
explained by yourself.

If, as you have written me on numerous occasions, you
are desirous that I receive the financial rewards, if any, as
a result of the publication of the work, I would like to have
you state so again in your next letter. I want you to know
that I will make whatever disposition of the money you care me
to make. Your letter to the Society for the Abolishment of
Capital Punishment was as you thought - very logical. I do
not see how they could take any other view of it. I will now
close this letter with the expectation of hearing from you
shortly. If there is anything that I can do, please do not
hesitate to notify me. I want to thank you very much for your
kind expressions of good will and confidence in my desires in
the past to do all that I possibly could for you. With kindest
personal regards, I remain,
                              Affectionately,

Please note the change of address Henry P. Leaser. (over) *OVER SIDE*

The following is the only letter from Henry Lesser to Carl Panzram which survived. Panzram sent back the letter to Lesser with Panzram's writing on the back of the letter including instructions on publishing and selling his autobiography.

Henry P. Lesser, Guard
c/o Atlanta Penitentiary,
Atlanta, Georgia,
August 4th, 1930

Mr. Carl Panzram, #31614,
P.O. Box #7
Leavenworth, Kan.

Dear Carl:-

I want to thank you very sincerely for the letters which you asked Austin McCormick, Assistant Director of Bureau of Prisons to hand over to me. He informed me of your attempt at suicide. I believe that you are under the impression that Mr. McCormick did not receive the material which you sent him some time back dealing with your views on crime and criminals. I know for a fact that he received it, and I am sure that he must have acknowledged it, although you may not have received the acknowledgement.

You asked me to submit a copy of your autobiography to the psychiatrists who declared you to be of unsound mind although aware of the difference between right and wrong, which made you legally responsible for your act.

I have already sent Dr. Carl Menninger, whom you already have met, a copy of your story. You say that you would like to write me about certain things. If you still care to, I will be more than glad to hear from you. I see no reason why your letters will not reach me, even though you send them directly to me. It seems that your life story will be published shortly just as it was written, so that society will know your side of it. I am telling you this because you always seemed to be anxious to have your version of things explained yourself.

If, as you have written me on numerous occasions, you are desirous that I receive the financial rewards, if any, as a result of the publication of the work, I would like to have you state so again in your next letter. I want you to know that I will make whatever disposition of the money you care me to make. Your letter to the Society for the Abolishment of Capitol Punishment was as you thought – very logical. I do not see how they could take any other view of it. I will now close this letter with the expectation of hearing from you shortly. If there is anything that I can do, please do not hesitate to notify me. I want to thank you very much for your kind expressions of good will and confidence in my desires in the past to do all that I can possibly could for you. With Kindest personal regards, I remain,

Affectionately, Henry P. Lesser

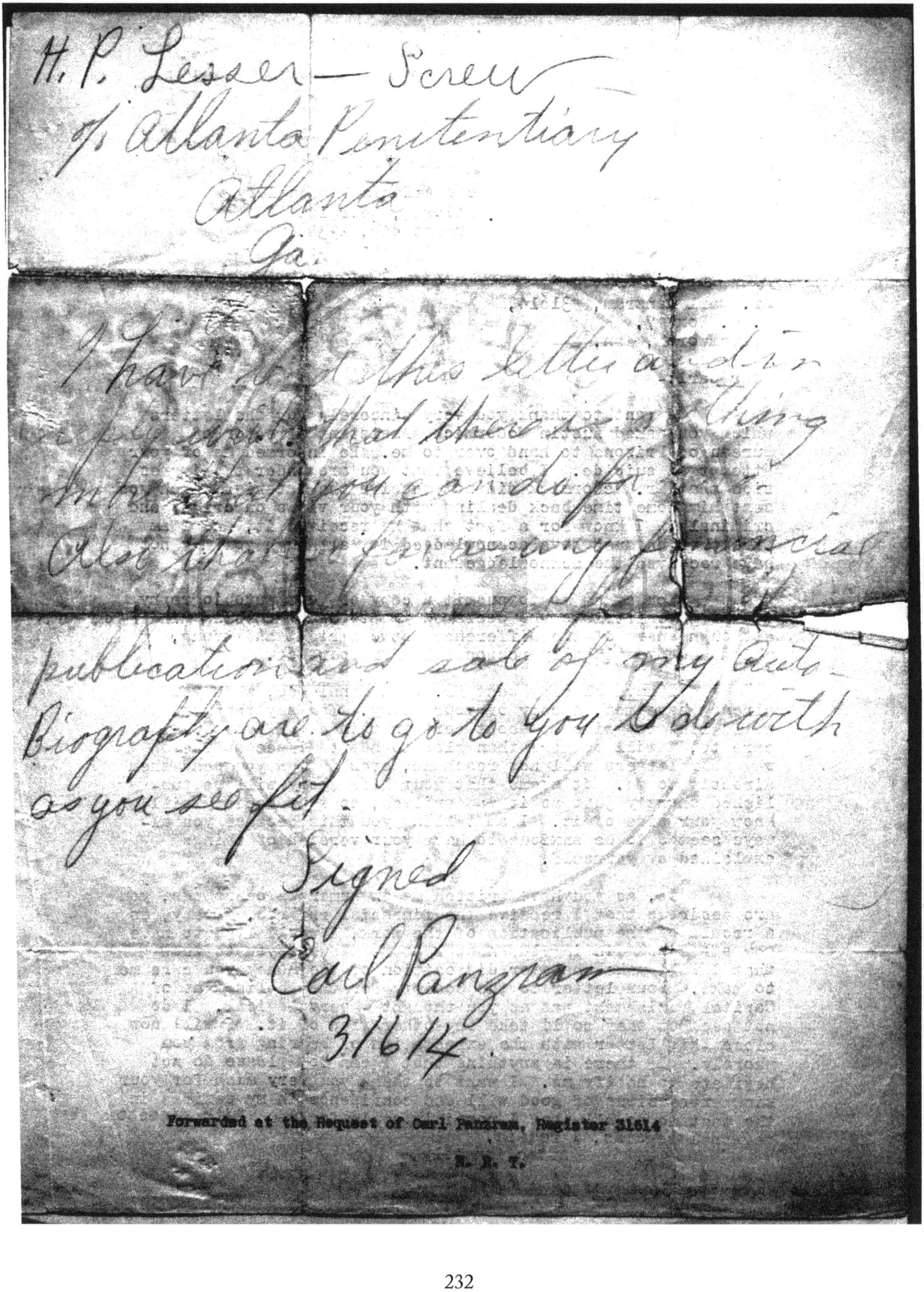

H. P. Lesser — Screw
of Atlanta Penitentiary
Atlanta
Ga.

I have read this letter and I r[illegible]
& fully accept that there is nothing
further that you can do for
Also that any financial
[illegible]
publication and sale of my Auto-
Biografy are to go to you to do with
as you see fit
Signed
Carl Panzram
31614

Forwarded at the Request of Carl Panzram, Register 31614

H. B. T.

This was written on the back side of Lesser's Aug. 4, 1930 letter to Panzram:

H.P. Lesser-Screw
c/o Atlanta Penitentiary
Atlanta
Ga.

I have read this letter and in reply write that there is nothing more that you can do for me. Also that as far as any financial (illegible words) from the publication and sale of my Autobiography are to go to you to do with as you see fit.

Signed
Carl Panzram
31614

August 22, 1930.

Mr. Clifton P. Fadiman,
Simon and Schuster, Inc.,
386 Fourth Avenue,
New York City.

Dear Sir:

Your letter of August 14th, with regard to the Panzram document was referred to me in the absence of Mr. Bates, who is attending the International Prison Congress at Prague. It will be referred to him on his return. In the meantime, I suggest that you send the document to me and I will see that it gets into his hands.

While my opinion is not requested, it so happens that I have been somewhat more close to the Panzram case than anybody else in this Bureau and that I have in my possession considerable material which he has written since the death penalty was given. I have talked to him and have discussed his case thoroughly with guards who have had him in charge and with psychiatrists who have either examined him or who have read his writings.

In my opinion, you would not serve any useful purpose by printing the manuscript which Panzram wrote while a prisoner in the District Jail. We feel certain that a great deal of it is fact and a great deal of it is fiction. What you describe as glacial ferocity is with Panzram partly real and partly posed. If his writings are published at all it should be done only as a part of a case history scientifically treated, interpreted by a competent psychiatrist, and furthermore, by a psychiatrist who knows Panzram. If you publish the book it should not be published as anything but a sensational record of real and imagined depravity with a frank surrender to public desire for the sordid and the sensational.

Very truly yours,

233854

A. H. MacCormick,
Assistant Director Bureau of Prisons.

A. H. McC-eb

234

386 *Fourth Avenue* NEW YORK

August 26, 1930

Mr. A. H. MacCormick
Asst. Director Bureau of Prisons
Department of Justice
Washington, D. C.

Dear Mr. MacCormick:

Re: CARL PANZRAM

I am very much obliged indeed for your helpful and discerning letter. It is not our intention to present the manuscript (which we are not yet sure we shall publish) as a true document. Undoubtedly a great deal of it is fiction and we shall not blink this fact. We believe, however, that the fictional portions are just as revelatory of the man as those which are factually true.

We are hoping to get hold of a psychiatrist who knows Panzram but so far have been unsuccessful. In the meantime we are securing the opinions of criminologists, penalogists, alienists, psychologists, etc.

As soon as carbons of the manuscript are available I shall send you one and shall hope to receive your considered opinion of it in due course of time.

Sincerely yours,

CLIFTON P. FADIMAN
SIMON AND SCHUSTER, INC.

CPF/CFW

Div. of Mails and Files

AUG 27 1930

235

Govt. Paid Postal Telegram.

Washington, D. C.

September 4th, 1930.

Warden,
United States Penitentiary.,
Leavenworth, Kansas.

President has denied application for clemency in behalf

of Carl Panzram.

Finch Pardon Attorney.

Copy to
Record Office.
Deputy Warden.

EXECUTION DAY

The dorm room at Leavenworth Penitentiary, where the Charles S. Wharton and other convicts witnessed the hanging of Panzram.

THE HANGING OF PANZARAN

SEPTEMBER 3. Very early this morning a truck drove up to the gate laden with lumber. It did not have to wait, it was expected; officialdom admitted it at once. Warden, deputies, chaplain and guards scurried to and fro, bent on mysterious errands. There were whispered consultations, telephone calls, anxious frowns and suppressed excitement.

But we knew! Before the truck came inside the gate the prison grapevine had telegraphed the message, "Here comes the gallows for Panzaran." Guards rushed the beams to the little walled courtyard behind Solitary, the same court-yard where Panzaran has had his brief hour of pacing to and fro these past months.

We knew! We saw the carpenters come from the outside to fit those beams together.

It is evening as I write, and by now the gallows has been completed. Gaunt, ugly, it rises fifty feet from where I sit; I can see it through a window—platform, stairs and crossbeams—hideous in the shroud of gloom.

September 4. Authority had an unhappy time today. It painted the windows of our parole room with Bon Ami so that we would not see the spectacle. Authority was nervous; more nervous than Panzaran who, I heard, sat reading in his cell, indifferent to the sound of hammer and saw.

But authority need not have worried. Its power was greater than it knew, for it is strong enough to kill everything in the breasts of men save selfishness and cruelty.

The convicts have been listless towards what is happening. Few among them would not gladly pull the drop to send Panzaran to his grave if by so doing they could get better food for thirty days or add three days good time to shorten their own terms of imprisonment. So far as I can judge, Panzaran's fate inspires far less pity than filthy jests in cell houses and parole rooms.

September 5. Today at six o'clock it happened. Yesterday, guards and officials gathered around the door of Solitary ward where Panzaran was chained in his cell. They were a worried lot, I was told, with solemn, apprehensive faces. Infinite precautions were taken to prevent any convict from witnessing the killer's end. In Parole One last night, the cots were taken from the side of the sleeping rooms which overlooks the courtyard and placed in a row down the inside corridor so that twenty men slept side by side after the doors were locked.

But they forgot one window. It did not look directly down on the yard, yet it permitted a slanting view. Through it we could see the gallows and the commencement of the ghastly death march.

When he came out of the back door we saw him, two hundred pounds of flesh possessed of but one virtue: brute courage. He was less to be pitied than the ashen-faced officials shrinking from the task they had in hand, terrified lest some convicts might set up howls of protest.

The man himself did not shrink. I was told that last night he ate every morsel of the sacrificial banquet pre-pared for a doomed man. After all, why shouldn't he?

He would be hurled into eternity hating, as hating he had lived. His hands were red with the blood of a score of victims; he never had shown mercy, never asked it.

There was no faltering to his step as he marched out of the door into the open courtyard. Then suddenly he bellowed 'BOO!' and whipped around to enjoy the fear he inspired, a frightful grin spreading over his face as everyone started

The courtyard behind solitary where the gallows was built for Panzram's execution.

in alarm at the sound. Apparently this was not enough to satisfy the brute in him, for as he passed out of our sight, I saw him wheel about again and spit full in the face of the Guards Captain.

So ended Panzaran. Thus was the murder of Warnicke expiated.

To my surprise, however, little was said after Panzaran became a broken-necked corpse, for as soon as he passed from the prison scene, none of the men took any further interest in his crime, his punishment or the revolting tales that were told of his moral habits.

Within an hour after he had been hanged that morning, I found my fellow inmates muttering ominously about the food they were likely to eat at early mess and about the vile meals which had been served us without a break throughout the preceding week. The tragedy of Panzaran had become as remote as the Punic wars.

When I marched out of the mess hall that night I expected the men about me to speak of nothing but the execution; instead, the one beside me grumbled fiercely:

"Veal cutlets! Where do they get their goddamn nerve! I call it pig slush!"

EXCERPT FROM:

TOM WHITE
The Life of a Lawman

By

Verdon Adams

Texas Western Press
The University of Texas at El Paso
1972

And then there was Carl Panzran. This man, whom Tom describes as the most thoroughly vicious human being he has ever known, had the dubious distinction of being the first person to be executed in a United States Federal prison.

As one listens to Tom White reminisce about the criminals he has known and worked with through more than fifty years of law enforcement work, he is ever more convinced that they are not greatly different from the rest of mankind. They seem to be about the same mixture of 'good' and 'bad' as other folk. There may be a bit more of the bad in them, as the term is usually defined — or maybe they just haven't been quite as lucky as some of us. Hopefully, most of those who are locked up deserve to be, according to our laws, but it would be a rash man who would say that there are not many on the outside who do not deserve it as much or more. Certainly there are no distinctive characteristics peculiar to the criminal's physical make-up. They come in all sizes, shapes, and colors. Indeed, the ability to maintain the appearance and demeanor of an honest, law-abiding citizen is the first requisite for success in many fields of crime.

But Panzran was different. Tom remembers very well the day he was brought to the Big L. Seeing him through his open door as the new arrival was being processed, he felt that he was looking at the archtype of what people refer to when they speak of a 'typical' killer, even though there is no such thing. Here was a man who personified, in appearance and manner, the qualities of viciousness and ruthlessness. Tom inquired about him and learned that the new prisoner was thought to have killed a number of persons, and had finally been convicted of premeditated murder. Among his victims was a woman whom he had not only beaten to death but had then pounded into an unrecognizable pulp. Later, while serving his sentence at Leavenworth, he killed a prison employee. For reasons know only to himself (if, indeed, even he knew them) he picked up a piece of iron pipe and smashed the skull of the laundry foreman while the latter was bending over a tub inspecting the work. For this killing he was sentenced to hang.

The law required that Panzran be executed by the Federal Government, because the murder for which he was condemned was committed in a Federal prison. A scaffold was built on the grounds of the penitentiary and the U.S. Marshal made arrangements with a firm in Kansas City to perform the execution. As a sidelight to this affair, Tom received instructions to cut off the end of the rope, including the noose, after it had served its purpose, and send it to Washington. He did so and, on a subsequent trip to the Capital, saw this memento on display in his Headquarters building as a grim reminder of the event.

The official history of Leavenworth Penitentiary gives the following account of Panzran's last murder and of his own execution:

It was shortly after this (the August 1st riot already related) that one of the weirdest criminal histories of all time saw its ending on the scaffold behind the laundry building. This was the case of Carl Panzran.

The thirties were a period in which criminals and criminal activity probably got more attention than at any other time during the history of the country. Leavenworth got its share of — unwanted — publicity.

On the night of June 19, 1929, the last of the spring breezes flowed softly through the open windows of 'D' cellhouse and wafted gently over the sleeping form in cell 130. In the half-dark of the prison night, the prisoner turned in his sleep, muttered, and turned again. The breeze flowed on and into another open window. It flowed as softly and caressingly over the form of another man sleeping in the city of Leavenworth, but he slept soundly and did not toss and turn. He wasn't planning murder.

At six in the morning of June 20, both these men rose and prepared for the day. The prisoner, Number 31614, doing time under his legal name of Carl Panzran for a change, stepped out of his cell and joined the blue line that marched silently into the dining hall for breakfast. After eating he returned to put the final straightening touches on his cell and waited tensely for the work bell to ring.

In the city, R. G. Warnke, Laundry Foreman at the United States Penitentiary, also sat down and ate breakfast. He ate leisurely and then got into his car for the short drive to the prison. Arriving at the front gate, he picked up his keys and proceeded to his place of work. It was about 7:30 when he entered the main room of the laundry and took up his daily tasks.

Panzran also arrived for work at 7:30, but he was more interested in finding the three-foot bar which he had seen in the shop a short time before. Having located it and put it within reach, he bided his time and watched for his moment. No one knows what went on in his mind during the next twenty minutes, but possibly he was thinking of the many terms he had served in prison, and brooding on the treatment he had received. Possibly he was thinking of the time only two short months before when he had tried to bleach three of his handkerchiefs in the bleaching tub. Foreman Warnke had caught him and told him he was not to use the bleach for his personal things. Panzran had been incensed and had asked for a job change, which was denied. Whatever he was thinking, he saw his chance at 7:49.

Foreman Warnke had made a round of the laundry and had stopped to checks some clothes in the rinser. He leaned over to pull some of them out, and Panzran gripped his iron bar and stepped toward him. Raising the bar high over his head, Panzran gauged the position of Warnke's head, then brought it down with all his might. Struck unconscious, Warnke fell across the bundle of clothes he had been inspecting, and Panzran struck him again.

A short distance away a prisoner named Kelly grabbed another prisoner and said, "Jesus Christ, look there." Panzran heard him and headed toward the two men, swinging his iron club. The prisoners fled before him and the killer returned to the fallen foreman. "Here's another one," he cried, bringing the bar down for the third time.

Certain that the man was dead, Panzran then ran toward the Deputy Warden's office, with the intention of killing him also. Prisoners and guards alike fled before him as he rushed in and out of the building which housed the Deputy's office. One guard tried to lure him into the open where the tower guard could get a shot at him, but the wily Panzran ducked behind some boxcars and headed toward the laundry.

By this time the guard force was alerted and had started to herd the men back into their cells so it would be safe to bring guns inside the walls. Panzran realized that he had only moments and after a last futile attempt to catch a prisoner, walked up to Guard Holtgrave and threw down the murder weapon. "I guess that's all I can get," he told the guard, "You can do whatever you want with me." Holtgrave immediately took him to the segregation building, where Guard Edmonds placed him inside a cell and locked him safely in.

At his trial for the murder, Panzran was defiant and boasted of having killed twenty-two people in his life. When asked if he had anything to say before sentencing was passed, he told the judge, "I wish all mankind had one neck so I could choke it."

He was sentenced to hang at the United States Penitentiary, thus having the wry distinction of being the first man hanged at the prison and the first legally hung (sic) in the State of Kansas since 1888.

On the morning of September 5, 1930, dressed in a neat blue suit, he ascended the scaffold which had been constructed in Kansas City and raised behind the segregation building. He seemed unafraid and other than letting out a boo and spitting at the guards around the scaffold he said no word. Two minutes after he ascended the gallows, his limp body was swinging from the hangman's rope.

As one of the principals in this ugly drama, Warden White can add a few details to the official account, and correct it in one small area. He tells us that, as the time approached for Panzran's execution, he asked the condemned man if there was anything he could do for him. He made only one specific request. He didn't want any of those God damned chaplains around at his hanging! It was none of their damned business, he had no use for them, and he wanted them kept away. Tom didn't say yes or no and, without making any particular point of it, chose to ignore this request. When time came to carry out the execution, he had both the Protestant and Catholic Chaplains on hand. Minutes before the time set for the trap to be sprung, the guards reported that Panzran refused to leave his cell. They asked whether they should use force. Tom replied that he would take care of it himself (even as his father would have done!), and went to the condemned man's cell. He told him his time had arrived and he would have to come along. The prisoner, in his usual profane language, refused. Tom then said, "This is your party and you've got to be there. You have two choices. You can either walk out there like a man, or you can let me take you my way." Panzran then said, "I told you I didn't want them God damned chaplains out there. I'll come just as soon as you get them out of there." When it was clear that he meant what he said, and absolutely did not want the clergymen present, Tom sent word for them to leave. When they were gone the prisoner accompanied Tom to the scaffold without further protest.

Anyone who might have expected a last-minute sign of repentance from this man was doomed to disappointment. As he stood on the platform, waiting for the hood and noose to be adjusted, he glared at the physician and other officials and witnesses and muttered: "All right you sons of bitches, you've come to see a show and now you're going to see it. They tell me when I drop down there and hit the end of this rope I'll crap in my pants. I just wish I could take them off so I could crap all over you dirty bastards." Those were the last words spoken by the man known as Convict Number 31614.

EXTRACT FROM ROBERT STROUD'S PRISON MANUSCRIPT
PART III LOOKING OUTWARD
CHAPTER XIX pp 455, 458-461

The Hanging

If the writer's memory serves him well, Panzeran was hanged shortly after six A.M. on August 22, 1930. His neck was broken and he was pronounced dead and cut down sixteen minutes after going through the trap.

Naturally, no convicts were present to witness the execution, which was performed in the little enclosed yard back of the Isolation building, where the men in Isolation exercised and played handball, but eight years later the writer had a ring-side seat at the hanging of Applegate and Seuy (?) in the same little court. His authority for what occurred in the Panzeran case is Dale Ballard, who assisted the hangsman.

All night long that last night, Panzeran walked the floor of his cell, singing a pornographic little song that he had composed himself. It was not much of a song, either from the point of view of melody or lyrics, but it undoubtedly expressed in not too polite terms the deepest craving of his heart. The principal theme was:

"Oh how I love my roundeye!"

Shortly before six A.M. the front door of the Isolation Building opened and about two hundred persons: Newspaper men; official witnesses; officials; and merely morbidly curious persons who had been able to wrangle passes, crowded into the Isolation corridor and grouped themselves in front of Panzeran's brightly-lighted cell, like a crowd of curious spectators at the zoo. (Note: This, or some similar occurrence, caused one convict to write a rather sarcastic poem entitled. The Leavenworth Zoo, the first line of which ran: "Have you ever been through the Leavenworth Zoo that is run by Uncle Sam." It is unfortunate that most of the lines are unprintable, and that an expurgated version would lose too much of the original flavor.)

Panzeran called White to his door:
"Are there any Bible-backed c___s___ here?"
"Chaplain so and so!"
"Right here, Warden! This is Reverend so and so whom I brought along, as he has never witnessed an execution and is very anxious to see one."
"Run the c___ s___ out! I don't want any Bible-backed hyprocrits at my funeral! I don't mind being hanged, but I don't want any preachers at my hanging. Run them out, and I will go out under my own power. It will not be necessary for anyone to put a hand on me. I don't want to cause any trouble, for I'm as anxious to get it over with as you are, but if you don't run those Biblebacks out, you are going to have one hell of a time getting me out of this cell, and you are going to have to fight every step of the way. I can't win, but I have nothing to lose, either. Every man I get one of my hands on is going to a hospital."
"You hear what he says,"said White, addressing the ministers. "You will have to leave!"
"Oh, Warden!" protested the Chaplain. "We are so anxious to see it. Why Reverend so and so came all the way from ____ at my invitation." The Chaplain named some little town out in Western Kansas.
"That has nothing to do with it. This man is going to die, but he still has the legal right to bar any person personally obnoxious to him from witnessing his execution, that is, anyone not absolutely essential to the function. I am here not because I want to be, but because it is part of my duty to see that everything is done in the proper manner. If he stated that my presence would be obnoxious to him, I would be morally and legally bound to delegate

my authority to someone else and honor his request. The guard will let you out."

As soon as the preachers were out of the building, Panzeran said:

"All right! Let's get going! What in hell are we stalling around for?"
Ballard, the heavy straps hung over his left arm, thrust his key in the lock and turned It over.

"You can forget the straps until we get to the gallows. I told you that I would not cause any trouble."

"Very well," said White.

As Panzeran stepped out the door, Ballard locked arms with him on one side and the hangsman on the other. They were both men better than six-feet, two inches tall.

"Let's go!" said Panzeran, leading the procession down the hall, almost dragging his longer-legged attendants along, like a bull on a leash.

He took the step of the gallows two at a time and took his place on the trap without an instants hesitation. Just before the black hood was flipped over his head the hangsman asked him if he had anything to say.

"Yes! Make it snappy, you hoosierfield c___ s___." and Panzeran spat in the hangsman's face.

So, maybe Carl Panzern did want to die, after all; maybe that had been his purpose all the time, but the writer, who has faced the same problem, could not think so. Not the least fact in forcing him to his conclusion was the tone of Carl's voice as he walked the floor and sang his little song, over and over, all night long. You see, the writer has walked the floor and sang, too.

In any case, a lot of convicts were sorry, sorry that Freddy was late reaching his office on that particular morning.

PANZRAM GOES TO GALLOWS CURSING RACE, INCLUDING SELF

Leavenworth Prisoner From D. C. Boasted Murder of 22.

Sentenced Here for Burglary. Called Meanest Prisoner by Peak.

A hangman's noose at Leavenworth, Kans., this morning snuffed out the life of Carl Panzram, a man who swore he hated all humanity with a consuming passion, including himself, and who was described by District Jail officials as the "meanest man ever held in the District Jail."

Panzram was hanged for the murder of a laundry foreman in Leavenworth prison, in June, 1929. At the time of the murder Panzram was serving a 25-year sentence for a burglary committed in the District of Columbia.

According to Associated Press dispatches from Leavenworth Panzram carried all his hate of humanity to the gallows with him, jeering at the crowd about the gallows and ordering the removal of two chaplains from the scene of the execution.

Cursed Own Parents.

A sullen, brute of a man, who cursed his parents for bringing him into the world, and who boasted that he had killed 22 persons during his lifetime, Panzram was described by Col. William L. Peak, warden at the District Jail, as the toughest customer he ever came in contact with.

Panzram made several confessions of murders to Col. Peak while being held here awaiting trial, and, Col. Peak said today, they were made with the utmost emphasis on the gruesome details of the deaths he caused.

Always sullen and baleful, Panzram was watched closely while he was in the District jail, for he made many threats he would kill guards, prisoners, even threatening death to Col. Peak. He never tried to kill himself, but begged the jailer to find some pretext upon which he could be killed by law.

Demands Death Sentence.

Before his trial out at Topeka, Kans., in the murder of the prison laundry foreman, Panzram, according to the Associated Press dispatches, wrote the

CARL PANZRAM.

judge who was to try him and demanded justice, which he described as "that I be found guilty of murder in the first degree and sentenced to die."

During his trial in the District Supreme Court on the burglary charge, which brought him a 25-year sentence in Leavenworth, Panzram bared all the hatefulness of his nature. With sullen calm he threatened court officers several times during the trial. Once he turned to Walter Shea, assistant district attorney, who was prosecuting him, and growled:

"And when I get out of this I'll come to get you."

When the trial was over and Panzram had been sentenced he growled at Chief Justice Walter T. McCoy:

"I hate the whole human race and would like to kill every person in the world."

Declared of Sound Mind.

Before a sanity board in Topeka Panzram freely boasted of 22 murders, and offered to tell the members of the board all about them. The board held him to be of sound mind.

Col. Peak this morning revealed that he accompanied Panzram on the trip out to Leavenworth, and "never had anything to do with a more sullen man."

Col. Peak said Panzram, throughout the trip, sat with his cap pulled far down on his face, would converse with no one and several times spoke only to throw the vilest sort of epithets at passengers on the train.

PANZRAN TO HIS DEATH ON GIBBET

Slayer of W. G. Warnke Defiant as He Marches Through Witnesses to Gallows

THE END CAME SWIFTLY

Two Minutes After Doomed Man Entered Execution Court, Body Had Shot Through Trap to Eternity.

Defiant to the last and unafraid, Carl Panzran, arch slayer who boasted of twenty-two murders, went to death on the scaffold at the federal prison this morning, paying with his life for the brutal murder on June 20, 1929, of W. G. Warkne, prison laundry foreman.

Panzran was removed from his cell at a few seconds after 6 o'clock. At 6:02 the trap was sprung and at 6:19 three physicians pronounced him dead. It was announced that his neck was broken. The hangman sliced the rope and the body was lowered into a basket. It was removed by Arnold Sumpter to the O'Donnell Undertaking company's chapel.

The handful of newspapermen, about thirty prison guards and other witnesses marched out. Reveille was sounding in the prison as the witnesses were marching out. There was no evidence of a demonstration and Warden Thomas B. White said he anticipated none. Regular prison routine was to be followed throughout the day.

As Panzran came through the gate from the isolation ward he was supported on either arm by a prison guard. United States Marshal Donald H. MacIvor, two deputy marshals and the un-named hangman walked beside him.

No Sign of Fear.

Panzran showed no sign of fear, but in the early morning light his face, cleanly shaven, appeared a pasty white. As he turned and saw the assembled prison guards he booed and spat at them. Nearer the gallows he repeated signs of his hatred.

Panzran walked erect with rapid strides. He mounted the gallows with firm steps and took his position on the platform. Only key straps were to be adjusted, the harness strapping his arms to his sides having been adjusted before leaving the cell.

Deft hands of a deputy marshal buckled the leg straps while the hangman taped Panzran's eyes, placed the rope and adjusted the knot behind the left ear. The deputy marshals and prison guards stepped back and the hangman jerked an iron lever that came up through the platform. Panzran shot through the trap and his head flopped to one side as his neck snapped. The body spun slowly and there was a pronounced quivering of the chest. No word had been spoken.

Requests Chaplains Retire.

As Panzran came through the gate from the isolation ward he saw the Catholic and Protestant prison chaplains in the assemblage. He requested that these be asked to leave the execution court. Prison authorities conveyed his wish to the chaplains and they withdrew.

Before beginning the death march Panzran was asked if he wished to make any statement on the gallows. He said that he would have nothing to say. He waived the reading of the death warrant.

"I know what it says and I am ready to go without that," he told the marshal. Previously he had said that he would go quietly, doing everything he was told. His only outburst was the booes he gave the witnesses as he strode from the door entering the court to the north wall where the gallows had been erected.

The gallows platform was 5 feet 9 inches from the concrete floor of the court, being erected according to regular building specifications. The drop is calculated by the height of the man to be executed. Before witnesses had left the court, workmen were dismantling the scaffold.

Hangman Keeps Identity.

In explanation of his purpose not to make known the identity of the hangman, Marshal MacIvor said the man was not a professional hangman, but one who had gained experience at many hangings. He said the man was engaged in business and did not wish his identity published, that the stigma of being a hangman be not attached to him. The man was allowed the customary government fee of $100 for his services.

Panzran spent a fitful night. Fortified with many cigarets he began his waiting for the morning. He conversed but little with the two guards who sat outside his cell. At the regular hour for retiring he prepared himself for sleep and retired to the mattress placed on the floor which has been his bed for many weeks. But sleep did not come easily to the man who was to die soon after the new day had broken. At times he apparently was sleeping restlessly. The pile of cigarettes which he had placed in a row on the floor grew smaller and smaller as the night wore on.

Eats Last Breakfast.

Soon after 4 o'clock the doomed man was aroused by the guards and new clothing was brought. He was dressed in a dark blue suit of pin stripe. New shoes were placed upon his feet. He ordered a substantial breakfast with steaming coffee. This was supplied him and he ate the food with an apparently hearty appetite. When the meal was finished the process of strapping his arms and placing handcuffs on his wrists was begun. A deputy marshal with watch in hand tolled off the minutes until 6 o'clock. As the hour mark was passed the death march was begun. Panzran, once a soldier, marched with head erect. To the witnesses it appeared that he was hurrying his guards along, so rapid was his stride.

Newspapermen and other witnesses had been given written invitations by Marshal MacIvor. These assembled outside the prison at 5 o'clock and soon were told to enter. Guards at the entrance checked each invitation with a prepared list. The witnesses then assembled in the warden's office where they remained until 5 minutes before 6 o'clock. They were then marched through the prison to the execution court.

Witnesses Show No Strain.

Few persons in the assemblage appeared under emotional strain. They examined the scaffold and its workings and conversed of inconsequential topics, seemingly wishing to keep away from the thing that was about to be done.

Continued on next page

"Here they come," spoke a voice and conversation ceased, as all eyes were turned toward those forming the death march. There was no sound until the thud of the falling body came, save the drone of an airplane that shuttled back and forth over the enclosure, only a few hundred feet in the air. Identity of the plane was not established. Those in authority expressed opinion that photographs were being taken.

After the body of Panzran had been removed to the undertaking establishment a post mortem examination was made by the three physicians who had witnessed the hanging. The body was then prepared for burial, which took place in the prison cemetery this afternoon, no one appearing to claim it. Panzran was said not to have any relatives.

Several persons called at the O'Donnell chapel with requests they be permitted to view the body. These requests were denied.

His Sixth Prison Term.

Panzran was received from Washington, D. C., where he was convicted of housebreaking and burglary and sentenced to serve twenty-five years. He was said to have begun his first prison sentence in Minnesota when 11 years of age.

Panzran was serving his sixth prison sentence, when he struck the laundry foreman with a heavy iron bar.

Panzran once was a prisoner at the United States Disciplinary Barrack. In the army only a month he was court martialed and sentenced to serve here.

Characterized as the "most criminally minded man in America," Panzran was convicted of the crime by a jury in the federal district court at Topeka, April 16, 1930. The verdict, murder in the first degree, made the death penalty mandatory. During the trial he spurned the attempts of attorneys to act in his behalf.

He repeatedly claimed he had murdered 23 persons.

A final effort to stay the hanging failed late yesterday when President Hoover, acting upon recommendation of the department of justice denied a plea for commutation of the death penalty. The president's action was on a telegraphic request filed by L. S. Harvey, a Kansas City, Kas., attorney. Panzran himself had made no application for clemency and Harvey refused to reveal the name of the parties he represented.

First Hanging Since 1888.

Historical records reveal that the hanging was the first legal execution within the boundaries of Kansas since 1888 when a federal prisoner from Indian Territory was hanged at Wichita. The last execution, under state statutes was August 9, 1870, when William Dickson went to his death here for the murder of Jason Barnett. Since that time, all governors have commuted death sentences until 1907 when capital punishment, except for treason, was abolished by statute.

In the past 40 years eight such sentences have been handed down by the Kansas district of the federal court. In every case executive clemency has been extended to the condemned men, two of whom are serving life sentences in the penitentiary here. One is Ono Manuel, a Mexican, who was convicted on charges of slaying a guard several years ago. The other is Robert Stroud, who was found guilty of slaying Andrew Turner, a guard, March 17, 1916. Two days before the execution was set to take place, the late President Woodrow Wilson commuted the sentence to life imprisonment. The gallows erected for his execution was kept for many years until it was ordered destroyed.

Dies on Gallows

Carl Panzran, slayer of W. G. Warnke, went to his death at 6 o'clock this morning in the recreation court of the federal prison isolation ward. He displayed no sign of fear as he walked briskly to the gallows. Unclaimed, the body was buried in the prison cemetery this afternoon.

NOOSE SILENCES FEDERAL PRISON SLAYER'S CURSES

EXPULSION OF MINISTERS IS HIS LAST WISH

Panzran Scowls Contempt for All Mankind as Trap Springs.

OFFERS NO REGRET

Execution at Leavenworth Marks First in Kansas in Forty Years.

BRAGGART SLAYER GETS HIS WISH; IS TO BE HANGED

TOPEKA, Kan., April 16.—(By International News Service.)—The hope of Carl Panzran, 23, inmate at the federal penitentiary at Leavenworth, Kan., that he be hanged for the murder of R. G. Warnke, a prison laundry employe, was partially fulfilled today.

A jury heard the evidence in the case and returned a verdict of guilty and added a curt "without mercy" to their findings.

The verdict of the jury making hanging mandatory. Federal Judge Richard J. Hopkins sentenced Panzran to be executed on September 5.

In the meantime, the court ordered that the braggart murderer must be held in solitary confinement.

Despite the fact he boasted of killing twenty-three persons—that he would like to kill thousands and then commit suicide—Panzran is sane to the extent that he knows right from wrong, a sanity commission reported.

The government proved that Panzran killed Warnke in cold blood and tried to kill others in the room—facts which the defendant not only admitted, but bragged about.

STATE OF KANSAS
State Board of Health—Division of Vital Statistics

STANDARD
CERTIFICATE OF DEATH

Do not write in this space

1. PLACE OF DEATH: County LEAVENWORTH
Township or City LEAVENWORTH No. U. S. Penitentiary St., Ward
(If death occurred in a hospital or institution, give its NAME instead of street and number.)

2. FULL NAME Carl PANZRAN
(a) Residence. No. U. S. Penitentiary St., Ward
(Usual place of abode) (If nonresident, give city or town and state)
Length of residence in city or town where death occurred 1 yrs. mos. ds. How long in U. S. if of foreign birth? yrs. mos. ds.
Was deceased ever a member of the Army, Navy, or Marine Corps of the United States? Not known
If so, state Organization Rank Period of service

PERSONAL AND STATISTICAL PARTICULARS

3. SEX Male
4. COLOR OR RACE White
5. Single, Married, Widowed, or Divorced (write the word) Single
5a. If married, widowed, or divorced HUSBAND of (or) WIFE of
6. DATE OF BIRTH (month, day, and year) Unknown
7. AGE Years 36 Months Days If LESS than 1 day, hrs. or min.
8. Trade, profession, or particular kind of work done, as spinner, sawyer, bookkeeper, etc. Seaman
9. Industry or business in which work was done, as silk mill, saw mill, bank, etc. Seaman
10. Date deceased last worked at this occupation (month and year) Unknown
11. Total time (years) spent in this occupation Unknown
12. BIRTHPLACE (city or town) (State or country) Unknown
13. NAME Unknown
14. BIRTHPLACE (city or town) (State or country) Unknown
15. MAIDEN NAME Unknown
16. BIRTHPLACE (city or town) (State or country) Unknown
17. INFORMANT (Address)
18. BURIAL, CREMATION, OR REMOVAL Place Date 19
19. UNDERTAKER (Address)
20. FILED 19 Registrar

MEDICAL CERTIFICATE OF DEATH

21. DATE OF DEATH (month, day, and year) Sept. 5, 1930
22. I HEREBY CERTIFY, That I attended deceased from September 5, 1930, to September 5, 1930
I last saw him alive on September 5, 1930 death is said to have occurred on the date stated above at 6.18 A. M.
The principal cause of death and related causes of importance in order of onset were as follows:
Dislocation cervical vertebrae
Strangulation,
Legal execution.

Contributory causes of importance not related to principal cause:

Name of operation Date of
What test confirmed diagnosis? Was there an autopsy? yes
23. If death was due to external causes (violence) fill in also the following:
Accident, suicide, or homicide? LEGAL EXECUTION 19
Where did injury occur? (Specify city or town, county, and state)
Specify whether injury occurred in industry, in home, or in public place.
Manner of injury
Nature of injury
24. Was disease or injury in any way related to occupation of deceased?
If so, specify
(Signed) M. D.
(Address) U. S. Pub. Health Service

Panzram's grave at Leavenworth USP. The name plate on the top of the grave-stone is missing. Only a blank stone remains.

PANZRAM'S GRAVE AT THE
U.S. PENITENTIARY, LEAVENWORTH KS
CIRCA 1992

R.Rains	9837 V.Kennard	9770 A.Dunlap	15708 G.Welty	M.Dillingham
7085 L.Thomas	9454 S.McGinty	13364 I.Love	15874 N.Marcus	42476 E.Ellis
7257 T.McMahon	9479 B.Francis		21067 A.Hill	26340 J.Guigia
7595 G.Lenzy	5333 L.Savage	10974 L.Schedler	23956 J.Alonso	46930 J.Fuller
7133 John Doe	9313 N.Simms	11856 R.Mason	26802 G.Ford	48603 E.Trevino
7422 K.Dodd	9573 W.Johnson	12248 R.Brownfield	32563 T.Walters	32930 C.Walker
5657 Maitland	7621 W.Beethem	3826 F.Ledbetter	20887 R.Leslie	28058 S.King
5743 W.Reid	6852 J.Matthews	22018 B.Hawkins	22998 W.Hedrick	48552 F.Miller
5846 J.Smith	23545 W.Gonzales	14761 T.Murry	29132 T.Bruner	32010 J.Kline	46770 F.Woods
M.Adams	G.Moore	26360 C.Johnson	28178 J.Murphy	27960	33485 E.Garcia
6147 B.Sales	23466 J.Cale	19685 W.Keenan	28132 P.Moore	36926 C.Martin
24591 R.Davis	16698 B.John	33001 C.Gardner	28907 C.Bunch	32179 J.Allen
19703 R.Gordon	31256 R.Webster		92415 T.Gilliam	33544 E.Pope
25537 J.Rage	32531 J.Flores	38394 R.Manning	29563 C.Hammond	31614 C.Panzram
4905 Lowery	33292 J.Thomas	38390 H.Jaeger	31251 F.Ellis	32558 C.Carrasco
26385 M.Lopez	27680 P.Petty	39747 E.Luna	4697 Z.Adams	30162 M.Martinez	14450 A.Curtis
26576-R. Quistierre	27965 E.Reed	27195 A.Moore	36197 T.Richardson	31900 F.Adams	48633 J.McDougal
27606 E.Wilson	3883 J.Holliday	3562 R.Wilkie	38665 J.Kaufman	27819 J.Woodward
27530 C.Reese	4521 L.Sims	2979 F.Conners	37144 W.Butler	17869 W.Buckner
25402 E.Moore	3074 C.Jesus	35912 R.Ault	25701 H.Benson	20626 P.Rico
3527 T.Carela				

LEAVENWORTH PRISON CEMETERY

The hood, eye band, and noose used in Panzram's execution on display at the J.M. Davis Arms & Historical Museum.

COLT'S
FIREARMS

SMITH & WESSON
FIREARMS

THOMPSON SUB-MACHINE GUNS

8/25/30

I N V O I C E

SOLD TO:

Mr. Donald H. McIvor
U. S. Marshal
Topeka, Kansas.

EXECUTION EQUIPMENT

‑

One 30 foot Plymouth Manila rope, with noose----$15:00

One shot-weighted black hood--------------------------- 7:50

One flexible eye-band--------------------------------- 1:00

Total------------------------$23:50

The above material was delivered to Deputy Marshal,
E. G. Harman, Federal building, Kansas City, Kansas,
8/25/30.

No. **417**   3/25/30   *19*

RECEIVED from M. A. Gill, 6900 Kensington, K. C. MO.

In good order the following articles:

One 30 foot hangman's rope with Noose tied.

One shot-loaded black cap.

One eye band.

Addressed to U. S. Marshal's office   , K. C. Kansas.

Retain this slip to compare
with Invoice.

Per C. G. Harman

Deputy U.S.M.

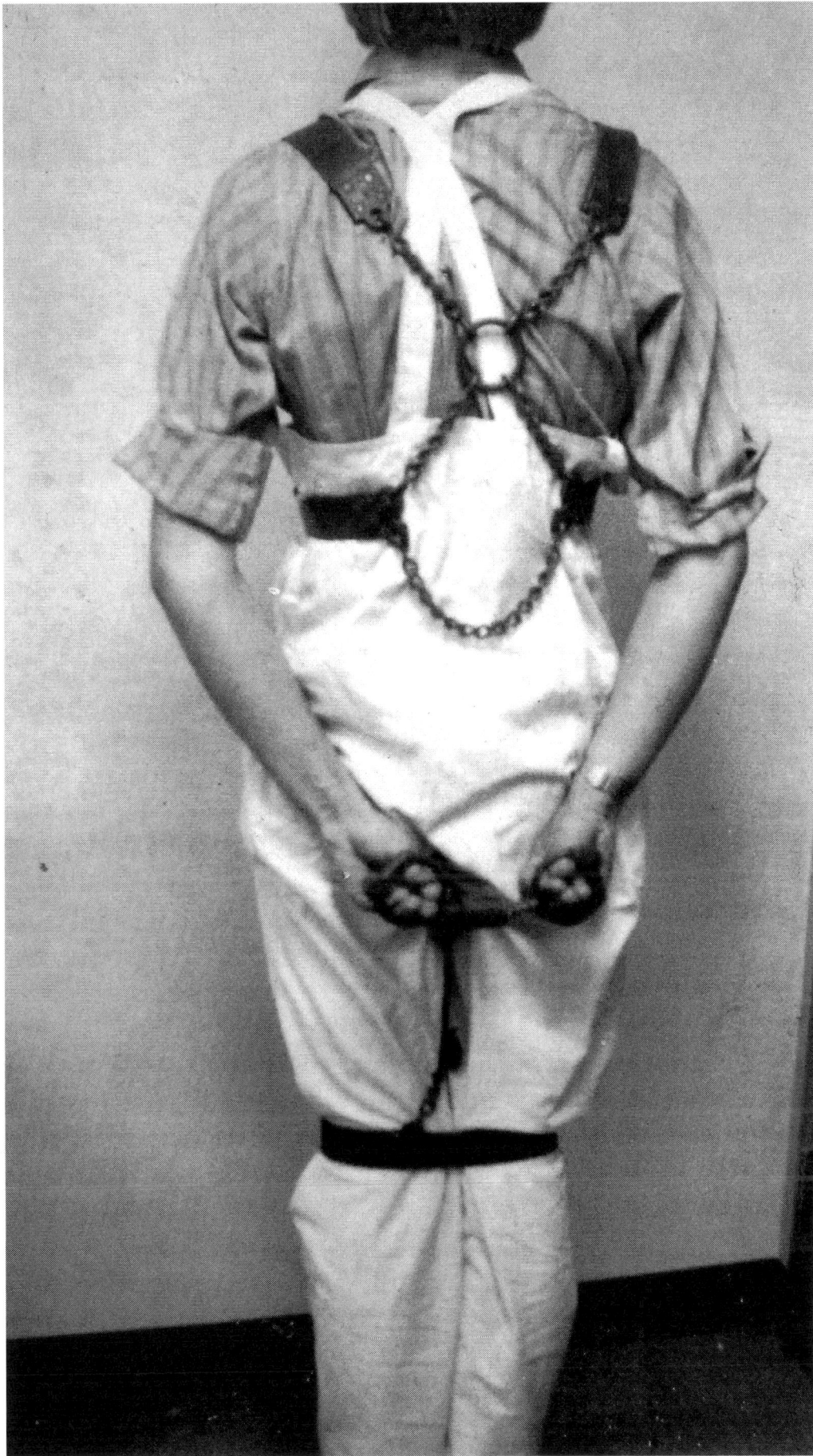

Restraints possibly worn by Carl Panzram during his execution. (J.M. Davis Arms Museum)

F 557 9-30 2M

WM. B. MILLS
SUPERINTENDENT

JAMES J. HEARN
JOSEPH A. LE STRANGE
ASSISTANT SUPERINTENDENTS

WILLIAM J. CONNELLY
INSPECTOR DETECTIVE DIV.

DEPARTMENT OF PUBLIC SAFETY
BUREAU OF POLICE
PHILADELPHIA

DETECTIVE DIVISION
THIRD FLOOR CITY HALL

Sept. 23, 1930.

MEMBER OF
NATIONAL BUREAU OF IDENTIFICATION

Warden of Federal Penitentiary,
Leavensworth, Kansas.

Dear Sir:

Will you kindly send us photograph and fingerprints
of one Karl Panzran who was hanged in your institution on Sept.
5, 1930.

One Karl Panzran is indicted in our city on a charge
of murder of one Alex Urszacki. Panzran made a confession to
Detective Sergeant Curran of the Homicide Squad, this city, in
Washington, D. C., on October 26, 1928, admitting the murder of
this boy; this was previous to his trial in Washington, D. C.,
on a charge of burglary.

It is necessary that we verify that the Karl Panzran
hanged by you is the same Karl Panzran indicted by us for murder.

Your assistance in this regard will be greatly ap-
preciated.

Yours very truly,

WILLIAM CONNELLY,
Inspector of Detectives.

258

HANG A MURDERER IN FEDERAL PRISON

Carl Panzran, Who Claimed to Have Murdered 22, is Executed

U. S. Bureau of Investigation

Department of Justice

SUITE L - FEDERAL BUILDING
KANSAS CITY, MISSOURI.
NOVEMBER 19, 1933.

Director,
Division of Investigation,
U. S. Department of Justice,
Washington, D. C.

RE: CARL PANZRAM
MURDER ON GOVERNMENT RESERVATION
K. C. File #70-47

Dear Sir:

There is being transmitted herewith a photograph of Carl Panzram, Subject in the above captioned closed case, together with a memorandum prepared by Mr. Merle A. Gill, Forensic Ballastician, of Kansas City, Missouri.

From a review of the closed case file it will be noted that Subject was convicted in Federal Court at Topeka, Kansas on April 16, 1930 on a charge of having murdered R. G. Warnke, a civilian at the United States Penitentiary at Leavenworth, Kansas; the death penalty was imposed and on September 5, 1930 at 6:01 AM Panzram was hanged at the United States Penitentiary at Leavenworth, Kansas.

There is being transmitted under separate cover the hood which Panzram wore at the time of his execution by hanging at Leavenworth, this original hood having been furnished to this office by Mr. Gill, above named. It is thought that this hood, together with the information of Mr. Gill's memorandum, may be of particular interest for the Division's exhibit in the new Department of Justice building at Washington, D. C., in view of the fact that there is not presently capital punishment in the State of Kansas and Panzram is the first man to be hanged by order of the Court in that State for some forty-six years.

If the Division desires, this office will make appropriate inquiries through the Capitol at Topeka, Kansas concerning just how many hangings or executions were had in the State of Kansas by order of the Court, in order that this information may be available in connection with this exhibit in the new Department of Justice Building.

Mr. Gill has also advised he is obtaining for this office a piece of the original rope used in the noose at the time of the hanging of Panzram, in order that it may likewise be transmitted to the Division in connection with the above mentioned exhibit.

RECORDED

INDEXED

DEC 7 1933

62-21811-19

DIVISION OF INVESTIGATION
NOV 22 1933 A.M.
DEPT. OF JUSTICE

It is respectfully suggested that if this hood or rope are used as exhibit in the Department of Justice building that a notation be made on exhibit, the same was furnished by Mr. Merle A. Gill, Forensic Ballistician, of Kansas City, Missouri.

Very truly yours,

M. C. SPEAR
ACTING SPECIAL AGENT IN CHARGE

MCS-jgw

Black hood used in the execution of Carl Panzran at
the Leavenworth Federal Prison on the morning of
September 15th, 1930.

The scaffold was furnished by the sheriff of Jackson
county Missouri and the hangman was H. S. Holliday,
deputy sheriff, Jackson County Missouri. The scaffold
was portable.

The hood is shot-weighted to prevent the skirt of
the hood from flying off of the head as the victim
drops through the trap.

The type of rope used in executions is 3/4" Plymouth
Manile having 36 threads to each strand. 3 strand rope
30 foot in length.   the knot has seven turns and
requires about 7 feet for the noose. prior to the
execution the rope is dropped through the trap weighted
with a 200 pound bag of sand. just before the
execution the rope is greased with hog lard to allow
it to slip freely within the knot.

The scaffold has 13 steps and the hangings are usually
on friday. The victim is dropped his length in inches.

In this execution the equipment was furnished by the
writer, equipment being purchased by the U. S. Marshal's
office.

Panzran was executed for the murder of a civilian guard
employed in the laundry of the prison.

Panzran admitted the murder of some 22 boys.

Apparently Panzran was "Stir-Bugs".

                              Gill

COPY

WORCESTER EVENING POST

October 7,1937.

Mr. J. Edgar Hoover
Director
Federal Bureau of Investigation
United States Department of Justice
Washington, D.C.

Dear Mr. Hoover:-

Thank you very much for sending us the copies of your
recent addresses. We are very glad to have these.

I noticed in that sketch of you running in the New
YORKER a reference to a man named Carl Panzram who was hanged. I also
read an article by you concerning sex criminals.

The record of Panzram might furnish material for quite
an article by you on this point. When he was under arrest in Washington
for burglary he was tied yp to the murder of a little boy either in Salem
or Peabody, Mass. I was then representing the Boston Traveler and the
Salem News in Washington and had occasion to interview Panzram in the office
of the jail superintendent. He was a sex pervert of the most brutal type
and finally confessed to the murders of five little boys in as many States
after assaulting them. As I recall it, each State concerned then held
back, waiting for another State to claim him. The Federal authorities
finally got tired and he was given a long sentence on the burglary charge.
He then killed either a guard or a fellow prisoner in a federal prison
and was promptly hanged. Otherwise, he would eventually have been released, undoubtedly to prey on more little boys.

With best wishes.

Yours sincerely,

W. G. Gavin
Editor and General Manager.

WGG/G

RECORDED
&
INDEXED

62 - 21811 - 21

FEDERAL BUREAU OF INVESTIGATION
OCT 9 1937
U. S. DEPARTMENT OF JUSTICE
FILE

I have lived 36 years in this world and soon I expect to leave it.

All that I leave behind me is, Smoke, death, desolation and damnation.

    signed.
   Carl Panzram.

Sept. 8, 1930.

Dr. C. B. Van Horn,
Topeka, Kans.

My dear Doctor:

I was so busy the day of the execution of
Panaram that I overlooked giving you our record clerk's
REVIEW of this man's sentence here upon which he had
the notation made as well as on the reverse side of
which he had his last will and testament. I had a
photostat in my office which I intended giving you.

I am now enclosing the full information
in connection with the study of this man's case.

Very truly yours,

TBN:M   Warden.
encl.

C. B. VAN HORN, M.D.

726-27-28 MILLS BUILDING
TOPEKA, KANSAS

Sept. 12, 1930.

Superintendent State Training
    School for boys,
Red Wing, Minn.

My dear Sir:

As attendant physician to our State Boys Industrial
School I am having constant observation of the varying types
of personalities among our entrants. In our psychological and
psychiatric studies we occasionally come on to some outstand-
ingly interesting cases. I have recently had an opportunity
to make some study of the case recently executed in the Federal
Prison at Leavenworth. This man, Carl Panzram, was first committed, according to our records, to your school about 1902 -
serving two years, paroled at the age of twenty-one,- and we are
anxious to know something of this fellows reaction to the confinement and treatment in your school. He was one of the most
pronounced types of psychopathic personality that I have ever
known and I am very anxious to get all information possible
regarding his family history, his early youth, his juvenile
court record and everything which you can give me of his history that will throw a light on the study of this perculiar man.
We see many of these perversed personalities in their beginning
and are now trying to trace this man's life back through his
checkered career. Much of this information we could not get
from him but the warden has given me a complete list of his
twelve commitments, the first having been in your school. I

266

realize that this is asking a great deal of you but believe that you will be willing to contribute all you can to the solution of the riddles in these boys lives. If you are interested I will be glad to send you what ever I find regarding his history. I felt in his first commitment we would be able to get more of both his immediate and remote family record, his environmental influences, first acts of delinquency, his mental ability, his early reaction to confinement or punishment, and so forth. I have a photostat copy of his last will and testament in which he bequeaths his carcass to the city dog catcher of East Grand Forks, Minn., to be used as dog meat. He terminates by leaving a curse to all man kind.

Thanking you in advance, I am

Very sincerely,

Dr. C. B. Van Horn.

CBV-EM

Panzram's last will and testament has never been located.

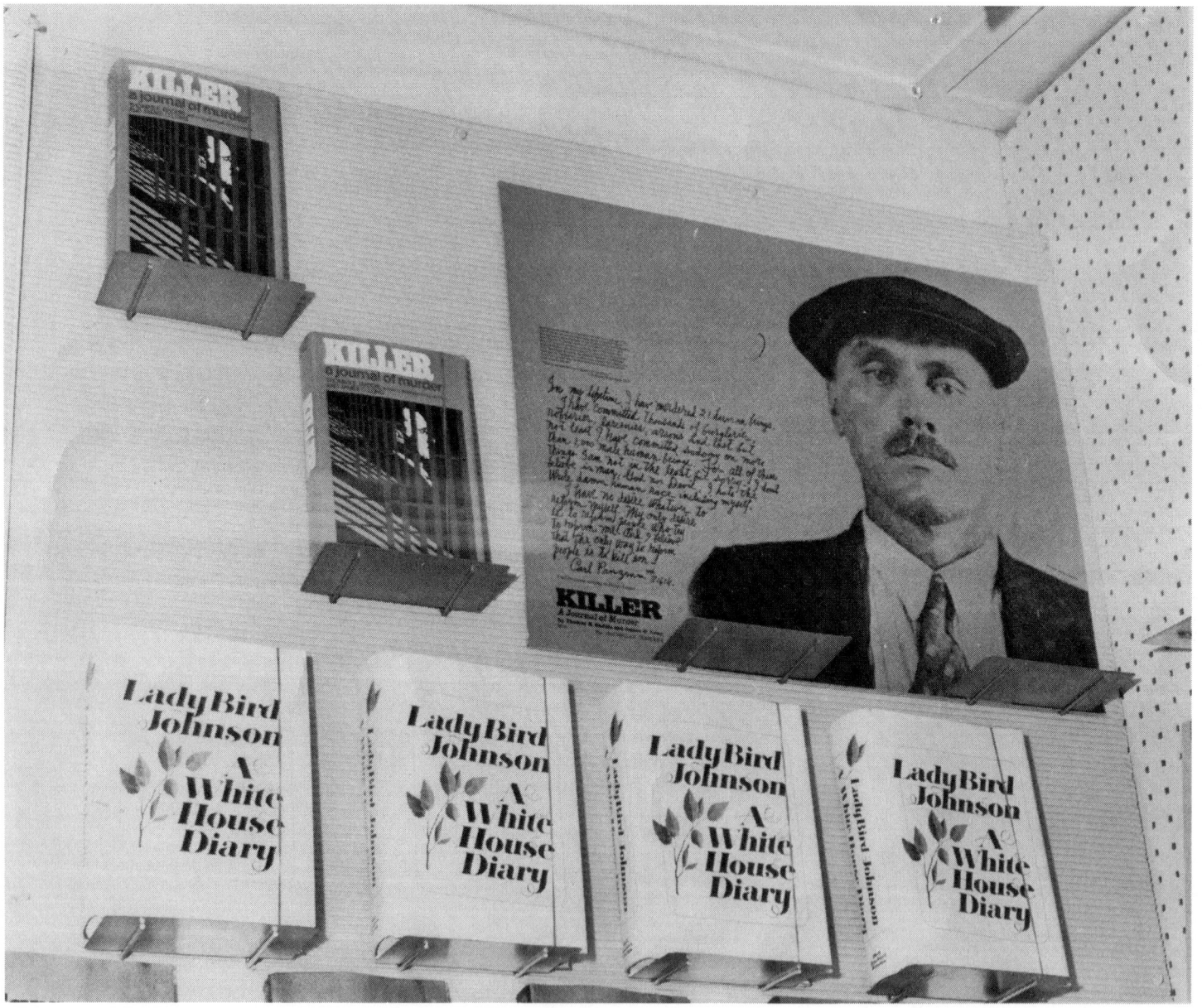

AFTERWORD

On Henry Lesser and Carl Panzram

Most join the prison profession because opportunities are close-to-home with good benefits and a public sector retirement. Not me. Curiosity was my singular motivation for pursuing this fascinating profession. I travelled far to pursue it and have been involved for more than four decades.

I was a misfit and bored with school during the eighth grade. In 1967 or 1968 I checked out my junior high school library copy of Thomas E. Gaddis' book, *Birdman of Alcatraz*, published in 1955. It enthralled. Also during my youth in the suburbs of St. Louis during the 1960s, my parents subscribed to the St. Louis Post-Dispatch. Much of the news was on crime and I developed an insatiable curiosity on what became of those sentenced to prison.

After graduating high school in 1972, I enrolled at the University of Missouri in St. Louis (UMSL) with aspirations to become a Certified Public Accountant. A few weeks into my first college math course I knew that becoming a CPA was not a viable career path. I changed my major to Administration of Justice and pursued my fascination for prisons.

I desired to experience traditional (fun!) college life and in the spring semester of 1974, I transferred to the main campus of University of Missouri in Columbia. While there at the ages of 19 and 20, I did an internship with the planning department of Missouri Department of Corrections (DOC) in Jefferson City. After charting the racial composition of each housing unit of the recently integrated prisons, I asked if I could obtain experience inside Missouri State Penitentiary (MSP). MSP was the oldest prison west of the Mississippi River and the end-of-the-line for the Missouri DOC. I was not aware of it then, but three years earlier Time Magazine described MSP as the "47 bloodiest acres in America." My unusual request was approved and without any training and with minimal supervision I went inside MSP on weekends and received an unconventional education on the realities of life inside a maximum security state penitentiary.

Also during that 1974 semester, on a spring Saturday morning I wandered inside a cigar store in downtown Columbia, Missouri. I do not recall why I went in since I did not smoke, but on their spinning red metal book rack was the paperback edition of *Killer: A Journal of Murder*, by Thomas E. Gaddis and James O. Long (the hardback edition was published in 1970). My fascination with prisons began as a child and I did not hesitate to buy it. I referenced it extensively in numerous college classes.

As the book detailed, in the late 1920s, Henry Lesser was an officer in the Washington D.C. Jail when hardened prisoner, Carl Panzram, was arrested and detained on a housebreaking charge. Officer Lesser sensed that Panzram was an atypical detainee. Days after his incarceration rogue jail guards brutally beat Panzram for a conduct infraction. That outraged Henry and led to communications with Panzram. Henry subsequently encouraged Panzram to write his story and that pencil-written biography formed the basis for Gaddis and Long's 1970 book. At the end of that fun spring 1974 semester I returned to St. Louis and resumed studies at UMSL. A year later during the spring of 1975, I visited the UMSL Placement Office looking for part-time warehouse work. The placement director was stapling a job announcement to a cork bulletin board for a paid Administrative Internship with St. Louis County Government. I never spoke with her before but she said it was a great opportunity. I applied and was invited for an interview, my first. In the reception area also waiting for his interview was the valedictorian from my high school from the year before I graduated.

I thought with competition of that caliber I would not have a chance to be selected for the internship. But the two interviewers were fascinated by my unusual experience inside MSP. I was hired and the valedictorian was not.

During the summer of 1975, I completed the internship for the Commissioner of St. Louis County's Department of Justice Services. I did research on the various agency components which include Prisoner Processing, the Jail, Probation Department and the Adult Correctional Institution. I got to know the agency training coordinator and he recommended that if I desired to pursue this profession I should go to work for the U.S. Department of Justice – Bureau of Prisons (BOP).

I followed his advice. In April 1976, after completing UMSL's degree requirements I was hired as a prison officer at the new Federal Correctional Institution in Butner, North Carolina. I did not attend UMSL's graduation ceremony since launching my career was priority.

The BOP hired me just after I turned 22. My experience with Missouri Department Corrections and St. Louis County's justice system made for a solid foundation. My fascination for prison history enabled me to connect on a sophisticated plane with older convicts and my curious nature contributed to developing rapport with seasoned staff.

Early on I had lofty professional aspirations and possessed a knack of cutting through bureaucratic distractions with creative problem solving. But to advance in the BOP during that era necessitated a masters' degree. In early 1978, I resigned my BOP position and drove 2,500 miles west to pursue a Master of Science Degree in Criminal Justice Administration at San Diego State University (SDSU). I went to school full time (it was the first time that I attended college while not working) until September 1978, when I was reinstated by the BOP as a senior officer at the downtown San Diego Metropolitan Correctional Center. I finished my degree while turning keys, primarily on the midnight to 8:00 a.m. shift.

In late 1978 or early 1979, SDSU Criminal Justice Professor G. Thomas Gitchoff learned that Henry Lesser was living in Los Angeles and we invited him to campus. On May 9, 1979, Henry came to SDSU and spoke with students, faculty, criminal justice practitioners and the local press.

HENRY LESSER AT SDSU

Henry Lesser with students at SDSU.

Henry Lesser at age 77 was a distinguished well-dressed gentleman. His build was slight, hair was gray and he wore glasses. He was modest and was not comfortable with the attention he received. Henry was in the spotlight because of his actions a half-century earlier when he went beyond the normative boundaries for jail officers and treated a vicious jail prisoner humanely.

For 40 years, from 1930 until 1970, Henry carried the Panzram manuscript and corresponded with renowned criminologists and writers with the singular mission of getting the story told. Following the class presentation, Professors Gitchoff, Ron Boostrom and I videotaped an interview with Henry (it was my first time on camera and it shows).

Henry was a kindred spirit. Like him, I am unusually curious and desired to improve the prison system. In 1979, I was walking the beat of a federal jail similar to what Henry did 50 years earlier in the Washington D.C. Jail. Henry spoke with crisp authority on current criminology trends. The other students and observers were captivated with the thoughtful man who a half-century earlier defied the brutal norms of other jail officers and treated Panzram with compassion.

An article about Henry's SDSU visit was published in the San Diego Union. It was the first public recognition that he received for his enormous contribution to criminology.

In September 1980, Henry returned to SDSU and donated the original Panzram manuscript and to the Special Collections and University Archives Department of SDSU's Library. At the same time he gave me boxes of his correspondence and a collection of historic criminology books.

In 2012 I donated all remaining historical materials to SDSU's Library. The comprehensive Carl Panzram / Henry Lesser archives are available on SDSU's website: https://library.sdsu.edu/scua/new-notable/panzram These materials are the most-accessed of SDSU Special Collections' vast holdings. People from all over the world have viewed these rare historic papers and the Henry Lesser video interview.

The BOP transferred me from San Diego back to St. Louis in 1980. I kept in contact with Henry through the mail (computers and email were not invented yet) until he passed away in 1983. I then wrote his wife, Esther, who later moved to Israel to be near their son. Their letters are in SDSU's collection.

Hollywood screenwriter, Tim Metcalfe, called in 1991. He got my number from SDSU and wrote the screenplay and subsequently directed the 1996 feature movie, *Killer: A Journal of Murder.* Tim and I corresponded and he invited me to the movie set in Groton CT (other scenes were filmed in a state penitentiary in Rhode Island). Tim's superb movie played in theaters in six cities and was released on DVD.

HENRY LESSER AND JOEL GOODMAN